Happy Birth[day]
All my [love]
Rachael xxx.

KIM PHILBY – OUR MAN IN MOSCOW

BY THE SAME AUTHOR

Three Faces of West

Stalingrad: Struggle in the East

D-DAY: Blood on the Beaches

KIM PHILBY
OUR MAN IN MOSCOW

THE LIFE OF A COLD WAR
MASTERSPY

CHRISTIAN
SHAKESPEARE

First published 2015

Copyright © Christian Shakespeare 2015
Afterword copyright © Christian Shakespeare 2015

The right of Christian Shakespeare as the author of this book
has been asserted in accordance with the
Copyright, Designs and Patrons Act 1988

No part of this book may be used, reproduced or stored in any form
whatsoever including mechanical, electronic recording,
photocopying or any other without written permission from the
author except for the use of brief quotations included in the book.

Every effort has been made to trace copyright holders.
If any have been overlooked, the author would be happy to
include them in any future additions of this book.

ISBN-13: 978-1508960256

ISBN-10: 1508960259

It's part of a writer's profession, as it's part of a spy's profession, to prey on the community to which he's attached, to take away information - often in secret - and to translate that into intelligence for his masters, whether it's his readership or his spy masters. And I think that both professions are perhaps rather lonely.

John Le Carré.

KIM PHILBY

"To betray you must first belong."
(Kim Philby)

CONTENTS

Preface

Introduction   1

1   Elitist to Marxist   8

2   Schnapps in Vienna, Vodka in London   16

3   Democracy and Fascism   30

4   Philby's War   40

5   My Friends, My Enemies   53

6   The Russian Defection   66

7   Lions, Bears and Eagles   82

8   Now I'm A Real Spy   100

9   The Balkan Bloodbath   119

10   Stanley and Homer   129

11   The Third of Five   153

12   Fight Like Hell!   168

13   The Innocence of a Guilty Man   181

14   A Gentleman in Foreign Lands   202

15   Hello Mr Elliott   220

16   Traitors and Suspects   231

17	Tea in Beirut	244
18	Hello Comrade Philby	265
19	A Lonely Old Spy	280
Afterword		297

PREFACE

Kim Philby was one of the Twentieth Century's most notorious double agents. A man who embodied the very essence of the quintessential Englishman; upper class, well educated, good family background, and certainly well connected.

But only a few individuals could ever really see the real man behind the mask, the man who privately threw off the velvet cloak of privilege and secretly embraced the coarse fabric of socialism and its chief doctrine, communism. Philby never joined the communist party in any country at any time so served well as background cover to worm his way into top secret positions. Even once he defected, he never formally became a member of the ruling party in the USSR. He was one of its most ardent advocates, yet remained politically on the fringes all his life, preferring to exist in a state of idealism rather than open support for the ruling party.

A great deal of what we know of Philby the man and Philby the spy comes from major sources such as newsreels, formal interviews only made possible toward the end thanks to radical reforms in the Soviet Union and from the accounts of his friends. However a considerable amount of material is also derived from official sources such as archives from intelligence files but only those which have been released. A lot of material on Philby and his accomplices in the wider Cambridge Spy Ring of which he was an integral part of, are still classified even today.

Material can be corroborated or purely circumstantial. The world of espionage and counterespionage is a black and white affair and those foot soldiers that are a part of it, the intelligence officers, can be famously guilty of a deliberate misrepresentation of events. More often than not this is only done to perhaps discredit opponents or to shift the blame from themselves. This can be especially true in relation to the Cold War of which Kim Philby and others were such a pivotal part of.

Propaganda fuels the so-called theories surrounding the true events of Philby's life, the true extent of his spying and the very intimate nature of the level of access he was allowed to see. Perhaps the real nature of his duplicity, including just how many people he sent to their deaths via the information he divulged to the Soviets over the years, will never fully be known. Perhaps Philby was just too good at what he did so that the true extent of the incompetence shown by the authorities will never be revealed for fear of intense embarrassment.

The case of Philby and the Cambridge spies will always be shrouded in a degree of mystery, with conflicting accounts and differing recollections – some intentional, others less so. The reality may be almost wholly different to what we know, or could be closer to the truth than what is believed. Based upon the available evidence the literature written on this man is extensive, but by no means exhausted. The many sides to the personality of Philby will always provide new material to study whether it is his friendships, his espionage or something entirely unknown previously. There is a very real sense for anyone who studies the Cold War or the story of Kim Philby and the Cambridge network, that there may be more shocking material waiting to be revealed. Whether or not such secrets will ever be divulged into the public domain remains to be seen if we are to build the complete picture on the life and work of one of the most proficient and duplicitous spies in modern history.

INTRODUCTION

The rain poured down in the middle of the violent storm which hung over the city in the cool January afternoon sky. A rather thin male figure, middle aged closed the door to his flat on the hill overlooking Beirut, the capital of Lebanon discretely and not wanting to draw attention to himself. Five flights of stairs separated him from his abode to the ground which he hurriedly descended as if he was fleeing for his safety from some great danger. The ground floor led out of the building and out onto the street named the Rue Kantari. Secluded just as the man wanted, there was only enough time to check that he was not being followed or observed which he probably expected to be given the circumstances surrounding him. His secret was out, and there was only now one course of action open to him.

The man had an appointment to keep tonight, on the 23 January 1963. Both he and his wife Eleanor was due to attend a dinner party held at the home of Glencairn Balfour Paul, a diplomat, the First Secretary of the British embassy in Beirut and family friend as they awaited the couple's arrival. After telling his wife he had to meet someone but would be back by six o' clock, he briskly walked through the rain soaked streets of the city, continuously assuring himself he was not being followed at any time, the man was not making his way to the residence of his friend and the dinner party he was due to attend, but toward a completely different destination; a bar in the town where a car woueventually pick him up, whisking him off toward Beirut's port and the docks on the Mediterranean coast.

In the lashing rain under that night's storm a large freighter was docked, she had already unloaded her cargo in haste when the man arrived who promptly made his way to the vessel which bore the name 'Dolmatova'.

The freighter weighed anchor as soon as the man arrived on board, its flag fluttering on the stern, solid red in colour and emblazoning a very provocative symbol in the corner; a hammer and sickle under a yellow edged star of the Communist Party; the flag of the Soviet Union. The Dolmatova, a Russian freighter hurriedly left the port and the city bound for the night waters of the Mediterranean Sea. Destined for the Black Sea port of Odessa, the passenger was a very special one indeed; a man born into privilege, subjected to high office and entrusted with the most sensitive of state secrets. Yet this was a man who both charmed and betrayed everyone and everything for an ideology, a criminal who sealed the fate of many people who did not share the same views he did, and a man who would betray any secret, even nuclear ones. After nearly twenty three years in the shadowy world of espionage and counter espionage, a world where nobody could be really trusted this man was about to come out into the cold. The passenger who fled Beirut and was now on board the Soviet ship was not some ordinary turncoat defecting to the other side, but a former senior figure of British Intelligence. His name was Kim Philby. Here was one of the men who were at the very forefront in the fight against world communism, but as of this moment he was on route to the state he was only supposed to help check the power of but had secretly aided.

1963 was the height of the tensions of the Cold War. Relations between east and west were blowing hot and cold with false assurances, contradictions and deception played by both sides, but this would turn out to be one of the most shocking and dramatic moments of the time. The effects of his departure by no means the first and not the last would certainly become the most controversial and would have incredible ramifications across the political divide and a revelation of just how many secrets were leaked. Yet Philby was not alone; his defection was just the latest link to flee from the group of privileged young men, all educated and all in respectable 'door opening' positions within the establishment and government. All exhibiting similar values in terms of speech, dress code and their 'old boys' clubs fuelled by the vice of heavy drinking these would form part of what would in time come to be known as the Cambridge Spy Ring, the ideological Socialist corruption of the upper middle-class in a devastating, almost abusive way. Motivated by the unfounded belief that capitalism was corrupt and that the communist model of the Soviet Union was a more fitting template for society, the members were driven more by political idioms rather than financial gain.

But why would they think this? In the sober days of the 1930's where the debauch partying of the roaring twenties had dissipated to be replaced by the political reality of a changing world in the face of rising fascism in both Germany and Italy. Therefore the elite classes saw themselves as increasingly vulnerable, especially in Britain. Stalinisation was well established in the USSR and this provided a magnet for impressionable young men going through the upper class university education system. For members of the Cambridge Spy Ring they looked not toward the bourgeois, oak panelled, alcohol fuelled lifestyle of the establishment where the whisky's and brandy's came as fast as the taps on the shoulders and promotions, but outward toward the creation of a more dynamic and modern society. Where such a society they believed lay was east in Stalin's Soviet Union. The 'Iron Man' in the Kremlin held a ruthless programme in the USSR, something the impressionable young men wished to imprint in the west with themselves at the forefront of this new revolution. The Cambridge

INTRODUCTION

Five's rejection of elitism in favour of Stalinism was ironically a form of elitism in itself, the old belief that they were born to rule. It was just that the model they desired to rule with was politically and ideologically different from the one they already had.

As such Guy Burgess, Anthony Blunt, Donald MacLean and John Carincross showed no outward signs that they were different to many of the other privileged young men who were staffing the Foreign Office or other high positions at the time such as the BBC and the diplomatic service. Yet each of them were all from the same Soviet mould as Kim Philby, all willing to throw away their gold plated careers and betray their principles and their friends for the red banner of communism. Despite their desire to rule under a new model each chose to become a traitor both to their class and their country.

This utter betrayal was a tempting prospect in the 1930's when Philby and others were turned. Communism held an almost hypnotic appeal over those who were young and impressionable even more so that this ideology seemed to be the only one strong enough to check and even stop the rampant rise of right-wing fascism boiling in central Europe. The zest of the allure of left-wing communism though could not be enough for these men to explain their duplicity considering each other's anxieties and competences, there had to be something else in their minds to turn their back on the life they were born into. This perverse fascination was profoundly shaken before the outbreak of the Second World War with the signing of the 1939 Nazi-Soviet Pact. This instilled a sense of shock in the minds of those secretly working for Moscow especially those who thought that Soviet Russia was the true enemy of fascism and the only state strong enough to fight Nazi Germany.

In the United Kingdom, The Daily Worker was the official newspaper of the Communist Party of Great Britain and an outlet for the virulent hypocrisy expressed in response to the politics of

INTRODUCTION

the time. Before the 1939 pact the paper promoted pacifism and anti-Nazism, however once both Berlin and Moscow were aligned it dropped this stance only to take it up once again in 1941 when Hitler invaded the Soviet Union. Even so through all these flippant policy U-turns the traitors of Philby and his ilk were both ingrained into and flaunting the privileges offered by the educational elite. Each of the Cambridge Five were untouched by embittered resentment, unhindered by state corruption or unashamedly blocked in ambition to achieve their goals even if those goals remained staunchly for the communist cause.

Philby himself was the most damaging of all the traitors becoming the most effective through his intoxicating appeal toward his peers. Philby the universally liked fellow, professional in attitude, competent in skill and methodical in approach was a man of utter contradictions. His wife regarded him as *"divine"* and his colleagues only saw the charming side of this amusing man. Nobody had any idea of Philby's real side, the only side he was truly faithful to himself, the side that was sympathetic to and aided his Soviet masters. His cover was perfect and he worked hard to maintain it through his interpersonal relationships with his peers and this provided the ladder for promotion and access to ever more sensitive secrets. In effect through Philby's manipulative charm offensives, the west unwittingly damaged themselves by allowing a Soviet agent, who was the last person they would suspect to leak secrets to Moscow.

His promotion through the secret service was rapid without attracting the slightest suspicion being seen as possessing the virtues of intelligence and sophistication. This rise effectively groomed Philby for consideration for the ultimate espionage job, to head the British secret service itself in a position known only as 'C'. What a major, somewhat audacious Cold War coup for Moscow it would be if Kim Philby, a Soviet agent was to become the head of MI6.

INTRODUCTION

This effort to ingratiate himself with high levels of the establishment bore fruit less than a decade before he was to finally defect in 1963, the British Foreign Secretary and future Prime Minister, Harold Macmillan stood before Parliament and innocently gave the intelligence chief a big vote of confidence. He stated that any evidence to implicate Philby to the disappearance and subsequent defection of two diplomats to the Soviet Union, Guy Burgess and Donald Maclean in 1951 did not exist. He was wrong; Macmillan was just the latest in a long line of individuals who quite understandably fell into the trap of believing the stories of one of the Cold War's accomplished liars.

The Cambridge Spy ring known in the USSR as the 'Ring of Five' or 'Magnificent Five' was one of the most damaging penetrations of top level security in the post war world. Both Blunt and Carincross aided Maclean and Philby in their quest to ensure that nuclear secrets were leaked in sufficient quantities and that it was real, to ensure the USSR catch up behind America and their Manhattan Project to become the second nation to obtain 'the bomb' before the United Kingdom.

Thanks to the intelligence that Philby and the Cambridge network had access to and what they were prepared to leak, the atomic balance had tipped away from the west and toward the east ensuring that both NATO and the Warsaw Pact (through the Soviet Union) were nuclear capable. The traitor's spying threw the world into a terrifying balance of power. Anthony Blunt himself was a member of the highest of social circles, a distant member of the British Royal family; a testament to how far up the establishment the Soviets had actually penetrated. Carincross was a Scottish civil servant who worked on the highly secretive ULTRA intelligence at Bletchley Park during the Second World War. He was secretly feeding his Soviet masters information about planned German attacks even though the Allies were double crossing the Russians in sending them intelligence that was late or already out of date.

INTRODUCTION

Maclean and Burgess, both were diplomats in the Foreign Office, one an alcoholic, the other homosexual, both attitudes taboo in the positions they occupied. But it was Philby, the senior officer, the man who was privy to some of the most sensitive information of the time who would go on to do the greatest damage to both international relations and to more personal relationships. Some of the intelligence he leaked became indirectly the cause of the Korean War. The very embodiment of treachery, he was revered by his employers, British Intelligence MI6 while all the time he was betraying the very colleagues who admired and stood by him in friendship, and sending others to almost certain death once they were deployed behind the Iron Curtain.

Not all of Philby's victims were professional in the espionage world; many were personal such as the women he married as well as his own children of which he had five throughout his life. Three of these children Philby had while with Aileen, his second wife who although neglected, died in 1957 aged 47 years old and just six years before Philby was to abandon the rest of his family too in his flight to the east.

CHAPTER ONE

ELITIST TO MARXIST

Harold Adrian Russell Philby was born on the 1 January 1912 in the Punjab, a region in the northwest of colonial British India. His father, Harry St John Bridger Philby was a prominent British explorer, writer and more professionally, an intelligence officer for the Colonial Office who converted to Islam. Married to Dora Johnston in 1910, their son was born two years later, the only boy in a family of four where Harold was to grow up with three more sisters. In his infancy, Harold was brought up by a nanny, employed by the family of Indian heritage meaning that the child learned rudimentary Punjabi as well as English, his mother tongue from a very early age. This meant that he could pass as Indian, even though his appearance was white even from this time, something similar to Kimbold O'Hara, the central character of Rudyard Kipling's award winning book *Kim* published in 1901. As a result of this his father referred to his son by a nickname after the Kipling character, 'Kim'.

Harold 'Kim' Philby grew up in a very honoured life, a life where attitudes to colonialism dictates the quality of existence and the advantages open to differing careers. As well as an explorer and writer, his father, John Philby was also a member of the Indian Civil Service, later to transfer to Kuwait, Iraq and Syria in the region of the Middle East spanning the Tigris and Euphrates rivers known as Mesopotamia. Well versed in the Arab and Islamic ways, Philby later transferred from the Civil Service to serve in Saudi Arabia as an advisor to King Ibn Sa'ud, the monarch of the third Saudi State.

The seeds of Kim Philby's double life were rooted within this privileged childhood and as so typical of subjects of the establishment, a bloated sense of their own ability, inflated by the self-belief that they were destined to rule over others in a quest to change the world.

However this Indian colonial lifestyle was not to last forever as the young Harold Philby himself now in England was schooled at Aldro, a boy's preparatory school founded in 1898 at Meads in Eastbourne and now in Surrey close to the town of Godalming where his father had once attended. Kim Philby stayed here until 1925 when at the age of 13 he moved onto the prestigious Westminster School in central London, independent and a major gateway to the Oxford and Cambridge Universities. While here he endured a rather basic lifestyle given the academic status of the school, living in a dormitory while studying in a small and often cool room, with no central heating and only an open fireplace that was lit to keep out the bitter cold of mid-winter. It was a rather Bohemianism life within the walls of elitism.

However Philby did have a strong educational ability that was able to commit himself to a task with vigour and concentration. He was not afraid of hard work and Westminster School embraced liberalism rather than conservatism and the regime reflected this. This meant that the teenager, while suffering inside from an absence of guidance from his father, could adjust well throughout his schooling. The teachers and contemporises noted that Philby possessed a range of aspects to his personality, amusing and distinctly charming every bit as much as he was intelligent, yet slightly rebellious, echoing only slightly the eccentricity of his father. One was Laurence Tanner, a fellow pupil who was born right in the heart of London, within sight of Westminster Abbey itself at 53 Vincent Square on the 12 February 1890. He attended the school between 1905 and 1909 and had happy experiences in the presence of the young Philby. He liked his friends who used their wits and embraced hard work, something which Kim was already practicing, made easier by the liberal regime of the institution. Tanner noticed the resemblance between the boy and his more illustrious father, picking up on his rebellious nature before the influence of heavy politics experienced at university. Admired by both teachers and fellow pupils, Kim Philby had the capacity to go far in whatever career path he was destined to choose.

This proved so for just three years later when at the age of 16 in 1928 Philby gained acceptance to Trinity College at Cambridge through winning a scholarship as he enrolled to read History and Economics at the university.

Soon after his enrolment, Philby found himself mixing in left wing circles, joining one of the many debating societies within the academic institution, the political group the Cambridge University Socialist Society. Most of his student friends already held left wing views and peer pressure was common, but Philby's friends he met here were David Guest and James Klugmann as well as three others, all privileged and all impressionable to radicalisation; Donald Maclean and Guy Burgess. The last one was the most privileged of them all, a distant relative to the Royal Family and already a convert; Anthony Blunt. Philby however was not mixed up in far left wing circles yet. Merely an activist and sympathetic to the left, rather than the more conservative right that his friends were born into, all were destined to turn their backs on the attitudes that brought them up. Dabbling in politics, utilised his activist responsibilities by canvassing for the Labour parliamentary candidate but lost when the local sitting Conservative politician

George Newton retained his seat which he had held since a by-election in 1922.

Philby never suffered any kind of sudden conversion to a political leaning, rather than declaring his allegiance, he simply became more and more sympathetic to more and more left wing views, gradually drifting toward the ideology that would dominate his life and grip his soul. Because of this change, Kim Philby never became a member of the Communist Party outright but instead found himself aligning his views which it promoted; the poor and disadvantaged were continuously being exploited for profit and labour by the rich and the elite.

By 1931 Ramsey MacDonald, the inaugural Labour Prime Minister, a man entrusted by the nation to carry out centre-left socialism in power formed a National Government, a coalition of four different parties and four different agendas in power. Philby saw it as nothing short of a disaster; the traditional Labour movement embodied the policies he so firmly believed in. The brand of socialism he so ardently identified himself with had now been utterly diluted to a point where he could no longer advocate it. Referring to it as the *"Labour disaster of 1931"*, Philby soon started seeking possible alternatives which carried his own beliefs, taking on a more active role in the Cambridge University Socialist Society to a point where he became the Treasurer in 1932 until 1935. This elevated position helped him to come into contact with other more radical left wing members of the Labour Party who were actively critical of the government; many members who expressed these views were sympathetic to communism. A growing appreciation of classical European Socialism from his extensive reading powered the discussions, sometimes heated debates within the walls of the society. Over the next two years Kim Philby would gradually shift his views from the centre-left socialist toward the far-left communist Marxist-Leninism.

One of these individuals who held such radical views and

invariably set him on a course toward the ideology was Maurice Dobb a British economist at Trinity College, Cambridge, and a lecturer in Economics. Dobb, who was the head of St. Andrews was a major Marxist economist, one of the most pre-eminent ones of the 20th Century and someone who Philby came into contact with while still a student. Dobb himself had a colourful background having joined the Communist Party of Great Britain in 1922 and was openly forthright about his views to his students. Marxist Theory was only beginning to flourish and Dobb's advocating for this only had a limited impact upon his students despite however passionate the academic was in promoting it.

Eric Hobsbawn, a historian on industrialisation, Marxism, nationalism and capitalism was Dobb's friend who knew about Dobb's activities in relation to being in touch with the Cambridge socialists and his membership of the Communist Party. However Dobb did stand out in both groups, being well dressed and sporting a rather upper class, bourgeois attitude made him appear, at least on the surface to be the very opposite of the blue collar stereotype that the Marxist movement typically attracted. Despite this Dobb was committed to his cause, acutely loyal to the Communist Party all his life as a radical academic. Not all of his students believed in his political views, some students were even angered, up to the point where some of them actually kidnapped their tutor and threw him into the River Cam. Dobb suffered this kind of abuse more than once, given the controversial nature of his views, but it didn't last; Dobb was unshakable from his Marxist beliefs, so much so that his tormentors eventually gave up trying to get him to convert to less radical views.

St Andrews was situated in Chesterton Lane and it was here that Dobb hosted on a frequent basis communist students for debates, so much so that it was known widely as 'The Red House'. Dobb's inflammatory rhetoric on Marxist theory coupled with the debates held within the halls of St Andrews made for a hotbed of political stirring. Young impressionable students were taught the message about the decline of capitalism, that Marxism was effectively classless meaning everyone was equal, and the high superiority of fashionable materialism. The result of this was a general world view and a very acute method to solving specific problems; it was basic doctrine of communism. People like Philby, who was taught by Dobb found the ideas and opinions (known as dialectical) relating to materialism appealing. Once he understood this philosophy, he was captivated like a religious convert; finally seeing where he realistically stood in life. Maurice Dobb had succeeded in converting Kim Philby away from his privileged, elitist upbringing and the perceived arrogance that came with it, to the radicalisation of Marxism.

Philby, while taking part in the rather heated discussions of the debating society, also began reading literature on European socialism all the time developing a fondness of the subject during his conversion to the extreme left. By 1933 Philby graduated with an upper second degree after gaining a third in the History paper in 1931 and a second in the Economic papers two years later. Philby therefore obtained a degree in Economics while at Cambridge, but he was not to pursue such a career instead upon his very last day at the university he made a profound decision; to throw off his last doubt and solidify his found belief in Marxism by deciding to embrace communism, for which he was sure he must now devote his life to for good.

Philby was like a man reborn, with a chilling devotion to the decision of his mind, an unwavering commitment to his untrusted judgement in the fanaticism that suddenly gripped him for which seemed totally logical. Communism was like a faith, and he was not going to lose it because of human cruelties or ill judgement on the part of his peers. Political policy and the evil perpetuated by the decisions taken in power would have no bearing now upon the effect for which the cause had on Philby's mind. To him there was a means to an end because there was logic to following communism. The west, the elitist, capitalist west was corrupt beyond the point of redemption, and the notion of communism was the only ideology strong enough to stand up to the spectre of fascism and Nazism growing on the continent.

Now radicalised he approached the lecturer he most admired, Maurice Dobb and asked him the very direct but discreet question on how he should go about it, stating that he wanted to devote his life to the communist cause. Instead of directing his former pupil to London where the headquarters of the Communist Party of Great Britain was situated, Dobb, who though that perhaps a recruit like Philby would be more effective in Europe, simply handed him an introductory note to the executive of the International Workers Relief Organisation. Philby was also introduced to the World Federation for the Relief of the Victims of German Fascism, a legal communist group located in the French capital Paris. It was operated by the German politician Willi Munzenberg a communist activist and a leading propagandist of the Communist Party of Germany who fled the Reichstag in 1933 after the Nazis came to power. The newly graduated Philby arrived in the city and immediately contacted the group on the directions given to him by Dobb who sent him to meet Louis Gibarti an agent of the Comintern (to broaden the influence of communism) based in Paris. Making his sympathies known, Philby was eventually put in contact with a communist organisation in Austria, which was then influenced by the Nazi government over the border in Germany and the capital Vienna was a maelstrom of anti-communist fascistic style turbulence. The underground there urgently needed volunteers to help smuggle wanted men, fellow communists and socialists, all wanted by the state prior to a crackdown on leftists by the administration of Chancellor Engelbert Dollfuss in 1934, out of the country to safety.

Kim Philby was now firmly to establish himself in the Austrian capital, to working tirelessly to aid the seemingly endless numbers of fleeing refugees out of Nazi Germany, those who were not wanted by the far-right wing state, and those liable for persecution.

CHAPTER TWO

SCHNAPPS IN VIENNA, VODKA IN LONDON

Kim Philby had arrived in Austria in 1933 and was instantly set up by Gibrati who arranged for him to live in the house of Israel and Gisella Kohlman and pay rent for lodgings. It was here he came into contact for the first time with their recently divorced daughter Litzi Friedmann (nee Kohlmann), who was also staying there while separated. Born under the name of Alice Kohlmann in 1910, Friedmann was a dark haired Austrian-Hungarian woman with Jewish ethnicity and drastic socialistic views. She had already joined the still illegal Austrian Communist Party and held low profile links with the secret service of the Soviet Union, the NKVD. Her Communist Party membership was a post which landed her in prison for some weeks although her association to the Soviets was not known. Despite this she retained her political stance, something which Philby upon meeting her admired greatly. Kim had only just arrived from Cambridge and was willing to learn German, Austria's official language.

He found her a direct, almost blunt type of person to deal with when upon their first meeting she could see him as both a useful helper and a source of potential party funds. She directly came out and asked how much money he had, to which Philby replied that he possessed £100. This, he hoped, would help him to last 12 months in the Austrian capital but Litzi surprised him by doing some quick sums. The answer astonished the young Englishman, announcing that his finances would in fact leave him with a more pleasing £25 in his pocket. But as forthright as she appeared, she was not going to let him keep it, boldly stating that he can give it to the International for Aid Revolutionaries who desperately required funds. Her demeanour pleasantly surprised Philby who admired her strong will and determination; he agreed to help her. Amidst an instant attraction, the pair started going out together as the young Cambridge graduate fell in love with the 23 year old Litzi who could see that Kim already held some very left wing views as an intellectual convert to communism.

Travelling as a courier between the city and the Czech capital Prague, out of the remaining £75 he purchased train tickets, discreetly channelling money through begging and other materials such as clothes to refugees fleeing Nazi persecutions. Other times he would aid in smuggling militants out of Vienna, all the time observing what the fight against fascism and the effects of the risks people took to fight it meant. He achieved this aim by using his passport as cover to evade the authorities who may investigate his actions which were becoming ever more drastic under the influence of Litzi. Kim Philby was being radicalised and his experiences in Vienna along with the struggle against the fascists only strengthened his conviction to the communist cause.

By February 1934 a suppression of all known radicals was initiated by Chancellor Dollfuss; the targets were communists and socialists. Mass arrests took place, 1,500 people in all were detained by the authorities causing turmoil throughout the country. Amidst all this, Friedmann knew the police were hunting her since she was a known communist and the only way for her to avoid arrest herself was to marry Kim. Philby realised that his passport would soon became a valuable document particularly in protecting Litzi Friedmann if she was his wife. Additionally it would provide a ticket out of the country in the increasing tensions occurring in

Vienna, including ever more valid threats against the Chancellor. Their relationship was at this time blossoming and on the 24 February he and Litzi formally married at Vienna Town Hall as much for convenience as it was for love.

At the same time they tied the knot, tensions broke out across Austria between a group called the socialist Schutzbund and the Social Democrats (which Philby himself was a sympathiser). Open violence occurred across the country, including Vienna resulting in the members of the Schutzbund exchanging small arms fire with the police while barricaded within housing estates as fortified strongholds. Such estates were ardent symbols of socialism throughout the city and now they were forming the front line of the February Uprising part of the wider Austrian Civil War of the early 1930's.

By March Philby left Vienna amongst the turmoil along with Friedmann as his wife back to the United Kingdom. Settling in the house of his mother Dora in London, this was where they were based now for the time being. It was here where Kim's mother could sense the change in her son, something had happened in Vienna, but he had changed in his attitude toward society. It prompted her to write to her husband, Kim's father, St John Philby, now based in Saudi Arabia, highlighting her concerns about their son's world view:

"I do hope Kim gets a job to get him off this bloody communism. He's not quite extreme yet, but he may become so."

Kim Philby's communist views were surfacing for those who knew him to see. Yet in time he would develop the skill to hide it so well, even from those who would go on to know him for most of his life and those who were supposed to be experts in the field of deception.

Soon the couple came into contact with Freidmann's friend, an Austrian born British woman by the name of Edith Tudor Hart who had fled to London the previous year along with her husband the medical doctor Alex Tudor Hart. Edith herself was of Jewish heritage, dangerous in the anti-Semitic atmosphere of Europe, but was also an ardent anti-fascist activist and committed communist. A photographer by profession, she was also, in the strictest confidence, a spy working for the Soviet Union and was therefore in the perfect position to help recruit such like-minded individuals. Litzi Freidmann radicalised Philby toward not just the communist cause, but also that of the USSR and Tudor Hart was the perfect gateway into the world of Soviet espionage.

However the open door into this murky world was through another. In January of 1934, just before the February Uprising that was to grip Vienna, an Austrian-Hungarian academic was sent to the British capital to study psychology at post-graduate level at London University. Travelling under his own name so his credentials would be valid, his name was Arnold Deutsch, also a Soviet agent and member of the NKVD, possessing a doctorate and working in academia as cover for his spying activities in the United Kingdom. Five months passed before he made contact with his compatriot and fellow communist Litzi Friedmann where upon meeting the topic of potential recruitment of others was discussed. Litzi knew of a perfect recruit; her husband Kim Philby.

Litzi knew just how passionate Philby was about the ideology and just how far she had radicalised him; enough for him to seriously betray his country and the establishment which was so fundamental to its way of life. She knew her husband's socialist views made him turn his back on the privileged and elite, and it was this elitism which could position Philby into acceptance into high flying jobs where an agent could gain access to the most sensitive of secrets. It seemed that Kim Philby could potentially be a useful asset if he could be turned. Also present was Edith Tudor Hart, the fellow spy who had known Deutsch since 1926 when the two worked together providing funding for communist parties outside the Soviet Union at the International Liaison Department.

As such this was a highly secretive organisation within the wider Comintern.

Tudor Hart agreed to the suggestion and ran a background check on the potential recruit. It proved favourable to them as nothing of concern was found which prompted Deutsch, thanks to his long association and trust of Edith, to authorise a preliminary meeting with Philby. This was to analyse whether or not he would be ideal as a Soviet spy, the usual course of action when recruiting operatives. However this time he agreed to meet Philby sooner than normal on recommendation from the checks and suggestion from both women.

By June 1934 Litzi, which Philby affectionately called 'Lizzy' arrived home one evening to deliver some urgent news to her husband. Informing him that she had arranged a meeting with a *"man of decisive importance"* for which Kim had no idea what she meant. Questioning her, Litzi refused to give details on the man's true identity nor the purpose or subject of the meeting; all she would divulge is the location, Regent's Park in central London.

Intrigued Philby attended the meeting as required, in Regent's Park on the 1 July 1934 to meet with the man, not large in frame, but stout in the body, and 5 foot 7 inches tall. Referring to himself just by the name 'Otto', the blue eyed, light hared man wanted to move toward asking Philby one direct question; would he be willing to spy for the Soviet Union? The way for Deutsch to achieve this was by talking to him at length about his background and family, reiterating that someone like Philby could do so much more for communism than just a sympathiser or normal party activist. The rhetoric struck a chord with the young Englishman. Already radicalised, Philby was beginning to allow himself to be seduced by Deutsch, who even though he was a communist, he possessed a more cultural streak every bit as passionate as his political one. He adored Paris, and often spoke about it affectionately, citing many cultural references as well as demonstrating a wonderful sense of humour to relax any nerves. This personality mix proved deadly as Deutsch started to play on Kim's passion for his chosen ideology in a sort of perverse, twisted emotional abuse. Yet the two men clearly had a lot in common, and Philby himself seems to have been captivated by the Soviet recruiter, noting that Deutsch made him feel like the most important thing, the only thing that mattered at that very moment through powerful eye contact. It was a useful and sweet seduction technique to dilute and wash away any clamour of doubt echoing in a potential recruit's mind.

In all the young man could not resist any longer. Finally he agreed and with that Arnold Deutsch had succeeded in recruiting Philby. From being a sympathetic communist at Cambridge to a radical communist in Vienna and London, he had now taken the final, ultimate step. Turning his back on everything he had known and understood, Kim Philby had committed himself to a life of lies and treason. Kim Philby was to be a traitor to the United Kingdom and the west and was to be a spy for, and therefore pledge his allegiance to, the Soviet Union.

Meanwhile Deutsch himself reported that Philby was ideal as an agent, citing his father's ambitious nature and almost tyrannically wanted to make something out of his son by repressing all of his desires. Deutsch also noted that Philby spoke with a slight stammer, something that would blight him for most of his life, but was not detrimental. On the contrary it only increased his difference being that he was shy and somewhat hesitant, something which actually could help his cover. Deutsch also reported to his superiors that Philby would be capable of handling finances in a rather careful manner and had a very great respect for honesty (which was a very ironic and one-sided statement). The NKVD man concluded his report by stressing Philby's total loyalty to the cause by stating that his turning was so complete that he would be willing to do anything asked of him without question with the upmost seriousness. Deutsch tried to paint Philby as a complete convert to communism, so much that he would be willing to betray his country to achieve his aims. It worked.

One of the very first acts Deutsch asked was if there was any other like-minded individuals Philby knew of and if so to make a list of their names. Kim knew his old acquaintances were of a similar disposition to himself and their very first person who came to mind was his old Cambridge University friend Donald Maclean. Both men had been a part of the Cambridge University Socialist Society and after education had entered the Foreign Office, an ideal position to be in for sensitive information to be leaked.

Maclean was still in touch with Philby who invited him to dinner. Over the table the two men conversed during which, Kim hinted to his old friend that there was important work to be done of a secretive nature of course, for the Soviet Union. This was inflammatory, but Philby tried to get around any reservations his old friend would have by wetting his appetite, tantalisingly stating that the people he could introduce Maclean to were serious indeed. Already sympathetic to the communist cause, Donald agreed to meet Arnold Deutsch, Philby's recruiter. To positively identify him, Maclean was told to bring with him a bright yellow book into a local cafe at a pre-designated time. This he did, and upon Kim Philby's recommendation, Donald Maclean kept his appointment, carrying out the instructions to initiate a successful contact with the NKVD man. As the two men conversed together, Deutsch found Maclean an impressive individual; Philby clearly had made a shrewd choice in bringing him into the fold. He came across as aloof but serious, and thanks to his background, he had useful connections; ideal for a spy. Just like Kim Philby, Arnold Deusch had succeeded in turning Donald Maclean to the east, persuading him to turn his back on the west and spy for the Soviet Union. Eventually he was issued a codename, something which was common practice for all agents. Maclean's was 'Orphan'. But there was one final thing 'Orphan' had to do to solidify his cover for his future spying activities; cut all ties with his communist friends and distance himself from the ideology.

It was through Philby that another old friend, now in the government, Guy Burgess was also met by Deutsch. Guy, a secretary to the Deputy Foreign Minister, was more volatile than either Kim or Donald which did not impress his potential recruiter. Deutsch sensed that his weakness was he exhibited a rather superficial nature and that could be a risk in letting something slip if things did not add up although he did note that the young man was smart. Maclean went around telling anyone he could that he had swapped the philosophy of Karl Marx for that of Benito Mussolini, desperately trying to position himself in anyone's eyes toward the Italian brand of right wing fascism. For his part Burgess did not buy this story, he knew his old friend too well and actually began to suspect that Maclean was himself recruited by the Soviets even going so far as to directly accuse his old friend. He knew that he had not relinquished his old communist tendencies and that only fuelled his suspicions when confronting Donald:

"Do you think that I believe for even one jot that you have stopped being a communist? You're simply up to something."

Burgess had found Maclean out, even though he had not said anything, prompting him to go back to Deutsch to inform him of the conversation. The Soviet controller had no choice but to also sign him up as well albeit reluctantly and with trepidation.

In turn Burgess suggested another of the old gang, his long-time friend Anthony Blunt. Blunt was the highest of all in the social hierarchy, being a member of the British Royal Family, portraying the image of a young artistic academic. He himself became influenced by the concept of Marxism under encouragement of his friend Guy Burgess. Both himself and Burgess were scandalously (at the time) homosexual and both former members of the much vaulted secret society, Cambridge Apostles (something who Philby and Maclean were also members of), and actually lived together in a non-sexual arrangement. This placed Burgess the recent communist convert, in a position to manoeuvre his friend to treachery. Blunt was an art expert and many of his critiques illustrated his defence of social realism exhibiting ever more savagery against anything depicted out of touch from the far left wing. In time he would even come to attack the work of even his favourite artist, Pablo Picasso, in particular his famous depiction of Guernica for its incorrect inclusion of communism.

While Burgess was busy recruiting Blunt for the cause, Kim Philby meanwhile had to make the most out of his spying duties, by creating as perfect a background as possible. This meant following Maclean in distancing himself, along with his wife from all their communist connections including friends with similar tendencies. In its place he was required to establish himself as more right wing in his views, something which he would find abhorrent but it was a necessity if he was to position himself to aid his new ideology. His new political image was now on the extreme; as a sympathiser to Nazism, a contemporary to the very ideology he was directly opposed to. Philby was informed by Deutsch that the bourgeoisie needed to be entered by people who were secretly anti-fascists in an attempt to justify what he was asking his recruit to do. Philby agreed to the guise even though he hated it as he was given a small gift from his master; a subminiture Minox camera, perfect for covert photography. Kim Philby now started to learn the trade he would execute so well, all under the guidance of Deutsch who issued him with the codename 'Sohnchen' and taught him the skills that would turn his young convert into one of the most damaging spies to the west and one of the greatest ever assets to the east. During his training, Philby learnt of safe places to leave messages, how to safely arrange meetings with contacts and how to tell if his telephone was bugged. Deutsch also taught him how to tell if he was being followed and how to lose the tail if he was.

With him learning the tricks of the trade, Philby's spying career began rather close to home. For his first ever assignment, he was to betray one of the people closest to him, his father. St John Philby was well known as a diplomat and the Soviets believed he was in possession of sensitive documents kept in the family home, in his office. Philby's task was to spy on his father and ascertain as much information as possible.

It was not long before Philby was told by Deutsch to get a job in journalism as this would be excellent cover for his Soviet spying activities. His background and education would be no problem in gaining employment and his first 'real' job was at the World Review of Reviews, a monthly publication concerning political and literary matters where he was employed as a sub-editor. According to his instructions to move away from communist sympathetic views as cover for his spying activities, he started to move toward more right-wing circles by moving on to the Anglo-German Trade Gazette. This was a magazine dedicated to improving relations economically between both Britain and Germany and was financed in part by the Nazi government. To keep up the pretence, Philby also enrolled in the pro-fascist society, the Anglo-German Fellowship which had been formed in 1935 to promote increased understanding with Adolf Hitler. Philby hated this; it was absolutely the opposite of everything he believed in, but his mentor, the ever persuasive Deutsch kept him on track by stressing that the very political nature of this radical group offered camouflage for the spy's real loyalties. Nobody would ever suspect Philby as a communist if he was part of and openly expressed Nazi-sympathetic, pro-fascist views. It was hard, but it was perfect for now as he was in a position to spy on the very group he had penetrated, and gain intelligence to pass onto the Soviets about pro-fascist activities in the United Kingdom.

Even though this was his cover for now, Philby still could not help but find it repulsive because he knew that he looked very much a pro-Nazi even to his friends no matter how conservative they were. However not all his friends found his political stance unrecognisable. Malcolm Muggeridge the writer and vehement anti-communist after witnessing the brutal hardships of Stalin's regime, was one of many who actually fell for Philby's deceptions. He could believe his pro-fascist stance, noting that he could see that he was attracted to the Anglo-German Fellowship calling it *"nonsense"*. Muggeridge noticed that Kim was a man with political subtlety with a keen eye for opportunities and becoming pro-Nazi would fit in with the perceived character that others saw in him. It was clear that Philby's cover and lies were working to the desired effect. Muggeridge also concluded that he admired Josef Goebbels, the Nazi propaganda puppet and was someone that he could work with while expecting him to actually become a National Socialist at any time. It was all Philby's lies and all part of his master cover story. To perpetuate the illusion, he rarely spoke about politics even though people could see that his sympathies lay vaguely on the left, but it was nothing more severe than the intelligentsia embraced at the time. It appeared to others that for Kim any such expression was more romantic, where it was more reckless buccaneering in the manifestation of drinking and womanising, more at home in the circle of Nazi bullies rather than radical communist patriotism. So complete was his cover because it reflected the politics of the time given the bandwagon interactions between the German and western governments that it was rather easy, if not morally repugnant for Philby to keep up his pretence.

By now a spy network had been developed through Deutsch who was responsible for recruiting a total of twenty-five men during his deployment in the United Kingdom. This included the Cambridge Five, otherwise known as the Cambridge Spy Ring; all influential individuals both in their professions and with each other. Donald Maclean, Guy Burgess, Anthony Blunt, were all part of this devastating group. But by far the most damaging would be Kim Philby. Different spies would have varying degrees of success, but what made the Cambridge Spy Ring so effective was that all members, including if not most of all, Philby were all driven by ideology. All were committed to the communist cause because they all incorrectly believed, perhaps blindly, in the myth surrounding the truths surrounding Stalin's rule in the Soviet Union. Communists, particularly those who tried to recruit into the intelligence services, portrayed the USSR as a social justice state which provided equally for all. In truth Stalinism was a vehicle for brutal dictatorial practices where anyone and everyone who did not fall into the party line were 'removed' one way or another. Soviet Russia also housed under Stalin, the largest gulag (work camps) in peacetime history. The gulags themselves were the very symbolism of the oppression through either threat or action Stalin imposed upon the Soviet state.

However these facts were not shared widely. Even Deutsch himself shared a similar vision to his recruits, perhaps helping to explain his persuasive nature, in the future where people would no longer be exploited under capitalism. The liberation message the Deutsch portrayed had a sexual as well as social and political implications, something which appealed to the homosexual Burgess and Blunt; a state where they would be free to practice their sexuality without fear or intimidation. Britain in the 1930's still held onto a rather rigid class system as well as strict sexual preferences; homosexuality simply was not tolerated in society, indeed it was an illegal practice, even if consensual. Philby however was strictly heterosexual, but still hated the inequality and lack of social mobility generated by the class system.

By 1937 things started to change. Philby's mentor Arnold Deutsch was recalled back to Moscow amidst a time when his own position in Western Europe was in danger of being discovered thanks to the high level defections of Soviet operatives Walter Krivitsky and Ignace Reiss. This was a time of great upheaval in the Stalinist brand of Soviet communism; Stalin himself was initiating the deadly Moscow Trials, part of the wider, lethal cleansing in the Soviet Union known as the Great Officer Purge for which Deutsch himself would eventually escape. He was replaced by Theodore Maly whose code name was 'Man', the Hungarian born Roman Catholic priest turned Soviet intelligence agent who would go on to be the controller of not only Philby, but his other friends in the spy network. By this time John Carincross, another rather uncommunicative student at Cambridge Trinity College was also recruited completing the Cambridge Five Spy Ring as well as another, an American known as Michael Straight. Deutsch had already initiated the recruitments but it was now Maly's job to handle the spies, all of them including Philby.

Philby and his friend's new controller was an imposing man, slightly grey in complexion and towering over them at six feet four inches tall, complete with gold fillings in his teeth. Despite this, Maly was rather gentle in his controlling and singled Philby out for admiration just like his predecessor Deutsch. In fact Maly saw Philby's capability to be inspirational, referring to him as a *"true comrade"*. Arnold Deutsch like them both, noting that they were both good people as well as being similarly intelligent and experienced.

However by May that same year, Maly was recalled to Moscow, just as Stalin's Terror was taking hold, leading to the Great Officer Purge for which himself would eventually be brutally interrogated and forced to confess to being a German agent, something which would see him executed the following year. Philby therefore as well as seventeen other agents including the rest of the Cambridge Spy Ring was to be handled by a Resident Spy (Rezident) with the Soviet Secret Police, known as the Joint State Political Directorate, the OGPU (superseding agency of the former GPU) by the name of Anatoly Gorsky whose code name was 'Kap'.

Philby was now firmly entrenched in the world of Soviet espionage. His cover of being pro-fascist was holding up and he had instrumental in forming the Cambridge Spy ring that was destined to penetrate and wreak havoc in the heart of the British government and security services. But now Kim Philby, as part of this world was to get his first foreign assignment as a fully-fledged Soviet spy. He was to be sent to Spain, where the fascist General Franco and the Nationalists was waging a bitter civil war against the Republicans in the country.

CHAPTER THREE

DEMOCRACY AND FASCISM

Both Kim Philby and his wife Litzi already had a taste of Spain having already travelled there on behalf of the NKVD as early as February 1934, while he was being radicalised and before he pledged his future to the Soviet Union. Even though the allegiance was sound, it was not long before Philby's marriage started to concern his Soviet controllers given his new right wing public image, his relationship with Litzi pointed to left-wing views.

Litzi was becoming a liability to Kim given that she was a constant reminder of his time in Vienna, thus posing a huge risk that his communist sympathising past could catch up with him to his friends and family. It could also be construed that he rescued this girl through his British citizenship from arrest for being a known communist and that his marriage was a way out to safety. It was vital that the Russians wanted to preserve the right wing illusion that Kim was building up meaning his relationship with the Jewish woman was going to hamper his progress and possibly expose him in the future. The Soviet control therefore decided they could not let this potential asset go informing both him and his wife somewhat uncompromisingly that perhaps it would be better if Philby acted as a sole operator, meaning he would have to dispose of Litzi as his wife. Something Kim discussed with his close friend Jim Lees.

Still in London Philby decided to learn to speak Russian and subsequently submitted an application to enrol at the School of

Slavonic Languages to do so. Elitist connections invariably helped his submission as his father was a friend of the director thus ensuring his son, of whom he had no idea as to his communist calling, a place. The school which had only been founded in 1915 by the future President of Czechoslovakia, Tomas Garrigue Masaryk also taught people in the fine art of diplomacy, ideal for a future career in either the Foreign Office or even the intelligence services. It was a goldmine for an aspiring communist agent, but only managing to learn Russian to only a rudimentary level, nowhere near fluent at all.

However upon the completion of his studies Philby managed to take a journalistic job working for the World Review of Reviews, a monthly periodical for which he wrote both articles occasionally serving as the acting editor. He followed this up with another assignment this time with a trade magazine called the Anglo-Russian Trade Gazette in 1936 which was by this time a failing publication and was in the process of converting its focus to cover business news with Germany instead. Through this was an opportunity to solidify his cover as a pro-fascist rather than his true communist tendencies and he subsequently tried to make contact with the German ambassador in London at the time Joachim von Ribbentrop. Through this courting of the Germans and as a result of his secretly hated membership of the Anglo-German Fellowship Philby made frequent trips right into the heart of right wing fascism, the capital of Nazi Germany, Berlin.

Things began to change in July that same year. Philby had been seeking ways to distance himself from Litzi and her well known communist stance to preserve his own cover but now far away political events swung an unexpected opportunity into his lap. In Spain a declaration of opposition a so-called *pronunciamiento* was issued by a group of Republican Army generals thus sparking events that would eventually degenerate into a vicious civil war in the country. Hitler's Nazi Germany and Mussolini's Fascist Italy supported the right-wing Nationals but the Stalin's Soviet Union supported the leftist Republicans under President Manuel Azana. Kim Philby acting under the codename agent 'Sonny' was therefore able to travel under the cover of a freelance journalist as a correspondent for the London newspaper The Times, a position he had held since May of that year and spy upon the Nationalists under the command of General Fransisco Franco. During this first covert assignment he was to record details including the moral of the troops, their strategic movements and to monitor communications of supporting troops to Franco, chiefly German and Italian forces sent by Berlin and Rome. His controller Theodore Maly instructed Philby to specifically look out for any security weaknesses through discovering how Franco was guarded by his entourage. It was clear that the NKVD wanted Philby to get as close to the Nationalist leader as possible. A typical article published by Philby for The Times dated 28 April 1937 is as follows:

"It is feared that the conflagration destroyed much of the evidence of its origin, but it is felt here that enough remains to support the Nationalist contention that incendiaries on the Basque side had more to do with the razing of Guernica than General Franco's aircraft. . . . Few fragments of bombs have been recovered, the facades of buildings still standing are unmarked, and the few craters I inspected were larger than anything hitherto made by a bomb in Spain. From their positions it is a fair inference that these craters were caused by exploding mines which were unscientifically laid to cut roads. In view of these circumstances it is difficult to believe that Guernica was the target of bombardment of exceptional intensity by the Nationalists or an experiment with incendiary bombs, as it is alleged by the Basques."

Away from this his initial public deployment as a journalist was too good to pass up and was noticed by Britain's own security agencies. Employing his services British Intelligence MI6 therefore approached hoping to use him as a part time spy reporting on the Nationalist activities completely unaware that he was actually spying for the Soviets.

Observing and secretly filing his reports he used very different methods to get information back to each of his masters. For intelligence bound for MI6 Philby simply delivered post through Hendaye a town in the north Pyrenean region on the French-Spanish border bound for the British embassy in Paris. But to send information to the Soviet handler in Paris Ozolin Haskins, a Latvian operating under the code name 'Pierre' he used a slightly more complicated plan, hiding his reports as coded words hidden in love letters written to Mlle Dupont, a fictitious girlfriend again in Paris. Philby did not know this yet, but the address he used for his 'love' was in reality publicly that of the Soviet embassy where his notes were easily intercepted by the Russians.

Interestingly both Britain and Russia wanted the same thing from Philby, reports on the performance of German military equipment sent to help Franco in the civil war. Both nations were especially interested in the efficiency of Germany's main battle tanks the Panzer's I and II as well as the Luftwaffe's chief fighter the Messerschmitt Bf109 deployed in the country. There was an additional worry for the British, the raging of the civil war, from which the initial revolution that sparked the conflict began in the south, could affect Gibraltar. Indeed if Franco won out and toppled the Republicans, would there be guarantees that he would not allow military access for German troops to invade the British territory in the event of a wider war?

So complete was Philby's deception that he was well liked and integrated extremely well with the Nationalists who suspected nothing of his spying on them. His penetration of the Nationalist movement was so deep that he achieved access to General Franco himself. This allowed him under his journalist guise to pose the question of whether or not his forces intended to allow German troops to take Gibraltar to which Franco assured the British that he would never allow the German army to cross into his country. British Intelligence was satisfied with what their mole had discovered.

Meanwhile Theodore Maly told the NKVD that he had already briefed in person Philby's requirement to reporting on Franco and his personal security for a proposed assassination attempt to remove him and cripple the right-wing movement. However Philby returned to London in May of 1937 and was secretly debriefed personally by Maly on the 24th. It was clear that Kim Philby did not possess the right qualities to become an assassin. Lacking physical courage though making up for it in a devotion to the cause whatever the price, he just did not possess the ice cold killer instinct, the ability to detach one's emotions from a situation in order to kill another human being. Maly therefore duly reported to Moscow that even though his devotion to duty shone through and he was willing to sacrifice himself if ordered he did not possess the right qualities necessary for an assassination attempt. The act to kill General Franco therefore was not a real possibility.

It was around this time a great upheaval began to intensify high up in the Soviet command. The political repression known as the Great Purge had been occurring in Russia throughout the 1930's but starting in 1937 this purge was to enter its most destructive phase known as Yezhovism. By now the Soviet leader Josef Stalin in his paranoia became irrationally concerned that Soviet agents deployed in other counties could be clandestinely supporting the Theory of World Revolution postulated by the Marxist revolutionary and theorist Leon Trotsky. A new section within the Soviet secret police by Nikolai Yezhov the head of the NKVD (of which Yezhovism is named after) set up the innocuous sounding Administration of Special Tasks. This new section was staffed by three hundred of the most loyal members of the Central Committee of the Communist Party whose job it was under the control of

Yezhov to execute sensitive duties without any hesitation. Therefore these three hundred men would not be allied to any one department of the NKVD and therefore free to operate totally autonomously. This allowed them to carry out assignments against any part of the organisation at will.

With this mandate the Administration of Special Tasks was therefore used to arrest the former head of the NKVD Genrikh Yagoda, an early victim of the purge widely known as Stalin's Terror. This extended to include all others who had knowledge of any conspiracy to neutralise the Soviet leader's rivals by any means. The Administration used the Mobile Group, a secret unit tasked with dealing with those within the Soviet hierarchy believed to be supporters of Trotsky. Under the command of Mikhail Shpiegelglass by mid-1937 the Mobile Group had summoned over forty intelligence agents working abroad back to the Soviet Union. Those who were ordered back to the Motherland were Philby's recruiter and first controller Arnold Deutsch as well as his current handler Theodore Maly amongst many others. Maly himself was certainly not oblivious to the bigger picture stating:

"If they don't kill me there, they'll kill me here. Better to die there."

Most were ruthlessly murdered as part of the Purge with Deutsch although interrogated, managing to escape the fate of execution. However as for Maly, upon his return to Moscow in the midst of Stalin's Terror he was positioned at the Lubyanka, the head offices of the NKVD which was becoming increasingly cramped due to the effects of the purges. Meanwhile the man who was handling Philby's intelligence gathered in Spain through their embassy in Paris, Ozolin Haskins under the code name 'Pierre' was himself assassinated by shooting as part of the Terror. Maly who still in Moscow hoped for a return west into Europe to resume his operations. However in July the defection of the Austro-Hungarian spy Ignaz Reiss, a recipient of the Order of the Red

Banner dashed his hopes. Reiss, who was disturbed at the Purge, informed Stalin of his flight through a letter which prompted the NKVD to assassinate him in Switzerland a few weeks later. Furthermore Reiss' old friend Walter Krivitsky a fellow Soviet agent and NKVD officer in Paris who had originally hesitated himself also fled which only served to fuel the rampant paranoia of the Soviet leader. All this spelt bad news for Maly who would eventually go on to be arrested and imprisoned. A year later in 1938 Theodore Maly would be subjected to Stalin's brutal torture methods in order to confess to being a Nazi spy after which he would be committed to a sentence of death under Article 58 of the Criminal Code and would be executed by a single shot to the head shortly afterwards.

By now Kim Philby found himself an outside victim of Stalin's Terror. His controller in Paris, Ozolin Haskins had been shot and Theodore Maly had gone back to the Soviet Union, it seemed that each of Philby's contacts was being systematically liquidated. Another agent, Boris Shapak was tasked with taking over the Philby network for the time being.

By late 1937 Kim was back in Spain reporting on the conduct of the war from the Nationalist side for The Times once more. Again he wrote glowing articles about Franco despite reporting undercover for the Soviets but in his official role as a reporter he found himself close to the city of Teruel in the east of the country by December. There along with other journalists he was reporting on the Battle of Teruel which was raging in the area at the time, one of the bloodier engagements of the civil war perhaps controversially along with the German bombing of Guernica. Covering the events of the battle, Philby found himself travelling in a car alongside journalists from other agencies including Bradish Johnson from Newsweek, Edward J. Neil from the Associated Press and Ernest Sheepshanks from Reuters. Travelling down a road and scoffing on chocolates a shell suddenly struck just in front of the vehicle and exploded killing Johnson outright and injuring fatally both Sheepshanks and Neil. Only Philby miraculously survived with only a light head wound.

It was a charmed existence and surviving the attack meant Philby continued his double life fitting in well with Franco's Nationalists. Therefore being able to conduct his subversive duties while promoting his cover as a journalist, even managed to get several pro-fascists articles and praising reports on Franco and the Nationalist efforts published in The Times without any trouble. It was this integration with Franco's men and the surviving of the accident which enabled him to receive from the General himself the Red Cross of Military Merit on the 2 March 1938. It opened a few doors for him around the fascists ironically helping his communist masters now that he was able to penetrate further. Before this the Spanish Nationalists criticised the British press for their left-wing and it seemed to them, a pro-communist bias but upon Philby being decorated personally by the leader he became known as the 'English decorated by Franco' which changed their attitude somewhat. It was this change that allowed Philby to entrench himself deeper in right-wing circles.

By now Walter Krivitsky who had already defected to France after Reiss' murder decided to flee from the country and the continent to the United States. There he testified in front of the Dies Committee set up to report on subversive activities, reporting on his experiences of being employed within Stalin's secret service as well as providing details of Soviet espionage within the United States.

Meanwhile back in Europe Philby's controller in Madrid Alexander Mikhailovich Orlov code-named 'Swede' also defected to the west. Orlov was a General in the NKVD whom Philby had met before in the French city of Perpignan but in 1938 he was made aware of Stalin's Terror through the subsequent disappearance, torture and shooting of close associates. Alerted by these incidents Orlov quickly realised that his turn would soon come, something which occurred when he received orders to travel to the Belgian port of Antwerp and report to a Soviet ship waiting there. Fuelling his certainty that he was about to be arrested as part of the Great Purge he travelled to Paris before fleeing with his family, a wife and daughter to Canada and its capital Quebec instead.

Orlov therefore left two letters before departing with the Soviet Ambassador, one addressed to the NKVD chief Nikolai Yezhov and the other for Stalin himself. Both contained threats that he was willing to reveal details of Soviet operations should anything happen to either himself or his family. To accentuate his threat Orlov cited the codenames of spies and moles currently deployed in the west. However to protect other members of his family still living within the USSR, he chose not to reveal anything about Kim Philby, something which appeased Stalin somewhat.

Now free from any threat of exposure and his cover intact Philby himself had now arrived back in London from Spain once more. It was here that he contacted Flora Solomon, born in 1895 in Pinsk, Imperial Russia and a long-time friend. Solomon had already seen Philby while he was working as a Times correspondent in Spain and would eventually go on to introduce him to her friend Aileen Furse who would eventually become his second wife. Now back in London and aware of her Russian ethnicity he tried to recruit her into the NKVD. However at this time another traitor Guy Burgess was also in contact with her effectively trying to get her to spy for British Intelligence MI6. However the Soviets were rather suspicious, suspecting Philby's motives and therefore rejected the recommendation as a provocation. There was a chance that had she have been recruited by both Philby and Burgess, Solomon would have effectively become a double agent.

Even now the Soviets didn't completely trust Kim Philby, never really going on to do so for many decades even after his defection.

Surprised at the effectiveness of his spying, for many years Moscow would still think somewhat ungratefully that he was still a double or even a triple agent secretly working for the British.

CHAPTER FOUR

PHILBY'S WAR

By 1939 the maelstrom in Spain had subsided with Franco's Nationalists crowning themselves in government, boosted by their victory and subsequent ousting of the Republican administration. With this the country became a right wing dictatorship and by July Philby returned to London having completed his assignment as a reporter for The Times. Just a few weeks later in August the world was shocked to hear of the Molotov-Ribbentrop Pact, the non-aggression agreement signed between Nazi Germany and the Soviet Union. These most polarising of ideologies were now bound in a political union in preparation for the cataclysm of the next conflict which would invariably overshadow Franco's fight to grab power.

The pact came as a shock to Philby who was back in Spain travelling with the aristocratic Frances Doble, an actress and recent divorcee. The two had embarked upon an affair together while he was assigned as a war correspondent during the war. It was all part of his cover as she was an admirer of right wing politicians such as General Franco himself as well as Hitler. For years he was instructed to behave like a pro-fascist to cover his real allegiance to communism only now to find himself supporting what were effectively both sides of the extreme left and right. The question: *"Why was this necessary?"* was one that troubled his mind. Matters further tailed off even more upon the outbreak of war, his Soviet controllers drifted away and consequently he fell short on clandestinely meeting up with them at various times.

Even though things were cooling in Soviet circles, on the 3 September 1939 the very day both Britain and France declared war upon Germany other aspects of Philby's life were taking another turn. His good friend the Russian born Flora Solomon, the first to be hired by the established British retailer Marks & Spencer and an influential committed Zionist introduced the clandestine communist to Aileen Furse. The two had known each other since the days of the Spanish Civil War and Aileen, a good friend of Flora was matched up with Kim at Flora's home in London the same day war was declared. Aileen was not typically confident but slim and attractive and a staunch patriot. However she came across as a bit out of date for the time, slightly awkward and somewhat lacking self-esteem in company with a sense of self destruction about her. Sometimes she even went as far as to self-harm to gain attention but despite this Philby saw something good inside her, noting that she was easy to laugh with and very open minded. Therefore he afforded affection upon the woman enthralling her with tales of his adventures in Spain as well as listening to stories about her work. In Aileen, Philby found an avid listener to his rhetoric and in turn the two developed a mutual attraction for each other. But even though there was an attraction between the two, on other levels she and Kim was not a perfect match for each other. Even though she was intelligent and loyal she was not particularly well-read and possessed little knowledge of the politics of the time seemingly exhibiting the hallmarks of progressive conservatism. This was the political persona Kim Philby himself was building up as a reporter for The Times and there was friction between him and Aileen's mother who knew her daughter's partner to be a former communist and did not want her daughter being influenced the same way.

Despite the mixed issues at home at work Philby's lifestyle was more ordered. Now with virtually no contact with Soviet intelligence he fell back upon his trade as a journalist, something he was acknowledged to be respected at. Now back with The Times, and based upon his revered work in Spain they dispatched him to the next theatre of operations, into France to cover the war from the Allied side from the perspective of the British Expeditionary Force. The BEF as they were known had been deployed to the continent as early as September 1939 shortly after the outbreak of war to reinforce the French army as the Germans were engaged in Poland. But this was a rather lacklustre time, it was almost as if there was not conflict at all, at least that is how it seemed in the west. Hitler at this time was more interested in carving up Poland and fulfilling the secret protocol of the Nazi-Soviet Pact in sharing the 'spheres of interest' previously agreed by Berlin and Moscow. Indeed Hitler would not even begin to turn his attention westward until the following year and even then he would be destined to strike north in Scandinavia against both Denmark and Norway, a first real test of the Nazi Blitzkrieg utilising the combined effort of all of Germany's military arms, the Wehrmacht, Luftwaffe and Kriegsmarine.

Philby therefore found himself as did thousands of others embroiled in what would become known as the 'Phony War'. Here he was established in the headquarters of the military staff, furnished in a military style uniform and positioned close to the British commander in France Lord John Gort who had been in place since the 19 September and would become embroiled in the Pillbox Affair. This was a row between the army and politicians on the criticisms made by the British War Minister Leslie Hore-Belisha on the lack of pillboxes constructed to impede the enemy. Tensions between Gort and the minister during the row would eventually lead to Hore-Belisha's eventual dismissal. Gort stayed in his post and Kim Philby war correspondent for The Times remained close by.

Autumn turned to winter then back to spring again until by the 10

May 1940 the Germans finally struck in the west after initially moving north into both Denmark and Norway on the 9 April. Pouring over the borders first into the Low Countries of Holland, Belgium and Luxembourg the Germans burst through the Ardennes forest, deemed impassable for tanks since 1919 and onto the French town of Sedan on the Meuse River. By the 13 May they were through, swinging north-west and heading for the Channel coast reaching the Aisne and Oise rivers around the towns of Hirson and Rathel by the 16th.

By the 21 May and with the situation dire in the face of the rapid German advance and constant retreat, Kim Philby found himself in the town of Boulogne awaiting evacuation from the continent. He previously had been covering the war from Amiens but managed to get out as the Panzer tanks were entering the city. By now the Germans had reached the Channel coast further south at Abbeville while further east the towns of St Quentin on the Somme River and Bapaume had been overrun. To the north Brussels, the Belgian capital, Charleroi and Maubeuge were also occupied. The trip back to England was successful as the Germans advanced upon Boulogne and Calais forcing an Allied evacuation under 'Operation Dynamo' from their beleaguered positions in and around the port of Dunkirk completed by the 4 June. By the middle of the same month with the British and a good proportion of the French armies forced out he was back. This time Philby represented both The Times and its rival paper the Daily Telegraph reporting on the general war situation deeper in France to monitor the focus of the combined forces of the Wehrmacht during the inexorable German advance south. To do this he was stationed in Normandy at the main port of Cherbourg and later to Brittany at Brest well away from the front lines for now even though it was rapidly closing in with the panzers under the Nazi blitzkrieg that was proving so unstoppable.

Here he remained filing reports for both papers even as Paris was first declared an open city and then occupied but not before he could arrange for the escape to Britain of his estranged wife Litzi who was living in the French capital just before it was overrun. Both, even though separated, remained good friends and would only divorce in 1946. Almost inevitably on the 21 June with the Weygand and Maginot lines already smashed and a Churchill proposal for a Franco-British Union rejected forcing the resignation of the Prime Minister Paul Raynaud, Philby finally fled France. He escaped back to Britain on a ship bound for Plymouth at the last moment, for it was, less than twenty-four hours later the French collapsed asking the Germans for an armistice on the 22nd.

With total Allied defeat in the west, Philby like many somewhat demoralised others found himself back in the relative safety across the Channel and it was here he wanted something that was a little more substantial than covering the war from a journalistic point of view. He wanted to become involved in the intelligence services.

Relying upon the activation of the old boy network he dropped a few hints here and there with a few 'select' influential friends. Waiting with a measure of patience Philby had no idea if his probing would ever come to anything; all pieces seemed to fit, a graduate of Trinity College Cambridge (the secret breeding ground of political communism and gestation of the entire Cambridge spy network), and his father had served in the Foreign Office. These were impeccable connections for those wishing to plunge into the murky world of espionage but the rigid class system was the ticket and the accent for which Kim Philby spoke was the knock on the door. But he would have to wait to see if anyone would let him in.

Because of his class a formal application was not required the right connections were a sure fire way to fast track and guarantee anyone into the secret service under the automatic assumption that they were indeed a patriot whose only wish was to serve their country.

The wait continued until one day when he was on a train journey in the first-class compartment running from Plymouth to London he unexpectedly found himself sharing with another journalist, a woman by the name of Hester Harriet Marsden-Smedley who worked for the Sunday Express. She was thirty-eight years of age, a veteran foreign correspondent and had already come under fire in Luxembourg when the Nazis invaded witnessing as they crossed the West Wall or Siegfried Line. Charmed by Philby's dashing figure she cut an upfront, no-nonsense attitude telling in in no uncertain terms:

"A person like you has to be a fool to join the Army. You're capable of doing a lot more to defeat Hitler."

Philby responded candidly with a stammer that he:

"Didn't have any contacts in the world."

"We'll see about that." She promised him. And that was that, this brief exchange marked the start of Kim Philby's spying and devastatingly traitorous career.

Belonging to the same elite class as Philby, the two shared many things and after her promise to make a few inquiries of her own for him the wheels of the network were beginning to turn. As one person whispered into the ear of another who in turn knew somebody else everything was moving fast it would not be long before the proverbial 'tap on the shoulder' would occur sooner or later.

But these wheels of the network were to come closer to home than he thought; from his old Cambridge friend and fellow communist spy Guy Burgess. He had joined the secret service in 1938 and was in Section D of MI6 dedicated to subversion and sabotage in the face of the Nazi threat and was close to Guy Liddell, recently promoted Director-General of B Division responsible for counter espionage. Burgess had wormed his way into the influential areas of the establishment despite being rather ostentatious who tolerated him purely because they saw themselves above others. This tolerance of Burgess' drunken debauchery and drug intoxicated lifestyle ingrained within the flair of his homosexuality was only maintained due to who he knew on the inside. They had no idea that the flamboyance of seducing frustrated sailors, posh boys and rough truck drivers also covered the real Burgess; like Philby under the cover of a journalist, Burgess the Soviet spy was seen by nobody in the service. Eccentricity was mistaken for patriotism.

Despite this Burgess wanted Philby, his old friend and fellow agent inside the service. Therefore he suggested such a notion to another colleague the grandiosely named Sarah Algeria Marjorie Maxse. Maxse was the chief organiser for the Conservative Party and an influential figure since she was also the chief of staff for Section D's propaganda school. She agreed and thanks to Burgess, Liddell who had also appointed Anthony Blunt fellow spy and Soviet agent of all people along with Dick White future head of the secret service, to grant Kim Philby security clearance. Incredibly even with his communist past at Cambridge the green light was given and the wheels were set in motion.

Philby's boss at The Times was Ralph Deakin who was the Foreign News Editor who summoned him to his office. Once there he informed his young star reporter that he had received a phone call from the War Office to enquire about the young man to determine if he was available for war work. This was Philby's access opportunity to penetrate the security services as the telephone call from the War Department invited him to tea at St Ermin's Hotel to meet the respected Maxse.

Upon his first meeting with her he found himself in the forecourt of the hotel close to St James's Park Station chatting to the elderly lady. She seemed very likable with an air of authority in her voice; Philby though was not aware of her precise position within the government but he could deduce that she was in a position to gain him employment in the service. Swiftly the conversation moved toward the inevitable subject of political work against the Nazis on the European continent, something which Philby had already taken a serious interest for at least the last decade, colouring this with various trips throughout the 1930's ranging from Portugal in the west and Greece in the east including many others between including Spain with Litzi Friedmann in 1934. Already he had formed some kind of ideas, many only partially thought through on how to be subversive toward the Germans and it was through these half-baked concoctions and experiences that he used along with his impeccable charm to coax Maxse (without mentioning his communist connections). Her similar ideas on Nazi subversion and political work had been fermenting in her mind a little longer than his but very few people had thought seriously about the subject with suited Philby perfectly.

The chat over drinks was going like clockwork, his enticing charm coupled with perfect manners befitting the company, surroundings and the class stood out. His stammer, so playful to those who heard it was enough to wash away even the slightest of doubts aided no less by his ferocious appetite for and capacity to consume alcohol. The culture of heavy drinking in the smoky clubs of the privileged where secrets were shared as much as the drink was something of a staple in the intelligence game, and Philby seemed more than qualified on this front.

The initial meeting concluded on an encouraging note and Philby's name was passed up the greasy chain of the ranks within MI5, Britain's internal security service who ran a background check against the potential new recruit. Unbelievably they found nothing against his name, not even his communist sympathising past or even his time in Vienna. Again it was the old boy network rolling in his favour, this time by Kim's father, St John Philby who had served with the deputy head of MI5 Oswald Allen Harker while in India in the early 20th Century. This connection for which Harker simply stated that he *"knew his people"* ensured that nothing untoward came up against him.

A few days passed before Masxe and Kim Philby met once more for a second meeting. This time though a pleasant surprise awaited him, his old Cambridge friend Guy Burgess who had been working for intelligence or the past two years accompanied Maxse. Totally unaware that she was surrounded by Soviet spies the interview itself was a little less sociable and a little more professional as she proceeded to put Philby through his paces. This did not matter as he began to show off slightly, encouraged by the presence of his old friend. The show of bravado included name-dropping which prompted an exchange of glances between his two interviewers for which Guy who wanted his friend on the inside nodded approvingly. Like so much in the espionage world it turned out to be a pantomime, the decision had already been taken, the old boy elite network had done its job and Kim Philby had already been accepted into the security service.

By the end of the interview Maxse informed her new recruit that before he reports to Guy Burgess at an address at Caxton Street in the vicinity of St. Ermin's Hotel it perhaps would be best if he give up his career as a journalist and leave The Times before moving on. This he promptly did without too much difficulty. Upon hearing that one of his best reporters was leaving Deakin sighed and huffed slightly like a man coming to terms with disappointment, but gave Kim no great offer to stay. The way was clear for Philby to leaver The Times at Printing House Square and report to British Intelligence in the appropriate, subdued manor for which his new position demanded. That weekend he decided to gain whatever he could from the experiences of Guy Burgess through the only befitting him, with sessions of heavy drinking. There was nothing outwardly unusual about this for nobody outside the spy ring knew about their real allegiances. To an observer they were just two old friends in the fit of socialising.

By the following Monday and nursing a slight headache from the liquid blowout, Kim Philby reported to Guy Burgess, himself slightly worse for wear to begin his (formal) intelligence career.

The organisation which he found himself in was MI6 known by its other name the Secret Intelligence Service or SIS for short. Philby was quite surprised at how easy he managed to penetrate the agency for the elite network had actually paved the way; as it turned out the only enquiry into Philby's past was made by MI5 itself which returned no results through their records. It actually made him hesitate in his thoughts, had he really made the grade? Was there another secret service pulling strings somewhere with hidden suspicions and agendas? Could he really have penetrated the British secret service after his communist sympathetic past?

There wasn't, and he *had* made the grade. Kim Philby was in, no conspiracy or suspicion. As far as his recruiters were concerned he was clean. Burgess escorted his ideological friend to the office which had been assigned to him, a bare rooms containing nothing else but a table, chair and a telephone. Leaving Philby alone for a short Burgess first disappeared only to return a brief while later with a sheaf of paper placing it upon the table after which he declared that his salary would be £600 per year the same as his, a handsome sum for the time as he placed the paper upon the table. This cash was to be paid in monthly instalments directly without any interference from the taxman engineered to prevent them from snooping. The pay scales of secret service personnel was wildly uneven with each financial contract negotiated separately in confidence between only the operative and their chief, it was an extremely sensitive and clandestine affair. Kim was happy with both the arrangement and the amount as he was taken to be introduced to his new intelligence colleagues.

The colleagues whom he met were all in the department termed Section IX otherwise known as Section D (standing for Destruction) and headed by Colonel Lawrence Grand, a tall but slim fellow whom Philby would meet a few days into his new job. Now in this department himself he quickly discovered that the objective of the section was to subvert the enemy by encouraging resistance throughout German occupied Europe and such ideas to commit such operations were not bound by caution in Grand's mind. He considered any idea no matter how large or far-fetched and Philby found him to be almost dream-like, not too dissimilar from those who would have approached him abroad.

By July the Germans had total military domination across the Channel and were making tentative moves to attack British shipping in the sea lanes from the air. It seemed that the Luftwaffe was preparing to fire the opening shots in an expected Nazi invasion of the British Isles. Yet the whole of the intelligence service was abuzz, that same month Section D was taken over by the SOE, the Special Operations Executive itself only formed on the 22nd and responsible for planting agents and conducting aggressive sabotage operations in occupied Europe.

This change was not suited to everyone in the department. Guy Burgess, his flamboyant lifestyle showing a distinct lack of respect for other was one who left the underfunded section as it was absorbed after being fired for irreverence.

Life in the SOE meant that Philby had to move around and he soon found himself back and forth around London to be moved to Station XVII at Brickendonbury Hall in Hertfordshire. This was the SOE's station for conducting explosive trials where during one demonstration conducted for Czech intelligence officers the resident explosives expert accidently set fire to a nearby wood almost incinerating the entire delegation. Philby was to act as an instructor for sabotage agents and it was here he met Tomas Harris, an art dealer with great distinction. This dark haired man, an English born intelligence officer who spoke fluent Spanish, destined to go on to distinguish himself working with the crucial double agent in Madrid Juan Pujol known by the codename 'Garbo' to the British and 'Arabel' to the Germans. Together they would go on to fool the Nazis who thought he was working for them by creating a fake network of agents designed to fool the German oversees intelligence agency, the Abwehr in Spain and beyond.

Philby first came across Harris while at the SOE facility after he was taken on at Guy Burgess's suggestion and known for being an inspired cook along with his wife. Harris occupied a sort of housekeeper role amongst the instructors within the confines of Brickendonbury Hall and was known for rapidly acquiring personal contact with the trainees who passed through the facility. Harris, Philby noticed possessed nothing short of an intuitive mind that was nothing short of brilliance, too worthy of the mundane work being conducted here.

Philby's war work in the SOE was stable enough but through the tense days when the entire country was under the dark threat of Nazi invasion and the fighters swarmed the skies over southern England in a bid to gain control of the air, his home life was flourishing. The relationship between him and Aileen was developing rapidly and the couple were soon sharing a home together, nothing luxurious just a simple flat in the city. His personal life was to settle down somewhat and over the next few years as the war progressed she would furnish him with a family a daughter, Josephine and two sons, John and Tommy between 1941 and 1944.

Kim Philby, still retained in the SOE was now appointed to instruct officers in the field of clandestine propaganda, considered suitable given his background in journalism. The location for this training role was based out at SOE facilities a so-called 'finishing' school in the village of Beaulieu in Hampshire on the edge of the New Forest and not too far from the south coast. Here he received tutorage from George Alexander Hill, an Estonian born intelligence officer and formidable linguist, speaking a total of six languages fluently. Hill was also a vehement anti-communist having fought against the Bolsheviks during the Russian

Revolution.

Meanwhile Kim Philby was seemingly building up the existence of a middle-class, slightly bourgeois life during the war years when fate handed him the cards of his true calling. His role of sabotage agent instructor caught the attention of his old masters in the Soviet Union and in particular the OGPU, the Joint State Political Directorate with its new London rezident called Ivan Andreyevich Chichayev code-named 'Vadim'. In 1940 he was the main liaison for the SOE Russian section who would go on to become the senior NKVD representative in the United Kingdom the following year until 1943. Aware of Philby's role within the SOE Chichayev re-established contact with their former agent 'Sonny'.

He still did whatever orders secretly came through from Moscow spying and reporting on his peers, even those in his personal life were not safe from his careful scrutiny for Aileen was described in a condescending way:

"Her political views are Socialistic, but like the majority of the wealthy middle class, she has an almost ineradicable tendency towards a definite form of philistinism (petite bourgeoisie) namely: she believes in upbringing, the British navy, personal freedom, democracy, the constitutional system, honour etc..."

Philby's spying had started up once more, and he never allowed his anti-fascist instincts ever to get hindered by the Nazi-Soviet Pact which contributed to his cover. Therefore he had no trouble reporting on any information he came across relating to anti-communism in the Soviet republics. Any movements in Armenia, Georgia, Lithuania, Estonia and Latvia aimed at liberating their lands by declaring independence from the USSR were swiftly crushed as thousands were mercilessly sent to their deaths. The intelligence Kim Philby provided resulted in the complicity to murder individuals thousands of miles away not just the culprits but their families as well. They would not be the last victims of Stalinist brutality based upon evidence gathered in the west.

CHAPTER FIVE

MY FRIENDS, MY ENEMIES

With the Soviet side of Kim Philby completely unknown to all but a very tiny few the SOE officer was still continuing his career as a member of Section D. By now the whole intelligence network was a web of agencies all relying upon each other in the war effort. Under Section D which was known as Section IX there was the 'Statistical Research War Office', a cover name for the top secret part of the agency based at Station X at Bletchley Park where the German Enigma codes were being decrypted. Another department based at 6 Chesterfield Gardens was known as Section V covering counter espionage under the command of Lieutenant Colonel Valentine Vivian the deputy head of MI6 itself.

Tomas Harris would prove to be the key for Philby's climb up the intelligence ladder as he transferred to MI5 going on to establish a group of fellow security service officers who gathered socially for boozy sessions of secret swapping at his home at 6 Chesterfield Gardens. For Philby, away from his secret spying activities this was a time for developing relationships within the service. One of the relationships he would develop would have a direct impact upon the future of his own intelligence career for during one of the many excursions he was taking back to London from Beaulieu during the tense days of 1940 he came across another intelligence officer from a background similar to his own. A class copy of himself, the young man was a rising star within MI6 and went by the name of Nicholas Elliott.

The two men shared many similarities for Elliott's father like Philby's was a respected figure in an influential position, and rather alienated from his son. Indeed Nicholas's father Claude Elliott was the headmaster of Eton, the English public school, gateway to Oxford and Cambridge and the breeding ground for the educated upper-middle classes where the expectation in life was to rule. He hated listening to music often complaining of indigestion as a result of hearing it. Extremely old fashioned for the time, almost echoing the hardy attitude of the Victorians in the previous century he firmly believed with a hint of brazen imperialism that the only way to get through to any foreigner was to shout loudly at them in English. He also dismissed as 'effete' any form of heating.

This then was the man who headed one of England's finest elite schools and bore a son who was destined to serve his country not behind the barrel of a gun, but in the smoke and mirror, cloak and dagger world of espionage. From Eton Nicholas too attended Trinity College at Cambridge, arriving as Philby was leaving but managing not to become embroiled in the heated arguments of the Socialist debating societies which his contemporary had been involved in. Cambridge at the time was an intoxicating melting pot of ideological beliefs with the rise of Hitler, the fight of Franco in Spain, both political extremes left and right fought it out in a game of wits and counter-argument. Nicholas Elliott graduated from Trinity College Cambridge in 1938 but with no idea what to do. Things were about to move along quite rapidly when during a cricket match at his old school Eton he was approached by Sir Nevile Bland an important diplomat and family friend of the Elliott's. Guided by a previous quiet word from Claude Elliott who was concerned about his son's future, he mentioned that he was about to take up a position at The Hague and would the young Nicholas like to accompany him? The young man in his naivety agreed and he was offered a position within diplomatic circles in the Netherlands as Honorary Attach at The Hague.

Bland himself vouched for Nicholas by stating to the Foreign Office in a bid to push the young man into following a similar public position he was alright since he knew him as well as the connection with Eton. Just like it did for Kim Philby, it was the old boy network rolling once again. He offered some casual if not some fatherly advice to Nicolas telling him that sleeping with the wife of a colleague was indeed a sackable offence within the diplomatic service. He also mentioned rather pompously that the young man follow his actions and that it was bad form to light a cigar before starting his third glass of port. Arriving in November that year Elliott began work which he found interesting but inevitably found himself getting caught up in more clandestine affairs at the time. These were varied such as travelling into Germany with an accomplice, a naval officer named Glyn Hearson, sneaking into the port of Hamburg and investigating while taking notes for around an hour before successfully retreating without being seen. It was a good job as they would have been executed as spies by the Nazis if they were caught by the authorities.

April 20 1939 was Adolf Hitler's fiftieth birthday and Berlin marked the occasion by staging a huge military parade through the city centre. For around four hours over 50,000 troops as well as waves of tanks, mechanized units and artillery pieces marched and rumbled past the main stand as well as the swell of crowds. The Luftwaffe roared overhead the delirious public with hordes of fighters and bombers in continuous fanatical salute to their Fuhrer under rows of fluttering swastika flags. This synchronised occult of lunacy was certainly an impressive if not imposing and intimidating sight and it was meant to be for this was supposed to be a powerful message, a message of German 'Ayrian' superiority and defiant might to the rest of the world. Just 21 years after the collapse in the last war, Germany was back. Nicholas Elliott was in the Nazi capital watching this spectacle with a measure of abject horror and was so outraged that he would have been tempted to assassinate the dictator from his hotel balcony if he had a rifle. Afterwards he left the city to return to The Hague with the firm conviction that Hitler's Germany who by this stage had absorbed both Austria and scandalously Czechoslovakia had to be stopped. He also knew now that the best way he could do this was from within the secret service. Nicholas Elliott wanted to play the intelligence game. This chance came about not long after back in Britain where at Ascot Racecourse he was sharing a bottle of champagne with Sir Robert Vansittart a major diplomat. Meetings with other figures within Whitehall followed and Nicholas Elliott with the blessing of Bland smoothly became a recruit into MI6 while still working as cover as the diplomatic attaché to The Hague.

Elliott's time as an intelligence officer would be marked soon after the start of the Second World War in late September 1939 with the Venlo Incident, a false flag operation where the SD, the internal intelligence agency of Nazi Germany and the SS set up and captured two British agents in the Dutch town of Venlo close to the border eventually using this as a pretext to invade neutral Holland in May 1940.

When Nicolas Elliott and Kim Philby met both were low level intelligence officers, but sharing a common educational and social background the two quickly became firm friends. The blossoming of such a friendship was helped by the tragic death of Elliott's friend Basil Fisher, a Hawker Hurricane pilot of 111 Squadron who was shot down and killed during the Battle of Britain on the 15 August. Philby filled the gap in Elliott's life and the two quickly became solid partners. But Philby in the SOE was still on the very fringes of the intelligent departments while Elliott was close to more established figures in the game.

The drinking clubs of the intelligence elite was the forum where to make friends and to acquaint with other associates to swap secrets and a way to promote ones-self in the business. The currency was alcohol, hard and lots of it for the capacity to hold drink was the measure of a man in this little bubble of the social elite. Philby used to indulge as much as he used to involve himself with such a group, affiliated with them through his friendship with Nicholas Elliott. Many of these fellows already inside the deeper areas of both MI5 and MI6 could be a door opening to some of the higher departments in these agencies. These influential figures of 'Young Turks' but known simply as 'The Group' of British Intelligence came from far and wide; Peter Wilson a journalist and future art auctioneer at the prestigious Sotheby's, Tim Milne a Royal Engineer recruited in MI6, nephew of the author A.A. Milne and former Westminster School mate of Kim and Lord Victor Rothschild, the aristocratic chief of counter espionage within MI5 and flatmate of two of the other members. Sharing with Rothschild were two 'friendly' faces within the group Anthony Blunt and the ever flamboyant Guy Burgess who sometimes arrived with a rent-boy in tow and both clandestinely linked to Philby unknown to anybody else. Completing the line-up was Richard Brooman-White, head of Iberian operations and Tomas Harris' boss and Guy Liddell head of B Division in MI5 a talented musician who contemplated a professional career he would sometimes play the Cello. He was the man who appointed both Anthony Blunt the Cambridge art scholar and another called Dick White whom would have an association with Kim in later years to senior posts.

This was the social gathering that convened at Harris' home at 6 Chesterfield Gardens filled with magnificent art treasures for bouts of drinking sessions fuelled by the liquidity of the brandy's and whisky's. Although included Philby was still an outsider of this exclusive club and served the drinks as much as he consumed it, savouring the atmosphere with a certain *Joie de vivre* in the upper class setting. Spies could not share their secrets nor their experiences with outsiders, especially in wartime so they tended to turn to the only people they could, each other. Alcohol served as the glue which bonded comrades together, helping to blunt the stresses and burdens of the war. Elliott noted that Kim was a formidable drinker which helped lubricate the easing of his acceptance amongst his peers. This was happening at a time when Britain was undergoing a strict policy of rationing. With the Germans on the continent and the United Kingdom destined to be subjected to blockades and attacks in the Atlantic by the U-Boats, the population was only allowed one egg, 50g of butter, 100g of bacon and ham, three pints of milk, 50g of tea and 225g of sugar per adult per week amongst others. Those however within the elite circle of friends did not share the shortages of the general population throughout the war and beyond. Indeed the friendship enjoyed between both men was synonymous with the lifestyle they held even outside of MI6 as both families took vacations together during breaks in the war work. Elliott therefore trusted, admired and revered his friend Philby and even looked up to him modelling his personality upon him even down to his dress sense. Both had items they both treasures, Kim with his Trinity College scarf and Nicholas with his umbrella complete with ebony handle, both icons of a close and flourishing friendship.

Philby made regular appearances at Chesterfield Gardens, it was clear he wanted more and intended to use his friendship with Nicholas Elliott as leverage to gain another job within intelligence. His flimsy argument for this was to complain that it was necessary for him to now more than ever escape the rhododendrons of Beaulieu and to find a better 'hole' as he put it rather hastily. During one of the regular visits to Chesterfield Gardens with its opulent décor in an atmosphere of haute cuisine and grand vin. Harris, even though he was now within MI5 and away from

Brickmondbury Hall still enjoyed a friendship with Philby telling him in a rather bourgeois manner that no good table could ever be spoilt by wine stains.

Soon he was to find himself moved inward, along with Nicholas Elliott whose two careers seemed to be moving forward in tandem. His best friend would soon be deployed to Istanbul to head up the MI6 there but Philby found himself in St Albans Hertfordshire just to the north of London and close to the centre of MI6 as part of Section V dedicated to counter espionage. Both he and his family moved into a cottage on the edge of the town. Nobody even suspected for a second that he was really a Soviet spy.

The halls of Section V were the place to build connections for Kim, anyone who might help with both his intelligence and secret spying career. The head of the department and Philby's boss was Major Felix Cowgill, the SIS representative on the Twenty Committee chaired by the academic John Masterman. He was an influential figure of the infamous Double Cross System where virtually all German spies dropped into Britain was caught, turned and used as double agents to feed false information back to the Abwehr. Cowgill was an experienced man, a former police officer in India who reported to his chief Sir Stewart Graham Menzies known as 'C'. A Major-General in the army and the head of MI6 (SIS) a man who enjoyed the privileges of both rank and title for he was certainly well connected, mixing with royalty, enjoyed riding with hounds and liked the days out at Ascot even more where he preferred the company of ladies to men but horses over both. Like many of the heavy boozers in the wartime intelligence business, he too liked a drink and lots of it but still managed to keep secrets to himself like a good boss should. The alcohol never loosened his lips which lay hidden behind his moustache. But despite all the finery in his life he was a military man and therefore a bit of an amateur whereas his rivals in other agencies were more of the consummate professional type. British Intelligence during the war was in a constant state of flux continuously reorganising to counter the ongoing Nazi threat but the right background could guarantee a place in these secret groups. Donald Maclean, Philby's Cambridge friend and fellow Soviet spy was an alcoholic shambles, yet he still found a place within the service due to his accent and connections. Maclean fit the bill and like Philby, the authorities knew nothing of his communism even though his instability could get the better of him.

Maclean's unpredictability accompanied by the raucous antics of Guy Burgess meant that they were in stark contrast to Kim Philby, the quiet gentlemanly spy who was coolly and quietly building up a network of friends within both MI5 and MI6, all the time manoeuvring himself into a position where he could do the greatest benefit to his real employers the Soviets. Such was Philby's schmoozing that Sir Stewart Menzies had to fight off the Foreign Office who wanted him in the diplomatic service. Menzies put up a spirited reply of his talented recruit by stating to them in a curt manner:

"You know as well as I do the valuable work which Philby is doing for me. The essential nature of Philby contribution to the war effort compels his present employers to regretfully refuse to let him go."

Yet even with this ringing endorsement of assurance from 'C' now that Philby was in the heart of MI6 there came increased danger for his intelligence would now be more valuable as it would be more sensitive meaning any defections could bring the real risk of exposure to the authorities. Even though he was busy covering his back with the officers of MI5, any such suspicions could result in them snooping in an unwanted manner and such worries would come about from all sides even from Moscow itself. By now they had penetrated the very heart of the British establishment with considerable ease; Philby in MI6, Blunt in MI5, Maclean and Burgess in the Foreign Office while John Carincross was in

Bletchley Park (Station X). Philby himself, still operating under the codename 'Sonny' worked feverishly in the department stealthily combing the files and reporting any useful information back to Moscow, particularly messages sent between London and the military mission in the Russian capital which were especially useful.

Every evening he would take home in his bulging briefcase laboriously copying out the files intended for Moscow While Aileen innocently prepared dinner and played mother to the children. Moscow Centre could not quite believe just how far they had infiltrated since these were some of the most impervious organisations in the world and now the Soviet Union had moles embedded in them. It made them rather suspicious as surely this must be a British ploy to deceive Moscow by some kind of subversion?

Moscow Centre decided to find out for sure and now called upon Kim Philby who was best placed to provide them with intelligence on details on all British agents that were currently operating inside the USSR, their assets, and what information had they gathered. Moscow pondered the question; was he a plant? Was he protecting his family for some reason? This request was to test Kim Philby's real loyalty, if he provided this crucial information then his dedication would become a little more assured, if not then Moscow would draw its own conclusions. Philby politely if not a little cautiously pointed out that his role was to catch spies not running agents. He informed the NKVD that that role was in a different department and away in a totally different building. However Moscow Centre was determined that this task must be conducted pointing out that he must use whatever plausible pretext he could to get hold of the relevant files. Philby it seemed was trapped into doing this no matter what.

Details of the information could be found within the inventory of all intelligence assets abroad called 'source books'. These were part of the massive MI6 archive called the Central Registry which was housed quite conveniently for Philby at Prae Wood just next door to the offices of Section V in St Albans. The guardian of this sensitive material was a red-faced ex-policeman and Special Branch member called Captain William Woodfield; slightly built with dark hair and bald on top with glasses and a long face. Despite being the keeper of the valuable information he had one particular achilles heel; he was a raging alcoholic with a fondness for rude jokes and pink gin. Woodfield's weakness was Philby's strength for after seeking him out at the local drinking hole, the King Harry Pub next to the cricket ground where he and Elliott played matches, to become best drinking buddies. Philby supplied Woodfield with plentiful quantities of his favourite tipple where the former police officer would get intoxicated by the MI6 man in an effort to groom him for what he wanted, access to those files. The audacious con worked and soon Philby, whom Woodfield trusted gained access to the source book document room. He had to be careful here for he knew one careless slip up could be costly. When Philby finally asked for the source books on Spain and Portugal Woodfield signed them out without question for there was no need to be suspicious of his motives of his best drinking buddy.

After all the Iberian Peninsula was familiar to Kim since he had been there before as a journalist, why wouldn't he have the right to study MI6 assets in the region for his work?

Now he had made his first move Philby probed a little further by proceeding to ask Woodfield for access to the source books on the Soviet Union. It was a risk asking for agent information so far from his own area but yet again the gin loving ex-policeman did not enquire and allowed the MI6 officer full access to sign out the files and its contents. With the information he gathered Philby sent a report to Moscow with the answer to their request on the number of British agents operating in the USSR. He answer could not be simpler, apart from a few minor informants, mostly Poles, there were none. Britain did not recruit any assets or had deployed any agents anywhere inside the Soviet Union and was not even a priority since it was tenth on the list. Efforts at this time were being overwhelmingly concentrated upon Nazi Germany and the threat from the other Axis powers during wartime. Moscow found Philby's report very suspicious, inflated by a sense of self-importance to the handlers and spymasters of the Lubyanka the USSR was a world power so it made perfect sense that the Allies must be spying on them in some capacity. Outraged the at being relegated in the British espionage target list, Soviet Intelligence who received the report drew two underlines accompanied by question marks in fiercely scribbled red ink. Clearly Moscow Centre did not believe him for he had to be lying citing that he must be tested for his loyalty many times given the failure to corroborate his explanations. This was typical of the relationship Philby endured with his handlers. Sometimes they would believe the plausibility of his reports other times not. The sheer fluidity of the relationship Kim Philby went through with Moscow was one that ebbed and flowed with the times.

Philby's actions inevitably put him under suspicion from the Russians but such was Moscow's paranoia that even when another of the Cambridge Spies, Anthony Blunt confirmed his friend's report that there were indeed no British agents inside the Soviet Union, he too came under scrutiny. The Soviets wrongly thought that the two must be in league together even though in reality the Foreign Office would go on to impose strict restrictions on espionage activities against the USSR once the two would become allies. Therefore the relationship was that where Philby actually reported the truth, his handlers refused to believe him simply on the grounds that what he reported was not what Moscow expected to find. It was a very cynical way to treat some of their most valuable moles in the establishment.

But Philby had other matters closer to home to worry about. Even though his access to the source books was an impressive feat of espionage (even though it went unappreciated by Moscow Centre), it almost exposed him in the process. Woodfield sent Kim a short note one
morning to ask if he could return the source books on the Soviet Union he had borrowed. For his failings as a drunk, Woodfield redeemed himself by being a meticulous record keeper and knew that there was only one file on the USSR in the archives, the one Philby had borrowed. Kim responded by pointing out that he already done so even though Woodfield said that Registry recorded that only one, the file on Iberian Peninsula had been returned. Philby was sure both had been returned but in a state of quiet panic proceed to scour his office for the missing Soviet source book. However it was nowhere to be found and by the Friday evening when Philby met his drinking friend at the King Harry Pub to discuss the mystery over a few pink gins he was to get an even bigger shock. Woodfield informed Philby that he would have to inform Sir Stewart Menzies of the missing file as per the rules and would do so by memo the following Monday. For Woodfield this was a simple routine enquiry and that it was nothing to worry about. But Philby knew otherwise. Quietly shocked, now this was serious for if Menzies ever got to hear of this it would invariably raise awkward questions. For 'C' may be able to understand if his young rising star of the intelligence service wanted access of the files on Spain and Portugal, but why would Philby require the source books on the Soviet Union? He knew suspicion would fall upon him and MI5 may come sniffing around; tricky questioning would be the least case, exposure and arrest would be the worst. However because this was the weekend there was little he could do so for the next two days Philby endured a sense of simmering and niggling panic at was he would have to say to his boss.

Monday came and nothing. As it turned out Woodfield's secretary had been off work ill with flu for a few days and only just returned. Explaining that Philby had in fact returned both source books she confessed to amalgamating the two together to save space. Woodfield offered his profound apologies over more drinks of gin for the confusion to Philby who was mightily relieved. This was a very close shave for Kim and indeed there was every chance he could have been found out there and then, but he was not and he was lucky in an extremely large dose. The matter was closed but the risks were stark at this level and would not be the last. Events in Moscow and the United States from a Soviet defector were to provide both an opportunity and another scare for him. And it would reveal the ruthless side of Kim Philby.

CHAPTER SIX

THE RUSSIAN DEFECTION

One such risk already presented itself even before Kim Philby joined the British secret service. In 1938 a senior NKVD intelligence officer defected to the west armed with valuable intelligence on the inner workings of current long term Soviet operations. The officer with the information to potentially destroy the Cambridge Spy ring went by the name of Walter Krivitsky. Born into a Jewish family under his real name of Samuel Ginsberg on the 28 June 1899 this tall, blue eyed and dark haired boy joined a radical youth movement at the age of thirteen. In 1917 at the age of eighteen he seized the popular and fluid teachings of Marxist-Leninism and soon joined the Bolshevik Party as a political organiser. After the maelstrom of the Russian Revolution, Krivitsky briefly worked as a journalist before operating behind White Army lines during the subsequent Civil War in the country. By 1920 he was attached to Soviet military intelligence headquartered in Smolensk for the Western Front during the Soviet-Polish War. He was involved in subversion aimed at destroying the morale of the Polish Army as well as providing intelligence for the Red Army general staff.

In 1923 along with six other officers Krivitsky was deployed into western Germany when the French Army moved in as a response to the Weimar Republic's inability to keep up reparation payments as demanded by the Versailles Treaty. Sensing an opportunity to create a communist revolution within Germany itself Krivitsky's mission was to liaise with the Communist Party in the country and organise resistance in the area to undermine the confidence of the Reichswehr and the police. However the attempt at a communist uprising was more difficult than expected as was the case in Hamburg when local communists took to the streets believing they were taking part in a wider nationwide revolt. Attacking the local police station and other major buildings the uprising soon began to falter as other working class groups failed to support them. The result was that the revolution was crushed within three days by the local police and army authorities and prompting the Russians to utilise the best men developed by the party intelligence and introduced them into the Soviet military intelligence.

The ultimate failure of the communist revolt against the Weimar Republic would eventually result in far right nationalists steadily grow and eventually take power throwing Germany into a right wing dictatorship under Hitler in the grip of the indoctrination of Nazism by the 1930's. Yet that same decade Stalin was busy satisfying his rampant paranoia by ruthlessly purging the officer class during the great Purge. Krivitsky himself now an officer within the NKVD would reflect upon the 'Stalin's Terror' by admitting:

"Already in December 1936, the terror was sweeping Madrid, Barcelona and Valencia. The OGPU had its own special prisons. Its units carried out assassinations and kidnappings. It filled hidden dungeons and made flying raids. It functioned, of course, independent of the Loyalist government. The Ministry of Justice had no authority over the OGPU, which was an empire within an empire. It was a power before which even some of the highest officers in the Caballero government trembled. The Soviet Union seemed to have a grip on Loyalist Spain, as if it were already a Soviet possession."

By 1937 over forty intelligence agents stationed abroad were summoned back to the USSR. Krivitsky was smart and he knew it would only be a matter of time before his own turn would come. In Paris Alexander Orlov had a meeting with Theodore Maly, Kim Philby's handler at the time who had just received orders to be recalled back to the Soviet Union. Stories were rife that senior officers had also been recalled only to mysteriously disappear. Once Maly amongst others had indeed gone missing and had not returned, Krivitsky solidified his belief that his own life was in danger bolstered by the belief that his friend and fellow dissident Ignaz Reiss was beginning to have serious doubts regarding the show trials being conducted in Moscow. His wife Elsa Porestsky noted that ordinary citizens were rather intimidated and only knew fear while party members dreaded the accusations. It was a testament to the iron fist which Stalin wielded over the state.

Reiss therefore suggested to Krivitsky that they should both defect before they are summoned as a show of demonstration against the purge of loyal Bolsheviks. Krivitsky pointed out that there was nobody they could turn to. If they defected to the west that would only serve to betray everything they fundamentally believed in whereas turning toward Leon Trotsky would confirm Stalin's suspicions about them. Krivitsky had a different idea; he thought the Spanish Civil War would empower the Comintern through the spirit of revolution and eventually drive Stalin from power in the Kremlin. In due course Krivitsky received the expected recall to Moscow and he used the opportunity to discover exactly what was really going on in the motherland. He found support for Stalin had largely disappeared with the people, party members and commissars, as high as ninety percent in most areas were opposed to the Soviet dictatorship. Both men met in Rotterdam on the 29 May 1937 with Krivitsky telling his friend that Moscow was nothing short of a madhouse denouncing the NKVD chief Nikolai Yezhov as insane. Reiss agreed saying that the Soviet Union had descended into a fascist state. Krivitsky stated that the USSR was still the sole hope for ordinary workers in the world and that Stalin and his brand of communism may be wrong and that the Soviet Union will still endure something which Reiss actually disagreed with, even his wife Elsa was a little suspicious on how Krivitsky was allowed to leave Moscow after being recalled unlike so many others who did not.

By July Reiss had defected informing his superiors Abram Slutsky and Joseph Stalin himself by letter pompously stating:

"Up to this moment I marched alongside you. Now I will not take another step. Our paths diverge! He who now keeps quiet becomes Stalin's accomplice, betrays the working class, betrays socialism. I have been fighting for socialism since my twentieth year. Now on the threshold of my fortieth I do not want to live off the favours of a Yezhov. I have sixteen years of illegal work behind me. That is not little, but I have enough strength left to begin everything all over again to save socialism. ... No, I cannot stand it any longer. I take my freedom of action. I return to Lenin, to his doctrine, to his acts."

By now Krivitsky was informed by the Trotskyite Mikhail Shpiegelglass that Reiss had gone over to the other side after meeting fellow Dutch communist Henricus Sneevliet in Amsterdam. Both Krivitsky and Theodore Maly tried in vain to contact Reiss who secretly had been ordered to beat Reiss to death with an iron bar once found, something which Maly refused to do. Reiss himself would be eventually found hiding out in a village close to Lausanne in Switzerland. One evening Reiss was out dining with trusted friend Gertrude Schildback in a restaurant outside of town. After eating they both left on foot where a car carrying two NKVD agents, Etienne Martignat and Francois Rossi drove by. One carrying a machine gun shot at Reiss, hitting him seven times in the head and five times in the body killing him outright before speeding off. Furthermore the police upon investigation of the hotel room he was renting found a box of strychnine poisoned chocolates intended to kill both his wife and son.

This put Krivitsky under intense suspicion and his Soviet superiors in particular Slutsky who ordered him to transfer all of his spy contacts to Shpiegelglass including Hans Brusse a Dutch publisher and fellow NKVD spy. Brusse confessed to Krivitsky that he had been ordered by Shpiegelglass to assassinate Reiss's wife Elsa and was told by the Russian to accept the assignment but to carry it out in a way that it would fail. He also suggested to Brusse that he should try to distance himself from the NKVD and its activities. The Dutchman subsequently agreed. Krivitsky now learned of Theodore Maly's imprisonment and execution as part of Stalin's Terror which ultimately proved too much for him, he decided to defect to the west, to Canada where he would meet with Paul Wohl a Jewish intellectual and old friend to comment quite freely on events happening in the Soviet Union. Wohl agreed to the idea and helped Krivitsk to defect, renting him a villa on the French Mediterranean coast in Hyeres a province just to the east of Toulon. Now Wohl arranged for a car to spirit both Krivitsky and his family, his wife Antonia Porfirieva and their son to Dijon where they boarded a train to the Cote d'Azur. Once Shpiegelglass realised that Krivitsky had fled, he immediately informed his superior Nikolai Yezhov who in response ordered the assassination of the defector and his entire family.

By the 7 November 1937 Krivitsky returned to Paris to meet the son of Leon Trotsky, Lev Sedov through Paul Wohl. Sedov was the leader of the Left Opposition in France who in turn put him in touch with various others through the French Socialist Party such as its leader Leon Blum who was a member of the Popular Front. After several weeks Krivitsky received the documents he needed and a police guard to boot. Following on from this he then proceeded to arrange another meeting with Hans Brusse filled with the hope that he just may persuade him to defect as well. However his Dutch friend was not convinced, revealing a letter which was a copy of a note the Russian had written to Reiss' wife Elsa. Krivitsky denied ever writing this but still failed to convince Brusse who in turn tried to get him to return to Soviet spying.

After this failure Krivitsky arranged for the French press to openly publish a statement condemning Stalin's policies in the Soviet Union. His justification for this was that the Soviet secret police, the GPU would stop at nothing to silence him with dozens of people all following Yezhov's orders to carry out their mission. Seeing himself as a revolutionary fighter, Krivitsky saw it as his duty to bring to public attention the truth about the Soviet dictator. Before long both Krivitsky and Wohl decided to try and move to the United States with Wohl going on first to settle and arrange for Krivitsky to follow. Gaining employment as a foreign correspondent for a Czech newspaper, Wohl obtained a US visitor's visa valid for just sixty days as a German refugee. By the 5 November 1938 Krivitsky and his family were ready to take flight, fleeing France aboard the liner Normandie. However upon their arrival in New York, the first port of call for so many immigrants wishing to settle for a new life in America, they were refused entry. Ellis Island, where many illegals were detained was now the home for Krivitsky and his wife but with a little help they were allowed to at an apartment at 600 West 140th Street which Paul Wohl had found for him. Immediately the two began writing articles about the Soviet Union and with contacts with journalists such as Isaac Don Levine they had access to the mainstream American media.

Levine realised that the information Krivitsky possessed could get him lucrative deals and in April 1939 the first of Krivitsky's articles were published in the Saturday Evening Post. What it revealed was staggering; the USSR was spying on the United States and moreover the NKVD was sending agents in and the FBI was doing nothing to stop them. It angered its head J. Edgar

Hoover to know that the organisation he was in charge of was being proved so impotent. Even though now Krivitsky was being seen as a bit of an expert on the Soviet Union through his articles they did cause some controversy especially from the pro-Marxist publication the New Masses who tried to discredit him by claiming he was not really a former Soviet agent. Even the monthly pictorial monthly magazine Soviet Russia Today attacked him by publishing an anonymous article stating that he has a bitter hostility toward the USSR along with a hatred of the Republican Spanish government. They also said he was a counter-revolutionary who had contempt for democracy and was allied to the Trotskyists, inflammatory rhetoric from former masters who would now rather see him dead.

Even on this side of the Atlantic Krivitsky had sceptics, receiving little support from the government of President Franklin D. Roosevelt, but his articles and the information he published did catch the eye of the FBI who wanted to interview him about his knowledge. On the 27 July 1939 the Americans asked Krivitsky about Emilo Klemer, a Jewish immigrant born in Romania and someone who was on the FBI watch list since they were convinced he was running a spy ring. Krivitsky confirmed that Klemer had indeed worked for the NKVD but was unsure of any espionage activities by him in the United States. In fact he emphasised that Klemer was a target for Stalin's Purges. The interrogator noted that the statement given by the Russian contradicted known facts already gathered by the FBI. It was hardly a ringing endorsement of his truthfulness. In any case Krivitsky went on to reveal that there were fifteen Soviet agents active in New York and naming one individual, Boris Bykov as the main spy in America describing him in detail as small, red hair and eyebrows with red-brown eyes. However the FBI was not entirely convinced of his account and their suspicions were further compounded by the fact that they knew that Louis Waldman, the lawyer acting on Krivitsky's behalf was known to the Americans as a socialist.

Following on from this Krivitsky began to associate with other organisations such as appearing in front of the Committee for Cultural Freedom, set up to oppose the rising idea of totalitarianism which was already in countries like Germany, Italy, Japan and of course Soviet Russia. Following this he also invited to appear in front of the House Committee on Un-American Activities known more widely as the Dies Committee at this time. For this the New Masses attacked him by saying that he entered the country under a cloud engineered by friends abroad and that his activities and status made him subject for deportation. Krivitsky argued on the 26 August that the Nazi-Soviet Pact has finally shown the world for what Stalin really is and that in a free world the master stroke of diplomacy is the death stroke of Stalinism as a force.

Another damming piece of evidence was revealed on the 3 September, the same day war was declared by Britain and France on Nazi Germany. Phillip Kerr otherwise known as Lord Lothian the 11th Marquis of Lothian, the British ambassador to the United States met with Isaac Don Levine and was told by the journalist that Krivitsky had revealed something worrying. He said the Russian knew of two agents operating deep inside the British government. The first was operating in the Foreign Office (he was talking about Cambridge Spy, Donald Maclean) and the second one was in the Foreign Office Communications Department who is *"selling everything to Moscow"* as he so eloquently put it. He also added that another called Ernest Holloway Oldham was also a Soviet agent but had actually died.

Concerned about this new intelligence Lothian immediately sent the information back to MI5 who already knew about Oldham who had been forced out as early as 1932. They proceeded to arrest John Herbert King, fellow spy and associate who was apprehended on the way to a Whitehall tea shop with a top secret message in his possession. He was travelling to meet with his Soviet contact at the time whom strangely they did not arrest as well. By the 25 September head of Section V in the SIS, Colonel Valentine Vivian interrogated King but failed to extract a confession. However perseverance prevailed and King eventually broke to confess that he was indeed a Soviet spy. This was absolute proof that the NKVD had penetrated the Foreign Office and Colonel Vivian wanted to hunt for others for he was sure there was possibly more in the department. Lack of evidence for prosecution prevented this and unknowingly to him it would have saved Donald Maclean from investigation and probable exposure. In the subsequent investigation two officers were dismissed. Lord Halifax the British Foreign Secretary at the time who would come close to succeeding Neville Chamberlain as Prime Minister as the King's preferred choice over Winston Churchill in 1940, ordered staff to be moved to make way for fresh faces. Walter Krivitsky was right in his intelligence that there were Soviet moles embedded in the British establishment, but the investigation failed to discover Maclean. If he had been found out at this time, the whole Cambridge Spy ring may have fallen apart. Instead he wasn't and the way for Kim Philby to enter the service was laid unwittingly clear.

By the 11 October Krivitsky appeared before the Diels Committee just as President Roosevelt was beginning to have doubts about the initial investigation. The President tried to intervene in stopping Diels from investigating communism citing that he could not foresee that the communists would pose any threat to the USA and even praising Russia as a great ally in the coming years. It was as if he could tell that the Nazis would someday turn on their Soviet partners and preferred that the committee confine their investigations to the fascism of both Germany and Italy in response. Krivitsky was questioned on whether or not Soviet Intelligence actually cooperated with both

German and Italian agents and were they facing combined efforts on the espionage front? Krivitsky revealed that there was an exchange of information between the USSR and the Axis even before the signing of the Nazi-Soviet Pact, going on in closed session afterwards to provide information on Soviet agents still active in the United States. This information shed light in the fact that the American Communist Party was in fact being controlled by Moscow and its leaders were treated quite well. Krivitsky continued to provide mounting intelligence on NKVD activities in America and that the OPGU was willing to assassinate him to make it look like suicide and urged Joseph Brown Matthews, the investigator on the Diels Committee to travel to Mexico city and warn Leon Trotsky who was now based there that his life would be in danger as well.

He was right about the Soviets as they were tracking him. Samuel Dickstein a Congressman was asked by Peter Gutzeit for a copy of Krivitsky's testimony on the closed session of the Diels Committee. Gutzeit had special interest in what Krivitsky had revealed for he was an NKVD agent himself, one of the individuals that the Russian had already alluded to. But Gutzeit was out of luck as Dickstein only provided a rough outline of what was said along with the politician insisting that no evidence of espionage was presented in the document. The NKVD found this report highly suspicious as it contained strong references to what was already in the press.

By November Krivitsky's accounts were published in a book entitled '*I Was Stalin's Agent*' in the US, Britain Sweden and Holland and contained accounts of Stalin's actions during the Spanish Civil War. The book strongly hinted that Stalin wanted to bring Spain under the communist influence, a reference to foreign expansionism in the mind of the Soviet dictator but speculated that the loss of the Republicans in which the USSR supported plus the effects of the Great Officer Purge may have caused Stalin to lose support. In effect this book was an assault on the Soviet leadership, Stalin in particular and his regime as power hungry undemocratic and bloodthirsty.

  The book and its contents certainly caught the attention of MI5 who asked Levine if Kravitsky was willing to travel to London to discuss details of Soviet agents operating in Britain. Levine hinted that even though Krivitsky was acting for purely ideological reasons, to aid in the fight against Nazism as much as denouncing the Soviet regime, the financial motivation for his services was still there. On the 19 January 1940 Walter Krivitsky arrived in Britain aboard the Duchess of Richmond which docked at Liverpool. Upon arrival he was greeted by Major Stephen Alley, a Russian born British intelligence officer who passed him on to Colonel Valentine Vivian for interview. In London he was questioned by both Vivian and the deputy Director of MI5 Brigadier Oswald Allen Harker who took notes, but Krivitsky began by wanting to know how the British would use his information since any detainments would inevitably be attributed to the information he possessed. He knew the Soviet government would be aware of his activities once action by the west was taken. It almost seemed like he was frightened and knowing that the Moscow wanted him dead he was rather anxious to know just how far the British were planning to use him. Vivian sought to reassure him by saying that under no circumstances would he ever be called as a witness in trial and that any information he divulged would be treated with the strictest confidence. Krivitsky began but was soon skirting around the real information that both men wanted to hear. However he soon revealed that he was aware of an organisation in the country whose mission was to gather covert information, stressing that he was by no means responsible for how activities against Britain were to be carried out. He also said there was an agent in the Foreign Office who had supplied the Soviets with extremely detailed and highly secret information naming the culprit to be John Herbert King. This seemed to be the same information that he had already divulged and Vivian pointed out to the Russian that the man in question had already been found and arrested based on intelligence he had given Lord Lothian last year. Krivitsky was told that King had confessed to being a Soviet agent and was now in prison serving a ten year sentence before being shown a photograph of Henri Pieck a Dutch painter who was secretly working for Soviet Intelligence under Ignace Reiss before his murder. Krivitsky confirmed that he was a real agent who was in league with King.

The information was not great but they persevered and the next day he was to undergo interrogation by MI5 in the form of Jane Archer. Born Jane Sissmore and married to an RAF Wing Commander John Archer, she initially joined MI5 as a clerk while studying law in her spare time. Becoming a barrister in 1924 she rose quickly to become the first female officer within the secret service and was given the task of interviewing the Soviet defector.

Krivitsky claimed that the Soviet idea was to cultivate agents from within but had a flaw. He went on to explain that the disadvantage was that Moscow would have to be patient to see results but even so the long game was a regular tactic used by Soviet Intelligence.

He revealed that the Fourth Department in the NKVD was prepared to wait for a decade or more to begin seeing results as they preferred their moles to come from a university education and obtain posts within either the secret or diplomatic services to access key information. Even though he did not know specific names he did mention a Scotsman who was educated privately who was an ideologist who whose spying was not for financial gain adding that both NKVD agents Thodore Maly and Arnold Deutsch was running things but both had returned to the USSR. He claimed the Scotsman who was a Soviet agent was working in the Foreign Office but again did not know who (Donald Maclean). He also mentioned that Maly was also handling a young English upper-class gentleman who worked for a British newspaper as a reporter covering the recent Spanish Civil War and who was a friend of the agent positioned within the Foreign Office. He revealed that Maly had sent this agent into Spain with orders to assassinate General Franco. He was talking about Kim Philby who by February 1940 was still a reporter for The Times at this time.

Archer subsequently noted that Krivitsky genuinely believed that Stalin would remain at the top of the Soviet Union, consolidating it through vicious and bloody purges of enemies and dissidents. She also reported the defector thought that perhaps invasion from a foreign power may cause his ousting. Krivitsky had an absolute and patriotic conviction that the only way that the people will be free was if Stalin was toppled from power and that it was his duty to fight him in any way he can.

Archer's interrogation technique was extremely efficient and had extracted a lot of information that should have led to the arrest of both Maclean and Philby. But in November 1940, with Maclean still in the Foreign Office and Kim Philby now firmly settled into MI6 she was sacked after denouncing the incompetence of the now Director of the security service Brigadier Oswald Harker. Harker was the previous Deputy Director General who had succeeded his predecessor Sir Vernon Kell after his dismissal as the head of MI5 in June 1940 but Krivitsky's testament was not convincing and his leads were not followed up. The internal wheels of MI5 actually prevented anything further from happening. Guy Liddell thought that Archer had in fact gone too far in her criticism of her boss but that did not matter anymore. Walter Krivitsky had the potential to smash the Cambridge Spy Ring but the pressure of fighting the clandestine war against Germany coupled with internal squabbles within MI5 resulted in Kim Philby's appointment to the intelligence service and the other members of the spy network continuing their undercover work for the Soviet Union. Philby's good fortune after the source book scare hit again and now he was in a position to inform Moscow of Krivitsky's actions himself.

Krivitsky returned to America and New York City and settled into a small apartment in the Bronk district at 36 West Gun Hill Road with his family to settle down. Even in this happy little suburban existence Krivitsky's greatest fear was for that of his wife and son rather than his own. He was used to living under the threat of death from his former Soviet masters but his family was who he most wanted to protect. His future plans were to buy a farm in Virginia after visiting another friend Eitel Wolf Dobert on his ranch north of Charlottsville in the same state in February 1941. That was on the 6th. Three days later on Sunday the 9th Krivitsky travelled to Washington D.C. and checked into the Bellevue Hotel at 5:49 p.m. After paying $12.50 for the room in advance he signed the register under the alias of Walter Poref. The staff noticed that 'Mr Poref' was trembling in a rather nervous manner. Despite this he was settled in his room and at 6.30 p.m. called room service for a bottle of sparkling water in a quiet fashion which was delivered by the porter.

Nothing was heard until the next morning when at 09.30 a.m. a young maid called Thelma Jackson knocked upon his door but did not receive an answer. Assuming the room must be empty and needing to be cleaned she used her hotel passkey to access the room where upon opening it she discovered Krivitsky laying on the bed. His body was the wrong way round with his head toward the bottom and covered in blood. It was obvious the Walter Krivitsky was dead.

The police assumed the case as it appeared was to be suicide; a certificate of such was recorded that same afternoon. Investigators also found three notes purporting to be from Krivitsky himself, one in English another in German and the third in his native Russian. The English letter addressed to Louis Waldman a leading figure of the Socialist Party of America wrote: *"Dear Mr. Waldman: My wife and my boy will need your help. Please do for them what you can. I went to Virginia because that there I can get a gun. If my friends should have trouble please Mr. Waldman help them, they are good people and they didn't know why I bought the gun. Many thanks."*

The second letter written in German was addressed to Suzanne La Follette, an American journalist and author: *"Dear Suzanne: I believe you that you are good, and I am dying with the hope that you will help Tonia and my poor boy. You were a good friend."*

The third letter in Russian was to his wife Antonia Porfirieva and read: *"Dear Tonia and dear Alek. Very difficult and very much want to live but I can't live any longer. I love you my only ones. It's difficult for me to write but think about me and you will understand that I have to go. Don't tell Alek yet where his father has gone. I believe that in time you will explain since it will be good for him. Forgive difficult to write. Take care of him and be a good mother - as always be strong and never get angry at him. He is after all such a such a good and such a poor boy. Good people will help you but not enemies of the Soviet people. Great are my sins I think. I see you Tonia and Alek and embrace you."*

The letters and the events surrounding his so-called suicide were dubious and were believed only by certain people while others were convinced that this man who only wanted to expose the totalitarian criminality of Stalinism and ensure freedom of democracy was in fact coldly murdered by the NKVD. Indeed the man who many saw as the killer, Walter's old acquaintance and the man he tried to turn, Hans Brusse was seen in New York at around the same time Krivitsky was there. The second German latter raised questions as he had only used the language previously when his English was still poor. As time went on as his language improved he began to use it less often. Another account speculated that Krivitsky perhaps did commit suicide under threat from the NKVD against his beloved wife and children. But another and perhaps more telling reason was that his location was discovered and that intelligence was used to tip off Moscow to his whereabouts and movements. Krivitsky's accounts were in the system of British Intelligence and could have been passed onto to Moscow by a mole that would have access to such information. A Soviet agent operating in counter espionage Section V would want Krivitsky and his testimony to expose certain operatives that were active within the establishment eliminated. They would see no problem in aiding their Soviet masters to achieve this aim. Such a man would have been someone just like Kim Philby.

CHAPTER SEVEN

LIONS, BEARS AND EAGLES

By 1941 the war was beginning to take a new turn as the Allies discovered that Germany was about to throw away the non-aggression pact with Moscow by intending to launch Operation Barbarossa the invasion of the Soviet Union. Philby leaked information and provided Moscow with advance warning of the impending attack as well as the intelligence suggesting that the Japanese was not going to follow Hitler's urging and attack north at Russia but south into Singapore. Stalin dismissed Philby's warning as a simple provocation, something he would continue to do in ignorance to the reality of the situation right up until the invasion itself but the information concerning Japan was more of use to him. The NKVD had a spy planted in Tokyo, a journalist called Richard Sorge, and he confirmed that Philby was right. It was a good thing as well since Hitler launched his much vaulted invasion of the Soviet Union on the 22 June 1941 with the Panzers smashing through Red Army front lines and fighting for the next four months ever eastwards. Even as the Russian winter broke early and savagely the German advance continued and was only checked and stopped by first the weather and then thrown back by a massive Soviet counter-offensive. This was conducted by reserve units from Siberia under the command of the celebrated commander Georgy Zhukov, a survivor of Stalin's purges. These reserves which the Soviets used to push the Germans back once they reached the edges of Moscow, only fifteen miles from Red Square and could actually see the Kremlin in the distance came about from the intelligence that Kim Philby provided. Had he not leaked this information, had it confirmed by Sorge in Tokyo, then these units would still be guarding a pointless border against Japan and the Panzers would be rumbling through Stalin's capital.

While the ideological clash between Nazism and Communism was raging upon the new eastern front in London things were moving at a different pace. In July 1941 Richard Brooman-White the man who had laid the path for Philby to enter the secret service was approached by his subordinate Tomas Harris to suggest whether or not Kim would make a decent head of MI5's Iberian section. Clearly the choice was logical as his trade was that of a reporter and he was there during the Civil War. His job would be to fend off any espionage attempts coming in from both Spain and Portugal which was at the time fertile ground for wartime clandestine operations. Indeed the Nazi foreign secret service the German Abwehr was rather weak in the Iberian peninsula, a contrast to the more brutal efficiency of the organisation that was established in the Low Countries. Brooman-White approached fellow officer Dick White now a senior officer in MI5 to recommend Philby to Major Felix Cowgill the head of Section V itself. Cowgill clearly saw the rising potential of the star of the security service and in turn recommended him for the job to Colonel Valentine Vivian. He was open to the idea but as head of counter espionage, decided to make a few background enquiries against the recruit. Vivian achieved this by approaching Kim's father Harry St. John Bridger Philby the noted and respected diplomat to enquire about his son. Over a rather polite and convivial conversation the intelligence officer asked:

"He was a bit communist at Cambridge wasn't he?"

To this slightly offensive question his father replied:

"Oh that was all schoolboy nonsense. He's a reformed character now."

And that was that. Vivian accepted the word of one of the most respected diplomats and explorers of the time and he saw no need to probe further into the young man's past. One can only imagine what he may have discovered if he knew the true extent of the real Kim Philby and what the reaction may have been. As such he was satisfied with the assessment and instructed Cowgill to go ahead with the appointment. By September the same year Philby was firmly established in Section V and responsible for offensive counter-intelligence thus giving him access to even higher levels of information. His appointment as head of the Iberian section was based upon his experience as a journalist in Franco's Spain and this enabled him to feed his Soviet controllers with ever more confidential secrets. The section liaised with a network of agents and operatives in Madrid and Lisbon as well as Tangier and Gibraltar because even though it was weaker than in other areas, the Abwehr was still a threat. That threat posed the most sensitive for the British around Gibraltar itself which was not only a major naval base but also controlled access in and out of the Mediterranean Sea, vital for both the Malta convoys and the North Africa campaign. The Germans watched this small British port on the southern tip of the peninsula with both cameras and radar in the hope to deduce Allies shipping movements in the region. Philby's Iberian section helped to counter this threat.

He was worshipped by his colleagues in Section V, the rising star of the intelligence game and the darling of the security services. But Philby had to be careful in counter espionage for if he did his job too well there was a danger he could disrupt real Soviet operations. Therefore he found himself in a position where he had to appear to be doing an efficient job but not get it quite right as so to protect his real interests. His MI6 fiends suspected nothing and even his Soviet masters saw him as the only individual in the entire organisation without any enemy at all and that is just how they liked it to be.

But Kim Philby was a contradictive character, one with a mirrored personality and the admiration and respect he commanded in MI6 was far from reciprocated. His real views were reflected in the secret reports he was constantly sending off to Moscow describing his so called 'friends' with nothing short of distain. He described one unfortunate person as: *"inclined to inertia"*, another as possessing: *"an inferior brain"*. Even his boss Felix Cowgill did not escape describing him as having: *"few social graces"*.

Perhaps one of the most disturbing of Philby's contradictions occurred one morning in 1941 Philby left for work as usual with a bulging briefcase full of the detailed inner workings of Section V laboriously copied out in small neat handwriting as well as further details on operations, failures and achievements. At the end of the day instead of heading home or to the bar beneath MI6 for another heavy secret sharing drinking session he took the train out from St James's Park underground station. Only boarding the second train after the first one had left, he waited until everyone else had got on before he did to make sure he was not followed, slipping on just as the doors were closing. Travelling two stops he got off and took another train back in the opposite direction. Finally back where he started he exited the station and caught a bus as it was moving. Finally assured that he was not being tailed by anyone he got off making his way to a local park for a pre-arranged meeting. Here Philby met a stocky built fair haired man, sitting on a bench. Shaking hands Philby handed over the briefcase contents, the documents on MI6 Section V including a description of his best friend Nicholas Elliott. Of his most devoted friend, a man who, when times got hard, paid Philby's children's school fees – Philby wrote: '*NICHOLAS ELLIOTT: Brown hair, prominent lips, black glasses, ugly and rather pig-like to look at,*' before giving away his exact role in MI6.

By December the Japanese finally launched their own assault on the US Pacific Fleet based at Pearl Harbour. This action inevitably drew the United States out of its policy of neutrality and into the chaos of the Second World War. When Hitler, although irritated by his ally's action himself declared war upon the Americans in support thus drawing them not only to the far east but into the European theatre. By 1942 Britain was becoming flooded by the tide of American G.I's all deployed to take the fight to Hitler. The intelligence world was also swept up in this as British Intelligence as the veterans of the spy game were now going to work alongside their incoming, overenthusiastic and rather naïve American counterparts.

For Philby this was also a time of career development as Anatoly Gorsky, who proved himself quite unpopular was moved aside for his replacement, a charming and Jewish man called Max Krotenschield, real name Boris Kreshin. Officially within MI6 his remit was expanded beyond Spain and Portugal to include both North Africa and Italy to reflect the rapidly developing events and the shift in focus of the war to the Mediterranean. With this came a promotion to deputy head of Section V under Felix Cowgill and as part of the job he came into contact with other officials in the business including some of the young Americans in the war. But despite this jump up the career ladder the distrust that the Soviets had of Philby was continuing to grow. Doubtful about the quantity of the information he was providing Moscow decided to transfer the entire Philby file over to an impartial desk officer in the Main Directorate of State Security, the GUGB, for an independent evaluation, a woman named Elena Modrzhinskaya. She was entirely sceptical of him and the whole network the Russians were running inside the British establishment noting somewhat cynically:

"Could the British Secret Intelligence Service really be run by

such fools that no one had noticed that precious information was leaking to Moscow?"

The skepticism she showed reflect the Soviet attitude toward an agent whom they accepted information from but thought doubtful. Steadily she built up a case against Philby using the argument that each of his previous controllers had been shot following confession to being Polish or German spies, (referring to the purges of Stalin), or had unquestionably defected to the west. On the matter that Philby had revealed startling information on German war plans but almost nothing on subversive activities, repeatedly stating that there were no British agents operating in the Soviet Union she commented:

"Could the SIS really be such fools they failed to notice suitcase-loads of papers leaving the office? Could they have overlooked Philby's communist wife?"

Despite the obvious hot and cold relationship Philby had with Moscow his MI6 career was taking a more upward trend with him expanding his influence to incorporate the inclusion of the American agents into the war. One of those enthusiastic young spies, destined to encounter and become embroiled in the charm of Kim Philby was man by the name of James Jesus Angleton.

Angleton had been born in Boise, the largest city in Idaho on December 9 1917 to Hugh Angleton and Carmen Mercedes Moreno a young Mexican woman. Hugh was a tall six foot four red faced farm boy and former cavalry officer who had served under General John Pershing but after his stint in the army, he worked for the National Cash Register Company as an executive and salesman. Carmen Mercedes Moreno was a devout Catholic and it was this religious belief that caused her to furnish her son James with the middle name 'Jesus' which he actually hated using even though he would become proud of his Mexican heritage as he grew older.

The Angleton family moved to northern Italy to settle in Milan due to the nature of Hugh's work in 1931 and right into the middle of the fascism of Benito Mussolini, something which appealed to the strict conservatism of James's father. By 1933 James was sent to England to continue his education at Malvern College in the county of Worcestershire. Malvern was an independent establishment and the highbrow elitism so typical of upper class Britishness at the time forced the slightly awkward young man to become acquainted with the trappings of prejudice and outright snobbery. He stayed there for three years serving as a prefect, a corporal in the Officers' Training Corps until finally leaving in 1936 after becoming a member of the Old Malvern Society. This was quite a feat for the pupil known as a 'half-Mexican Yank'. His formative years there made a lasting impression upon him; here was an American boy, schooled in the ways of the British and was seen as 'more English than the English'. Angleton liked his education here, his impressionable mind imprinted in the disciplines in life for which he would hold dear and come to regard with a sense of duty.

By 1937 he returned to the United States and enrolled at Yale University in New Haven Connecticut. By now this tall, thin and intelligent many he had begun to exhibit his own, quite unique style finished off with a slight English accent, a legacy from his college education. However he was slightly odd only tending to excel in subjects which fascinated him and even go so far as to skip classes in subjects which did not. This erratic approach to university education was smoothed over by the fact that his tutors actually quite liked him even though he had trouble completing the school papers. Some of his peers thought he was lazy, others thought the problem was more psychological.

By 1941 he had moved on to Harvard Law School where he met fellow student Cicely Harriet d'Autremont the granddaughter of a wealthy mining and lumber magnete. She was utterly struck by his handsomeness and charisma, falling in love with him at first sight.

Two years later Angleton had been drafted into the US Army and a few weeks after, in April 1943 the pair was engaged. His father Hugh, the ultra-conservative disapproved of the relationship but could do nothing to stop the wedding which took place on a small scale on the 17 July at Battle Creek, Michigan.

As part of his war work, Angleton became included in the Office of Strategic Services, the OSS, (the American version of the British SOE) which was the United States wartime intelligence agency that would eventually evolve into the CIA. The OSS which had been created by President Roosevelt to replace the former Office of the Coordinator of Information (OCI) and had the responsibility for collecting intel on any nation at war with the USA. Here he worked on the staff of his superior Colonel William Donovan a lawyer by trade and an efficient intelligence officer. He was a ferocious worker, devoting almost his entire time to the espionage work, filling out reports nestled in piles of papers with a kind of odd enthusiasm that made him a dedicated and capable man. Another aspect of the OSS's work was to organise espionage and more underground guerrilla tactics when fighting the enemy and it was this aspect of the organisation that would have a profound impact on Angleton's career and life.

He impressed his senior officers, gaining promotion to the rank of second lieutenant within six months and with it came a new appointment, as chief of the Italian Desk for the European Theatre of Operations. Despite his slight awkwardness he was known by his colleagues as an officer that was well respected with a quiet manner and voice to match. Quietly laughing when he found something amusing he never stepped out of that very British manner instilled in him at Malvern, never boisterous nor condescending, his manner exuberated the softness of a man who could get a point across in subtlety. The uncanny ability to dominate the topic of conversation without ever having to raise his voice to anyone was something which impressed everyone.

The atmosphere that James Angleton was to be deployed into though was one of absolute uncertainty. As the summer months drew to a close in 1943, with the tide of the war finally turning against the Third Reich the Red Army in the east was finally on the offensive. The gruelling and savage battles around first Moscow in 1941, then Stalingrad and Kursk coupled with the barbarism committed behind the front in the murdering of civilians caused an apocalyptic death toll. The Soviets were suffering terribly from both Stalin's brutal orders of no retreat and the Nazi's utter hated for what they saw as 'sub-humans'. The fight had been long but rapidly depleted, gradually demoralised and no longer willing to believe in the 'final victory', the Germans were generally retreating. This changed the game for the intelligence services and MI6 in an 'official' cooperation with their allies, provided the Soviet GRU with a report on the movements of German agents operating in both Bulgaria and Romania. Both countries it seemed looked destined to be invaded by the Red Army as the Soviets approached the border from the Ukraine. However the NKVD upon receipt were not satisfied with the Allied findings suspecting that only partial intelligence had been disclosed. Amidst a continuous mistrust of the west which would lay the foundations for the tensions post war, they duly complained to the SIS attaché to Moscow, Cecil Barclay. Noting the Russian's concerns he referred the complaint back to London where Kim Philby was in position to overhear in secret discussions within the halls of Section V regarding the matter.

This was a chance to test agent 'Sonny's' loyalty that the suspicious Elena Modrzhinskaya had been waiting for. The British had managed to decode an intercepted telegram from the Japanese ambassador to Berlin, Hiroshi Oshima to his foreign minister in Tokyo. Philby copied the information and passed it in secret to his NKVD controller. However what he did not know was that Moscow already had another copy from their own spy in the

Japanese capital Richard Sorge. When those at Moscow Centre compared both versions they noticed the final paragraph concerning information indicating that Hitler may be willing to seek peace with the Soviet Union was missing from Philby's account. Why was this? The Soviets thought. Why did he leave this crucial bit of intelligence out? Did agent 'Sonny' secretly want Germany to defeat the USSR? Philby's controller demanded an explanation for the lapse for which he explained that radio reception used to intercept the message was poor quality with the final part, referring to Hitler being virtually unintelligible. It was not enough for Moscow who refused to believe him preferring instead to accept Modrzhinskaya's version. Quite cynically she came to the conclusion that Kim Philby along with Blunt, Carincross and Burgess were really MI6 double agents and Donald Maclean was genuine but was being manipulated by the others. It was totally incorrect but the NKVD was in a precarious position over the issue, what if they were wrong? Modrzhinskaya had made a powerful argument in discrediting the Cambridge spies but if they reached the wrong conclusion then they would be in fact throwing away some of their best and most productive agents in the west. In the twisted logic of Stalinism that was a death sentence usually by firing squad. In the end the Soviets decided to compromise; they would keep contact with Philby and the rest reasoning that if they were indeed double agents as many of them thought, they must divulge some real intelligence sometimes to maintain credibility. Any pieces no matter how small were treated as valuable if verified as genuine, so therefore they decided to play their own little deception game with their agents. Moscow would pretend nothing had ever happened and that they were as creditworthy as ever before, reinforcing their position that they trust Philby and his friends implicitly.

For James Angleton this was the world he was about to have thrust upon him and the nature of the man he was eventually going to meet. He seemed the most appropriate choice to be sent to work for the Italian section of X-2 C.I, the American version of the British Section V. The job required a move to the United Kingdom, a country which he was already familiar with the customs, manners and reserved social acceptances for this man who was 'more English than the English' exhibited some of them himself. Therefore James Jesus Angleton arrived in London to accept his new post and to be trained in counter-intelligence by the veteran British secret services on the 28 December 1943 and into a country that looked more like huge military base in the gearing up for the launch of the much anticipated second front-the long awaited invasion of Normandy.

The trainers of the rampant anglophiles in the OSS included James Angleton, now newly arrived was Dick White of MI5 and another senior officer of Section V the deputy head, Kim Philby. It was not long before James Angleton was seduced by the charm of Section V's head of the Iberian section, it would by the start of a long and loyal friendship between the two men.

"Once I met Philby, the world of intelligence that had once interested me consumed me. He had taken on the Nazis and Fascists head-on and penetrated their operations in Spain and Germany. His sophistication and experience appealed to us... Kim taught me a great deal."

Even though Philby was Angleton's counter-intelligence instructor, just like the reserved Nicholas Elliott, the American was consumed by the inexorable charm of his superior. Looking upon the Englishman as a mentor and confidant virtually to the point where he saw him as a brother, both men found a mutual respect and admiration for each other.

The relationship was slightly tainted when Philby failed to pass on information on a British agent that had been caught in occupied Europe and subsequently executed by the Gestapo. This agent known as 'Schmidt' was also involved in the Rote Kapelle or 'Red

Orchestra' an anti-Nazi movement in Germany who worked as cover for both subversive operations on behalf of the west and to the Soviet Union. However such was Philby's standing in the intelligence community, Angleton's suspicions no matter how slight were virtually ignored and it was not enough to damage the burgeoning friendship the two men enjoyed.

Philby was building up quite a circle of colleagues he considered as friends in order to extract information out of them. One of his warmest friendships came from one of his subordinates in Section V, Graham Greene. He liked his boss even though he, like his peers had no idea of just who he really was. Under Cowgill, Philby was in charge of a small but dedicated group of people in including Greene such as the aristocratic Victor Rothschild, Stuart Hampshire, Gilbert Gayle and Hugh Trevor-Roper, possibly one of bluntest men in England. All did not rate Major Cowgill that highly as he was up against formidable intelligence and combativeness. Trevor-Roper for instance, a man who would go on to forge a respected career as a historian after the war, sometimes conflicted with Cowgill's approach in a clearly unequal struggle branding him as a: *"purblind, disastrous megalomaniac."*

From Roper's point of view the appointment of Kim Philby in Section V was treated like the heralding of the Messiah. The appointment astonished him somewhat since Roper had an old friend from Oxford University who knew of him and his communist past. Roper just assumed that because of his induction into the secret service, Philby must have shed the left-wing sympathies he once had. This was a strict requirement for the fanatically anti-communist old boys of MI5 and MI6 and none more so than Felix Cowgill. Roper picked up on the fact that many in the security services, including Cowgill himself suspended any convictions to the charm of Philby and that indeed he had many qualities that would prove extremely useful to the service. Even though Roper was perfectly aware of Kim Philby's communist past, due to the reputation he had built and the high regard he was held, it never occurred to him that his motives were more ulterior. Such was the rampant anti-communist attitude he was at least glad one ex-comrade had made it through to temper political prejudices with social ones. Philby himself in private was just as caustic as Trevor-Roper was in his remarks about their boss saying: *"As an intelligence officer, he was inhibited by lack of imagination, inattention to detail and sheer ignorance of the world."*

Philby had a point in this scathing opinion. Cowgill showed a fierce loyalty to anyone within his department and sharp suspicion against anyone else; an abrasive attitude to take in stark contrast against the smooth and slick demeanour of himself. As the war progressed Philby and his counter-espionage efforts were certainly exploiting the inefficiency of the Abwehr. Its head, Wilhelm Canaris was beginning to be seen as by the Nazis as both inefficient and disloyal in equal measure. Himmler wanted to oust the Admiral and seize control over the whole organisation. While turbulence flowed through the chaotic German intelligence network, Philby received a request to grant security clearance on a document. This document indicated that Canaris, who was making frequent trips to Spain where most operations were being conducted from, was willing to meet with his opposite number 'C' Sir Stewart Menzies. Roper noted that Philby strictly forbid the circulation of a report such as this instead utterly dismissing it as pure speculation.

However as the disorder of the Abwehr rolled on, the turn of Germany's fortunes in the war as a whole provided the Allies with a priceless opportunity. Philby himself would make the most out of it. Something was about to happen which would not only ensure the ideological division of Europe after the war but define it. The preliminary drawing of what Winston Churchill would refer to as the 'Iron Curtain' was going to be drawn across the continent. While the Allied leaders of Churchill, Roosevelt and

Stalin met publically at various conferences to exhibit a united front and decide the fate of the continent after the war, the real divisions fuelled by mistrust and suspicion were really deciding it through the intelligence services. This opportunity came in the spring of 1943 when Philby learnt of a German defector turning up and tentatively approached the British intelligence services. The defector's name was Erich Vermehren.

Vermehren came from a family of lawyers who expressed anti-Nazi feelings to a great extent. Erich actually refused to join the Hitler Youth – virtually a crime in Germany at the time which considered him in the eyes of the authorities as *"unfit to represent German youth"*. This restricted his opportunities under the oppressive regime of National Socialism meaning he could not take up a scholarship to Oxford University. The Nazis even prevented him from leaving Germany itself into neighbouring counties by revoking his passport. Vermehren embraced Roman Catholicism having converted to it in 1939 and met a senior member of one of Germany's leading Catholic families, Countess Elizabeth von Plattenberg, a similar minded woman who also loathed Hitler. Falling in love the two married just two years later and engaged in subversive anti-Nazi activities such as distributing the *'Mit brennender Sorge'* a letter circulated to all bishops of Catholic churches in preparation for wider distribution to the public on any particular matter. It was a practice that was banned in the Reich. It was not long for this illegal activity to get the attention of the authorities and Elizabeth's parents were soon arrested by the ever vicious Gestapo, the secret police subdivision of the SS. Their incarceration mercifully did not last forever since the Countess used her influence to secure a release after only three weeks but the Nazis were not going to let this go quietly. They questioned her on her activities despite the fact that quite unwillingly the couple found themselves involved in the regime itself.

Since Erich was excluded from military service through injury he therefore managed to obtain a draft into the Abwehr through his connections of his cousin Adam von Trott zu Solz and the Istanbul station chief, Paul Leverkuhn who was Nicholas Elliott's counterpart in the city when he was posted there by MI6. The couple felt that it was likely that their lives would be at risk should they stay within Germany and that this would be an adequate way out. Wilhelm Canaris was by 1943 making tentative peace approaches toward the United States through Franz von Papen, the former German chancellor and the man who helped Hitler into power in 1933. Now ten years later he was the ambassador to Turkey, and was the cousin of Elizabeth Vermehren. Now thank to this German version of the old boy network, she managed to secure a posting for her husband as a junior agent in surreal espionage world that enveloped Istanbul.

Vermehren managed to obtain leave and travelled back to Berlin where together they made the momentous decision to defect to Britain even the priority was to get Elizabeth out of Germany and away from the peering eyes of the state police. To get her safe passage to Istanbul she managed to take advantage of a friend, the Archbishop Francis Spellman's impending visit to Turkey to go on the trip in an official capacity. Travelling by train to Istanbul they were however stopped at the Bulgarian border where Elizabeth was arrested by the Gestapo and taken to the German embassy in Sofia. Despite this Erich was allowed to travel on to Turkey without his wife. But what the Nazis did not reckon was that their ambassador in Sofia was a family friend who smuggled her on board a diplomatic plane bound for the Turkish city. As Elizabeth was clandestinely making her way out, her husband was making his own moves. He had made tentative approaches to the British MI6 in Istanbul and its station chief there, Kim Philby's friend Nicholas Elliott who was already aware of Vermehren through files on him and his activities.

Their defection was prompted by the arrest of a friend based in the German foreign ministry Otto Carl Kiep in connection with anti-Nazi resistance fermenting within intellectual circles. The Vermehren's received a summons by the Gestapo to Berlin. They had no intention of returning knowing that to do so would be virtual suicide. In February 1944 the couple formally defected to Britain. MI6 took care in the way the 'fade' spy jargon for disappearances and defections, was engineered. The Nazis had a long history for punishing family member of those who stepped out of line so the Allies made it look like a kidnap to help dilute the response somewhat in the Reich. Under the strictest secrecy both Erich and Elizabeth were transported out via the long and tortuous route of Izmir in Turkey, Aleppo in Syria, down to Egypt and its capital Cairo before moving west to Gibraltar. From there they were spirited away to England. By now the build up to D-Day was beginning, the Germans were seriously on the defensive on the eastern front, fighting was raging in Italy and the invasion of the west would soon begin. The news of the Vermehren defection would both undermine the German intelligence service and wreak havoc within it. Upon the news which was broken by the British propaganda, Hitler reportedly flew in an absolute rage. This was compounded by the fact that the Nazis believed they both escaped with knowledge of the security codes used by the Abwehr. All this did was to increase mistrust of both the organisation and of Canaris himself. It ended with the formal abolition of the Abwehr on the 18 February and was replaced by the security organisation of the SS, the RSHA under the control of Heinrich Himmler. As anticipated, the Nazis vented their fury upon the traitor's family members through arrest and internment. Mercifully all of them including Erich's brother, sister and parents as well as Elisabeth's younger sister all survived the sharp hand of Nazi brutality to see the end of the war.

But as for the defectors, now safely in England, were given

accommodation in the South Kensington apartment of Dora Johnston the mother of the MI6 officer Kim Philby. Here they were free to inform the intelligence services of a list of Catholic figures inside the Third Reich who, interestingly for Philby, were opposed not only to Nazism but to Communism as well. These individuals wanted, as did the Vermehren's, a free Germany that embraced the Christian faith once Hitler had finally been defeated. The list that Erich provided to MI6 was not included in official intelligence sharing with their Soviet allies. They did not want the spread of Communism to reach as far as central Europe, Philby however did. To ensure that the ideals for which he secretly stood for would reach as far as it could he willingly and secretly provided Moscow with this list of these Catholic individuals who wanted nothing more than to see their country free of any ideological shackles. Philby's act ensured that when the Russians finally reached Germany as it looked increasingly likely the Red Army would, the Soviets would eventually liquidate these people. Kim Philby had unofficially signed the death warrants of the Vermehren's friends, effectively being complicit in their eventual murder.

The Soviets now asked Philby through his handler Anatoli Lebedev if he could arrange for a transfer within MI6 to a different department. As the Nazi threat was receding by the day, the spectre of the old enemy of Soviet espionage was gradually looming ever larger. Despite the official alliance between east and west the mistrust was growing and the intelligence community was on the front line of this new political situation. In MI6 a different section called Section IX dealt with the innocuously sounding 'Soviet Affairs', in reality it was set up to deal with Soviet espionage and if Kim Philby could get inside this he would be in a vital position to tell Moscow no only what Britain was doing, but what Britain was actually thinking to counter Soviet operations. Indeed Lebedev thought that Philby would be offered a senior position given his rising status in the service. Over several meetings both men discussed the possibility of Philby succeeding Cowgill as head of Section where it would be possible for him to influence some quite important decisions. It was clear and vital now for Moscow that their star agent Kim Philby became head of Section IX Soviet Affairs regardless of whether or not it would eventually merge with Section V. The Soviets wanted him in directly in the centre of British Intelligence.

CHAPTER EIGHT

NOW I'M A REAL SPY

Kim Philby's influence was noted by his peers in the rest of Section V. The same year as the Vermehren defection another German by the name of Otto John informed the Allies of a major conspiracy fermenting within not just inside German society but also in the German military leadership. Setbacks in the war caused dissent in the Wehrmacht ranks and doubts in Hitler overall as a leader. Officers who secretly believed that the Fuhrer was only going to lead Germany to ruin formed a conspiracy which included a plan to activate the battalion of soldiers stationed in Berlin under the command of the obedient automaton Major Otto Rehmer in a 'state of emergency' to seize and arrest senior Nazis. The plan could only work though if Hitler was removed as head of state and that meant killing him. This would be the conspiracy known as the infamous July Bomb Plot, the closest and most serious attempt to end Hitler's life while at the *Wolfsschanze* or Wolf's Lair in Rastenburg, East Prussia. 'Operation Valkyrie' as it was known would eventually end in failure; the subsequent arrest of the persons responsible including Hans Oster, Ludwig Beck, Henning von Trescow, Friedrich Olbrecht, Friedrich Fromm and the main would be assassin, Count Claus von Stauffenberg. Hitler furiously ordered that those responsible should be: *"hung like cattle."* Some were publically humiliated through being berated by the 'Hanging

Judge' Roland Freisler in the arena of the 'People's Court', others were ruthlessly shot like Stauffenberg. Those who hung were strung up with piano wire suspended from meat hooks. The executions were filmed for the morbid pleasure of Hitler to see. Anyone connected with the plot, or suspected to be were rounded up by the Gestapo and the SS. Even the much admired and public hero, Erwin Rommel did not escape, preferring to commit suicide by cyanide poisoning rather than face trial and execution. The plot would also spell doom for the former head of the now defunct Abwehr Wilhelm Canaris who would be beaten and interred in Flossenberg Concentration Camp where he would eventually die days before liberation from American forces. Just like Stalin had purged his administration during the terror of the 1930's, Hitler was doing the same in Germany in 1944. The Third Reich's death throes were marked by an utter purge of any remaining sanity still left in the leadership.

As the Allies learned of this intelligence from Otto John and the amount that was passing over Kim Philby's desk in Section V, his colleagues in the section noted he was being rather stubborn in his arguments considering the value of such important information. Here was the Nazi regime looking like it would implode and Kim Philby was displaying a healthy amount of intransigence. If anything it made him stand out from the rest of the ex-policemen and burnt out army officers, not to follow the strict line, not to be automatic in his orders and in his problem solving. Even Hugh Trevor-Roper, the usually masterful ringmaster of scathing sarcasm would go on to say: *"he alone was real. I was convinced that he was destined to head the service."*

However Philby's ambitions lay in positioning himself to obey his Soviet controllers. He needed to ensure the removal of Major Felix Cowgill to get the top job and it was a task that required cold determination, no sentimental remorse and no hesitation out of a sense of loyalty. Carefully and surgically Philby began to build tension between Cowgill and his superiors, making him look like the antagonist. The tension building between Cowgill and Valentine Vivian amongst others all played into Philby's hands, and it made his image shine. If ever Cowgill needed to go, Kim would be the most obvious choice as successor to head Section IX.

The subversive deception effort took its toll and indeed paid off by September 1944 when the Director-General of MI6 Major General Stewart Menzies still known as 'C' asked Philby to come and see him. Duly he informed his rising star that it was he and not his immediate boss Felix Cowgill that was to be offered the job as head of MI6's Section IX and responsible for Soviet counter espionage. Naturally Philby was delighted for this was a major coup for Moscow since it gave their spy access to highly sensitive documents that he would be quite willing to share. As a result of this new promotion and the endless, priceless opportunities that came with it, Moscow, no matter what the reservations about him, decided to reward him by a change of cryptonym. Agent 'Sonny' as he was known as would no longer be used. Instead Kim Philby would now be referred to by his new name, agent 'Stanley'.

Of course his MI6 colleagues knew nothing of this and when Cowgill became aware that he had been overlooked in favour of his deputy he immediately tendered his resignation. This at one stroke agent 'Stanley' managed not only to manoeuvre himself into a position where he had access to important Soviet material, but he managed to get rid of his immediate competitor to boot. However his appointment did not please everyone. Charles Arnold-Baker, a German born (Wolfgang Werner von Blumenthal) British academic and historian expressed reservations about Philby's appointment. He saw the Soviet Union as the clear post war threat to the west and in conducting interrogations of Germans, especially those who had served on the Eastern Front, reported that there was a high anti-communist feeling especially in the western USSR. These reports were buried by his superiors in the service mainly because they were Soviet spies themselves. He expressed suspicious doubts about Kim Philby being appointed to the role, but negligently he was ignored.

Therefore the man charged with the responsibility of being the head of Britain's anti-Soviet spy network was himself a Soviet spy. Philby was now in place to willingly inform Moscow of any current and planned operations to counter the threat. The Kremlin was to receive everything their enemy was doing, every effort, every plan to counter the spread of communism and any planned operations inside the USSR itself. The amount and quality of intelligence within reach almost seemed like striking gold, not only at Moscow Centre but also for Philby himself. He also by 1944 received a new controller. Max Krotenschield the man who had handled him since the unpopular Anatoly Gorsky had been moved on in 1942 was to be replaced. The other man to control agent 'Stanley' was called Anatoli Lebedev.

But almost straight away after his new appointment, Philby was to receive a threat. Something which had the very real potential to expose him and the entire network; once more it came about in the form of another defection, an ever growing risk the higher up the chain he climbed.

In August 1944 with the Germans now stretched on all sides, the Allies in France and the Soviets on the offensive under Operation Bagration in the east, a letter was received by Chantry Hamilton-Page, the vice consul in the British embassy in Istanbul. The note written in rather poor English was from a fellow consul from the Soviet embassy in the same city called Konstantin Volkov. It appeared he was requesting an urgent appointment with the diplomat who chose not to take it seriously. Hamilton-Page just assumed the letter was nothing more than a prank, simply ignored it and, due to him being prone to memory lapses, simply forgot all about it.

It was not until early September, the 4th to be exact when a nervous looking Volkov turned up in person at the embassy with his equally shaky wife, Zoya in tow for a personal meeting with the vice consul. Surprised the British agreed to meet him, ushering the couple into the vice consul's office. What he had to reveal would truly be explosive and had the potential to tip the balance of power toward the west. In his meeting Page did not speak Russian so he brought in the First Secretary at the embassy, John Leigh Reed to translate. Volkov explained to Page over the course of the next hour that his diplomatic posting was just a cover as he was in fact the deputy chief of Soviet intelligence in Turkey. He proceeded to say that he had spent several years in Moscow working for the NKVD in the Lubyanka headquarters on the British desk prior to this current posting. He therefore had vital information on what the Russians knew about British intelligence operations and after a strongly heated row with the Russian ambassador over a trivial matter, had decided to defect to the west to get even.

He was willing to reveal details of Soviet espionage networks both in Britain and here in Turkey including information leading to the real names of three Soviet agents operating within departments of the British government and security services. He was also willing to reveal details of the Lubyanka including financial details, training and guard schedules. He was also willing to divulge information on Soviet interceptions on British communications as well as providing wax impressions of keys that would access the files inside of the NKVD headquarters. On top of all this he would also make known the layout of the Lubyanka's burglar alarm system. On the 13 September Volkov returned to the British embassy this timed armed with a letter assuring that he knew of and would reveal the names of 314 Soviet agents in Turkey and astonishingly another 250 in Britain. He also said that in a suitcase located in an empty Moscow apartment were copies of documents that were delivered by Soviet spies in the United Kingdom (possibly including the ones copied out by Kim Philby when he was in Section V). He mentioned in teasing tones to wet the appetite of the British and to make them think seriously about his intentions that the three agents in the UK government were working in important positions. Two were in the Foreign Office, referring to Donald Maclean and Guy Burgess while the third was the head of a counter-espionage organisation in London. This was obviously Kim Philby.

His conditions were that in exchange for the vital material he requested £50,000 in funds, a considerable amount by today's standards justifying this amount by telling Page:

"I consider this sum as a minimum considering the importance of the material given to you, as a result of which all my relatives living in the territory of the USSR are doomed."

This had to make the British think seriously about his offer, it stood to reason. If he was some kind of clever ruse, why was Moscow willing to expose potential spies, if there were any that high up in the establishment? Surely this man had to be real. Volkov added to his list of demands political asylum in Britain under an assumed identity for he knew all too well what the NKVD would do to protect their secrets. He further added that once he had made it to Britain he would reveal the address of the Moscow flat and MI6 could go and retrieve the suitcase full of papers.

Volkov had also warned that not only did the NKVD have a spy inside the embassy but wire telegrams could also not be trusted as the Russians had cracked the British cipher codes and were reading their information. Based upon this claim he recommended that all messages regarding himself should strictly be written down and closely guarded. Any communications should be delivered via the immunity of the diplomatic bag and done through Chantry Page on routine business as so not to arouse suspicion. He told the British that his deadline for this deal would be no more than twenty-one days, after which he would assume the offer rejected if he did not hear from his counterpart by this time and take his information elsewhere. The request was delivered to the new British ambassador to Turkey, Sir Maurice Peterson who refused to deal with the Russian. He wanted nothing to do with spies of any kind since the Albanian valet of his predecessor Sir Hughe Knatchbull-Huggessen, called Elyesa Bazna was actually a German agent during the war with the codename 'Cicero'.

Instead he ordered John Leigh Reed to just pass the information onto MI6 as soon as possible and let them deal with the matter putting it somewhat undiplomatically:

"No one's going to turn my embassy into a nest of spies. Do it through London."

The diplomats agreed to this request, heeded Volkov's warning and sent the report written by hand by John Reed through the old fashioned way of the diplomatic bag. The whole thing was done so sensitively that not even Cyril Machray, the MI6 station chief in Istanbul (Nicholas Elliott had previously occupied the role), knew nothing of the matter. It took another ten days before news of Volkov's defection reached the halls of MI6 and the desk of Sir Stewart Menzies. Upon reading the report, 'C' summoned his trusted colleague and head of Soviet counter intelligence Kim Philby, one of the very men known by the defector to his office and passed the file onto him.

When Philby laid eyes on Volkov's information he was quietly shocked. Reading it with a rapidly filling sense of cold dread his eyes ran over the report:

"In support of his request for asylum, Volkov promised to reveal details of the headquarters of the NKVD, in which apparently he had worked for many years. He also offered details of Soviet networks and agents operating abroad. Inter alia, he claimed to know the real names of three Soviet agents working in Britain. Two

of them were in the Foreign Office; one was head of a counter-espionage organization in London."

Philby knew who the three men were. He knew he was one of them. Through his knowledge of the copied documents Philby had produced for the Soviets that could be recovered, this man had the very information that could be traced back to him and destroy his and his friend's careers. Guy Burgess was by now in the news department and Maclean was First Secretary of the British embassy in Washington D.C. but this could have them thrown into prison or worse still condemned for treason. Britain still carried the death penalty at this time and treason was one of the offences which warranted execution by hanging.

It was clear that Konstantin Volkov had to be silenced. But Philby had to be careful about the whole affair, rejecting the idea of caution just in case Volkov's approach should prove provocative toward him in some way. He concluded that it could possibly lead to his exposure later on. The only real way forward was for him to not show any outward signs of concern and indeed act as if this was some kind of interesting breakthrough. To solidify his deception he told Menzies that he was sure they were onto something of great importance, actually boosting the value of his potential exposer's claims. But Philby's motives were seriously ulterior. He couldn't just ignore and dismiss Volkov's claims while informing the NKVD who would just deal with him might arouse suspicion and fuel the idea that there actually was a mole in British intelligence. Based on what Volkov had already said, any amount of suspicion and the hounds of MI5 would investigate and eventually identify himself and his friends. Therefore he needed time to work and the initial enthusiasm he displayed to his superiors feigned the idea that he needed time to work on the case. He told Menzies a pack of lies saying that he required time to study the memo, dig into the background of this potential defector, and to make appropriate recommendations for action. Menzies agreed asking Philby to report his findings the next morning and also to keep things to himself. Philby was more than happy with that, the less people knew about this the better.

Unsurprisingly he worked late that same evening. Gripped by feverish panic he contacted his old friend Max Krotenschield informing him of the impending disaster in a hastily arranged meeting. Max desperately tried to bring Philby back to a state of calmness, reassuring him in a very English way:

"Don't worry old man, we've seen a lot worse. The score will be settled in our favour."

It was as simple as that. Philby knew that the ongoing Volkov affair would endanger the rest of the Cambridge network putting Burgess, Maclean, Blunt and Carincross all in danger as well. That night wireless monitors in London detected a sudden increase in coded radio traffic travelling first from London to Moscow, then on from Moscow to Istanbul.

The next morning Philby subsequently approached 'C' and informed him that because this thing was best kept to minimum, it should be someone experienced that would travel to Istanbul to meet Konstantin Volkov in person with a view to getting into one of the safehouses in the city before extracting him without the prior permission of the Turks to Egypt. Menzies agreed stating that he knew the ideal man to facilitate Volkov's arrival, the head of SIME – Security Intelligence Middle East, Brigadier Sir Douglas Roberts. He was on London at the time on leave from his base in Cairo. He was also fiercely anti-communist and a veteran officer. Born in Odessa to an English father and Russian mother he spoke the language fluently, and was the only intelligence officer to do so. Philby did not reckon upon this as he realised that he would certainly be able to smuggle the defector out quite easily. All he could do was hope that the Soviets would be able to do their work faster than MI6.

However there was one very important chink in Roberts' armour. Even though he was a veteran and extremely capable officer he suffered from aviophobia, an irrational fear of flying. When asked to head to Istanbul to pick up on the Volkov case, he stipulated that his contract expressly prevented him from taking a plane.

Another choice was none other the Philby's best friend, Nicolas Elliot, now stationed in Berne, Switzerland, already had contacts in Istanbul from his previous posting there and was experienced in extracting defectors from the Vermehren's. This was Philby's worst nightmare Elliott must *not* get involved in this so the time for a less subtle and more direct approach was needed. He simply put it to Menzies that it should be himself to travel to Istanbul instead to meet Volkov in person. Knowing that failure to prevent his defection would inevitably lead to his own arrest he certainly took him time about it. No stone could be left unturned undergoing a crash course in wireless tapping to get around the now known penetrated communication systems in the embassy before stalling for another three days. When his flight bound for the Egyptian capital eventually took off it was then diverted to Tunis causing even more delays to his arrival.

Finally on the 26 September 1945, twenty-two days since Volkov's contact, Kim Philby eventually arrived in Istanbul. Despite the obvious risk, when he arrived at the British consulate he asked Chantry Hamilton Page to contact the Soviet embassy to set up the meeting with Volkov himself. Here he also met John Leigh Reed who curiously asked him why on earth did MI6 take so long to respond. Philby blatantly lied to the diplomat with no hesitation or remorse:

"Sorry old man, it would have interfered with leave arrangements." He stated pompously. Reed just thought that the man he was dealing with a both incompetent and plain irresponsible. He had no idea that the man he was talking to was one of the Soviet spies Volkov had been alluding to. Philby did

not care what Reed thought as long as it did not interfere with whatever he had to do to silence the defector. There was a risk that the presence of Philby in this matter may have compromised his position but a stroke of luck came his way. The Soviets were aware of Volkov's deception when it was discussed earlier at the British embassy with Sir Maurice Peterson. They were tapping into the British telephone lines and listening to everything. Since the Russian insisted all messages be delivered by diplomatic bag, the delay would give time for Moscow to uncover Volkov's plan and if this was the case, any action and possible blame would therefore by deflected away from Philby himself. Nonetheless Hamilton Page proceeded on the MI6 man's instructions and tried to phone the Soviet consulate with Kim himself standing over him to establish contact with the defector but strangely found that he had difficulty getting through to him in person instead reaching the consul general. Page tied a second time and eventually after a bit of frustrating persistence from a lengthy pause he was put through to someone identifying himself as Konstantin Volkov. Immediately Page was suspicious. He had spoken to Volkov many times, the voice on the other end of the line was not his, he was sure of that. Whoever Page was speaking to at the Soviet embassy was an imposter.

Slightly irritated by this lack of progress at this vital time, he tried a third time but again he got no further than the switchboard operator who said he was out. Philby, still in the same room as Page must have been secretly delighted. Once again he tried the following day only to be told this time by an official that Volkov was no longer in Istanbul but in Moscow. Page noted that there seemed to be some sort of interference from the other end, hearing a scuffling noise before the hard click of a phone receiver slammed down. The line then went dead. Angered by his failure to get through to anyone, Page disappeared. He arrived back in one hour apparently still as angry as before viciously slating his Russian counterparts:

"It's no bloody good. I can't get any sense out of that madhouse. Nobody's ever heard of Volkov."

Page had decided to personally travel to the Soviet embassy to speak with the consulate-general yet had gotten nowhere and had arrived back with nothing. Philby informed Page quite cynically that it was the defectors own fault simply because he had insisted on the diplomatic bag to communicate. He was using Volkov's own preventative method in alerting the Soviets to his plans as an excuse to why he disappeared. In truth the Soviets had indeed whisked Konstantin Volkov and his wife away to Moscow, heavily sedated and bandaged aboard a transport plane unable to escape, even his family disappeared into the murk of Stalin's Russia. In Moscow Volkov found himself in the torture cells of the Lubyanka, undergoing brutal interrogation until finally he cracked. He admitted that he did intend to defect and expose the names of hundreds of Soviet agents active abroad, including those of Kim Philby and the other Cambridge Spies. It was enough for the authorities as Konstantin Volkov and his petrified wife Zoya were both executed for treason by the Stalinist state.

But the blame game between the British authorities continued, Philby maintained his argument that the diplomatic route took too long to alert MI6, Reed however rejected this argument saying that MI6 simply took too long to reach Istanbul in order to interview and possibly facilitate an extraction for him from Turkey.

Even though the Soviets were tapping the British phones and had broken the codes, Philby himself did all he could to warn Moscow of the threat to both himself and the entire Cambridge Spy Ring. His utter laziness in getting to Istanbul would have given time for the Soviets to act, despite the anxiety Volkov caused him from the threat of exposure. Due to the high level information he was willing to leak, Philby showed absolutely no guilt or remorse for the fate of the defector. He did not care if he or his family was liquidated as he knew deep down he would be describing him as:

"A nasty piece of work who deserved what he got."

There was no doubt however that the whole episode was frightening for Philby and his apparent disappearance was secretly a huge relief. He had almost been exposed for what he was; a traitor and so were the rest of his Cambridge friends. In part Volkov's fate was already unwittingly sealed by the people he was willing to help when they passed his file onto Philby. The complete unawareness of the British intelligence services to unwittingly make the Soviets aware through Philby possibly let to the defector's downfall.

Satisfied that the threat had passed, he sent a telegram back to Menzies innocently explaining that Volkov had simply vanished and requested that the case be closed pending his report. Philby put forward several explanations (except for the real one) as to the sudden disappearance. Perhaps he had gotten drunk, spoke too much and was overheard. Perhaps the tapping of the embassy telephones and cracking of the British codes help the Soviets to deduce what was going on. Anything to deflect the possibility that the tip off came from London, and himself.

With a measure of a bad impression from Istanbul about the episode he returned back. But on the way he stopped off in Rome for three days to see his old friend James Jesus Angleton, who by now had been stationed in the country as part of the counter intelligence department X-2 for the region. The Americans were aware of the whole Volkov situation but Philby was not quite sure how the affair was being viewed in the United States. After the stress of the past he needed to good blowout to relieve some of the tension he had felt and his friend greeted him warmly having no idea what he had just gone through although he expressed sympathy that such a promising defection had failed. Angleton for his part now married, confided in his friend that he felt guilty for not seeing his wife because due to his work. Philby proceeded to get extremely drunk in the reunion which was punctured by secrets and lubricated by liquor. By the end of it, Angleton bungled Kim onto a plane to fly him home.

This was at a time when the catastrophe of the Second World War was in its final throes. The Allies were flooding into western Germany and the Soviets had overrun most of Eastern Europe, eastern Germany and had surrounded Berlin. By the end of the war, with Hitler finally dead from his own hand, Nazism had been destroyed, the twisted dream shattered in the rubble strewn ruins of Berlin in the heart of a devastated and scarred Europe. In the Far East the Japanese Empire was brutally brought to its knees when the Americans dropped two of the new atom bombs over the Japanese cities of Hiroshima and Nagasaki to herald the dawn of the nuclear age. Where the war stared with bullets and tanks, it would end in plutonium and radiation. The divisions between east and west were now becoming a gulf. 'Uncle Joe Stalin' was fast becoming the enemy as he refused to relinquish the lands his Red Army had bloodily fought over and wrestled from the fascists. Instead he preferred over the coming years to oversee the installation of communist puppet states throughout Eastern Europe known as the 'Eastern Bloc' The dividing line which ideologically cut Germany in half along with the rest of the continent would eventually be referred to as what Churchill would go on to say the 'Iron Curtain'. This therefore would see the period of suspicion and tension that would eventually become known worldwide as the Cold War.

One of the first defections of the new situation came on the 5 September 1945 from another Soviet official, and Kim Philby could do nothing to prevent it. Igor Gouzenko was a cipher clerk who defected to Canada, approached the Royal Canadian Mounted Police and claimed political asylum. He claimed to provide hard evidence of Soviet spy networks established in the west. This prompted activity in the government with the Canadian Prime Minister Mackenzie King meeting with Norman Robertson, the Undersecretary for External Affairs to discuss the situation. Robertson claimed that intelligence revealed by Gouzenko indicated the presence of active Soviet spies operating in both America and Canada with some being based close to the US Secretary of State Edward Stettinius.

The clearly meant that Gouzenko's information was obviously useful to both countries, furthermore it would also be in the Britain's interest to seize upon it by whatever means in order to pass it onto her allies. The Canadians however were slightly cautious about it. Not wanting to antagonise Russia they needed to proceed very carefully given the potential for awkward political issues in the future. King saw it as vital that the Canadian government not to be seen mixed up in this matter, for this may give the Soviet Union the wrong impression and sour relations between the two.

Gouzenko was subsequently taken into protective custody, arranged by William Stephenson, the head of British Security Coordination who actually aided in the Russian's defection to the west. As such both he and his family were moved into Camp X a World War II paramilitary and training camp based near Whitby in Ontario. There they lived under guard as two intelligence agents interviewed him about what he knew. Gouzenko claimed to have evidence of a major spy ring in Canada which would lead to the eventual arrest of 22 home grown agents and a further 15 Soviet spies in the country. Meanwhile due to Stephenson's involvement, meant that the Soviet counter-espionage section of MI6 became inevitably involved. The case was passed onto its chief, Kim Philby. Menzies asked his opinion on the matter for which he replied that the Gouzenko defection was certainly important. Privately he resented it, knowing that it was an utter disaster for the Soviets, and this time it was completely out of his hands. He knew the Canadians were closely guarding the defector and so the long practiced ritual of liquidating traitors by NKVD assassins was not going to be an option. As such Gouzenko was free to dismantle the entire network in Canada. By the 17 September Philby in a measure of frustration reported back to Moscow exactly what Gouzenko was informing the west telling them that as a result of what was going on British counter-intelligence were going to begin taking effective measures against Soviet espionage operations based on the information the traitor was divulging.

Philby himself in his MI6 capacity dispatched Roger Hollis, journalist, fellow intelligence officer and the future head of MI5 to Canada instead of himself, possibly out of fear that the defector could very well recognise him and expose him as a Soviet spy. With Hollis gone and unable to determine what indeed was being said or to affect it, the wait was a nervous one for him during which time he wondered if it may be time to make a break for it and defect himself to the USSR. However what Gouzenko was revealing was something different. He was a member of the GRU, the Soviet secret police, not the NKVD so had little information regarding espionage in Britain. He leaked information regarding what the Soviets knew about the American atomic programme. He revealed that the Russians knew how much enriched material the US had giving the opportunity for Soviet scientists to calculate how many atom bombs the Unites States could produce, and therefore the size of their nuclear arsenal. The source of this information came from a spy working in the Anglo-Canadian nuclear research laboratory in Montreal. He was referring to Alan Nunn May a physicist and a previous fellow Cambridge student who also spied for the communists now back in the UK from Canada. May had a habit of contacting his controller in London by meeting outside the British Museum while carrying a copy of The Times. Based upon Gouzenko's information the authorities planned to intercept both May and his controller and capture them.

However when the trap was set it turned out that neither May or his handler appeared. It was the work of Kim Philby who had secretly tipped off Moscow Centre about May and indeed all Soviet agents which Gouzenko was referring to and was now in danger of being under surveillance from the British and American authorities. May himself would eventually be arrested in March 1946 and subsequently confess to spying. Another agent under threat from the defector's revelations was Klaus Fuchs the German born British theoretical nuclear physicist who was working on the Manhattan atomic bomb project at the time. Fuchs, was supplying technical details on the design of nuclear warheads but would eventually go on to be caught and convicted of spying based on evidence that Gouzenko had supplied.

Despite the duplicity Philby was engineering throughout the intelligence world, his private life was flourishing. By now he had three children, Josephine born in 1941, John in 1943 and Tom in 1944. By 1946 he was willing to marry Aileen Furse and approached his old flame and first wife Litzi Friedmann whom although separated remained on good terms. She granted him a divorce on the 17 September 1946 clearing the way for him to marry Aileen just seven days later. At the age of thirty-five, she was only a year older than Kim himself and was seven months pregnant with their fourth child, a daughter they would call Miranda at the time. The wedding which was witnessed by his friend in intelligence Tomas Harris and their mutual friend and one time possible Soviet recruit Flora Solomon, the darling of Marks & Spencer. Alileen was a patriot and was initially had some doubts over where her husband was disappearing off to at various times. Her now husband just said it was off to do with work, which was in reality a half-truth since he would go off and meet with his Soviet handlers. But now those reservations were starting to wain since she just assumed it was something to do with the Foreign Office and essential for war work. Now the war was over she assumed things would start to change and for her part she was to provide a domestic setting for the family. The reception after the ceremony was unsurprisingly a drunken affair, filled by many of Philby's compatriots in the intelligence world. The boozy wartime drinkers never left their old habits behind them.

This happy time of contentment was also boosted by another rise in his career. That same year he received, as did many of those who fought the war behind desks, bars and aliases received awards from a grateful but weary nation. Along with his friends Nicolas Elliott and James Angleton he went to Buckingham Palace to receive an investiture from the King, George VI. He was awarded the OBE, Officer of the British Empire in thanks for his war effort. However this award disappointed Philby somewhat, even his friends thought that he may have received a knighthood. On the way to the ceremony he, while walking up the front yard of the Palace stopped for a moment, turned to Jim Angleton and uttered the phrase:

"You know, what this country needs is a good dose of socialism."

It puzzled and made the young American anglophile equally suspicious. It was an odd moment and one where, just for a second Kim Philby opened the door ever so slightly into his real world. For a split second, the real Kim Philby appeared then disappeared once more.

What his closest friends did not know was that the newly appointed Kim Philby OBE was also recognised for his help by another grateful nation. The Soviet Union, now realising thanks to testimony from his handler, that agent 'Stanley' was indeed sincere awarded him with the Soviet Order of the Red Banner for his work over ten years to the communists.

With this Kim Philby became the only person in history to receive decorations from the world's three great ideologies, the fascists in Franco's Spain, the communists in Stalin's USSR and the OBE from the democratic British. But nobody could ever know of this unique accolade.

Philby's private life was settled, his intelligence career on the rise, and his espionage career bearing fruit. Things were looking up as the next phase rapidly loomed. The life of this Cold War spy though lay not in the west, but to the east, in familiar waters once more.

CHAPTER NINE

THE BALKAN BLOODBATH

By 1947 Kim Philby's career took a dramatic surge as he was appointed head of British Intelligence for Turkey in February. He was to be based in Istanbul, the social city of intelligence agencies since the war and the gateway to the east. Moving out with Aileen and their children his official capacity, as was so often the case, that of a diplomat. His title was that of First Secretary at the British Consulate. This was nothing more than a front to cover his real work of liaising with the Turkish security services on various matters and handling British agents while on operations.

It was during this time that the west decided to check the threat of Soviet communism by attempting to roll back the Iron Curtain in Albania. The Balkan subversions were designed to achieve its ultimate aim, the overthrowing of Enver Hoxha, the socialist dictator of Albania since 1944. As Philby was now situated in Istanbul he was in perfect position discover the Anglo-American plan to stage uprisings in the country by acting officially as the main liaison officer between the British and the US intelligence agencies. He was also in position to leak details of the conspiracy to Moscow.

Philby by now had a new controller, Yuri Modin, a man who would handle not just himself but go on to be responsible for the entire Cambridge network. Initially he was wary of the double agent and his motives, having only Arnold Deutsch's testimony to rely on but believing incorrectly that his real interests lay with western intelligence. Philby's duplicity was so complete that he even managed to fool his Soviet masters with his quintessentially English demeanour with Modin commenting on his recruit:

"He was so completely, psychologically and physically, the British intelligence officer that I could never quite accept that he was one of us, a Marxist in the clandestine service of the Soviet Union."

However Moscow Centre knew a little more than Modin did. They knew just what the quality and quantity their network was producing, they therefore instructed their man on how to handle their star agent forbidding him to be seen with him in public. Modin was forbidden to share a drink, dine with or even be seen with Philby in any capacity. Yuri found it difficult to measure the Englishman in this situation, preferring to base his judgement upon him solely by his performance. Modin soon found that Philby consistently provided intelligence of high quality concerning western operations and of the kind that was so secretive that there really was no other means to obtain them. The Russian noted that the Englishman, who was so complete the quintissential officer, was positioned so comfortably that he could have commanded anything he wanted out of life.

Albania and its one million strong population was still the poorest nation in post-war Europe, fractured by regions and ethnic groups. However one around one percent of the people owned around ninety-five percent of the land that people lived and worked on. During the war many Albanians fought as nationalists against German and Italian occupation of their country and the most successful group was the communist National Liberation Front.

After the war its neighbour Greece wanted the lands it claimed when it counter attacked in 1941 after the Italian led invasion from the country. Greece had conquered a quarter of Albania and now demanded the territory for herself even though Yugoslavia wanted Albania in a wider Balkan confederation. The Albanian leader,

King Zog was not recognised by the Allies and the country itself was largely forgotten by the wider events of the Second World War. This meant that in the early, tension filled days of the Cold War, Britain planned to parachute in agents, well trained in subversion to both trigger and facilitate a popular uprising. This would, they hoped, lead to wider national revolt throughout the communist eastern bloc and eventually a civil war in Albania itself. MI6 was enthusiastic in such a plan to roll back the Iron Curtain and weaken the communist influence in the Balkans but Sir Steward Menzies was less so and only agreed to it to appease those who were in the organisation that were former members of the SOE.

Britain wanted their chief ally, the United States, the arch enemy of communism to both provide regional bases and finance the entire plan. Such coordination required meetings with the officials concerned in the whole Albanian subversion to work out the logistics of the operation and the Joint Intelligence Committee convened in March 1947 chaired by the senior diplomat, intelligence officer and future ambassador to the Soviet Union, William Hayter. The meeting was to be held in Washington D.C. and read like a who's who of the espionage world in the early Cold War. The host delegation included the head of the US State Department's Policy and Planning Staff Robert Joyce, and Frank Wisner of the Office of Policy Coordination. Frank Lindsay and James McCargar made up the rest of the American intelligence contingent. Their British counterparts present included Foreign Office staff Earl Jellicoe and Gladwyn Jebb. SIS representatives included Peter Dwyer, an expert on the Balkan region, and of course, Kim Philby who was assigned to liaise with McCargar on joint operational matters. Such was the high level classified nature of the meeting it would have presented a goldmine for any eavesdroppers. But the Soviets in Philby did have that ear, listening, watching and reporting everything that was planned and discussed.

Amongst the Albanian population itself, there was no shortage of patriots who wanted to free Albania from the communists and western recruiters found no shortage of people from the different factions willing to participate throughout Greece, Italy and Turkey. Groups willing to fight and topple the communist regime consisted of a mixture of monarchists called Legalitati and members of the National Front called the Beli Kombetar as well as other smaller groups. They were to form the agitating vanguard for the operations the west was planning and that Philby was secretly feeding to Moscow which was named by the Americans as 'FIEND' and the British codenaming it as 'VALUABLE'.

Initially volunteers were trained and dropped off close to the Albanian coast to initiate an uprising. Things got off to a reasonable start, the first three missions were essentially free of any kind of unwanted attention from the communist authorities before larger numbers were to be trained and sent in under Operation Valuable itself.

However world events began to turn regardless of whoever was trying to influence it. Albania geographically and politically remained autonomous from the Eastern bloc, buffered by Socialist Federal Republic of Yugoslavia. This separation of Albania from the communist Balkan states was only possible because FPR Yugoslavia was expelled from the communist bloc due to the poor relations with the USSR in June 1948. This was known as the Tiso-Stalin split and marked the time known as the Informbiro Period.

Operation Valuable became even more of an opportunity to take advantage of the fractious nature of the precarious communist governments in the Balkans, topple Enver Hoxha's seemingly isolated Socialist administration and restore the monarchy under King Zog. Around a dozen Albanians were selected for the operation and were shipped to Libya to receive adequate training in the use of radio, codes and firearms under the tutorage of Colonel Miller, a US Army officer known by his nickname of 'Ace'.

Throughout the whole of 1947 the man were deployed into Albania, being dropped into mountainous regions of the Mati. Contacting residents of local villages, their initial attempts were rather unsuccessful in goading the people into dissent. It was hoped such dissatisfaction would eventually spark an uprising and eventually a full revolt but it was not happening. Sabotaging local landmarks such as copper mines and the oilfields of Kucova did not manage to achieve many successes that the west actually desired.

Kim Philby was responsible for facilitating the infiltration of six groups of guerrillas into the Soviet states of Georgia and Armenia via Turkey with the cooperation of the local intelligence forces. The Turks escorted the groups to the border with Georgia and allowed them to cross. It wasn't long before the sound of gunfire was heard from the Soviet side. They had been ambushed.

A further effort was to be launched again from Turkey via a seaborne landing, but the operation never got off the ground. The ship that was to be used to transport guerrillas never departed port.

The subversion efforts connected to Operation Valuable was quickly turning into a farce. Every time missions were being deployed the local authorities were there to meet them. Over the past two years the west's attempt to roll back the Iron Curtain by overthrowing the Hoxha dictatorship in Albania were getting nowhere. King Zog the former leader of Albania was now approached while in exile in Egypt. The west wanted him to recommend men required for the job, commandos better trained than the guerrilla volunteers they had previously sent in to counter the threat posed by the communists. Getting the support of the former monarch would not be easy as the negotiators, the Americans Robert Low and Robert Milner accompanied by their British counterpart Neil McLean (known as Billy) found out.

Nobody was willing to declare King Zog as the head of a provisional government in exile meaning that bringing him into the fold was virtually impossible if he was not recognised as the legitimate head of state.

By August 1949 the world learnt the Albanian exiles had managed to form a general committee, coalition of all the political classes via an announcement that was made from Paris. The purpose of such a union which was named the Free Albania National Committee was to stir up anti-communist feeling and therefore ignite rebellion in Albania itself. In truth the whole organisation was a political front created by both American and British intelligence agencies both MI6 and the relatively new CIA for subversive paramilitary operations. This was the first major organised operation to truly topple Enver Hoxa and finally remove him from power. Thirty fighters of the republican Beli Kombetar were armed and assisted by David Smiley, the deputy commander of a tank regiment stationed in West Germany. For Smiley this was like a negative; he had already had previous experience in Albania helping Hoxha and the communists to overthrow occupation and gain power in the country during the war but now was taking part in the act of trying to remove him.

Prior to deployment, the fighters had been trained in radio operation, techniques on how to obtain intelligence and general guerrilla tactics for the previous two months in Malta in an old fortress named Bin Jema and nicknamed 'The Pixies' by MI6. Even though there were some difficulties, one being language was the biggest. The trainers did not speak Albanian, the Albanians themselves spoke no English and most were poorly trained to start but some of those who were sent in were former resistance fighters during the war. But there were also misunderstandings about the overall objective of Valuable. One fighter though his task was to enter his homeland, make his way to his home village, try to promote the idea of an uprising then exfiltrate the country altogether. Nine out of the thirty were sent out on the 26 September, the beginning of Operation Valuable itself aboard a trawler in British Navy service which sailed north prior to a Greek style second vessel called a caique called the Stormie Seas departing from Malta three days later. After making a brief stop in Italy both ships met at a pre designated point in the Adriatic Sea on the 3 October where the nine aboard the Navy vessel transferred to the Stormie Seas which was to take them to the Albanian coast. They landed south of Vlora where the US believed the Soviet Union was building a so-called warm water port; a submarine base at the nearby Karaburun Peninsula. A few hours later where some of the men were deployed in the south to investigate this, the rest were taken further to the north. But things were starting to turn sour. The communist Albanian security forces, the Sigurimi, intercepted the raiding parties, firing upon them to cause casualties. Three of the guerrillas were killed from the first group that had landed while another one had deserted to find his family and another man was shot from the second group. Four surviving members managed to get away and cross the border into Greece in complete disarray.

In response Earnst Bevin, the British Foreign Secretary who wanted to replace King Zog once Hoxha was overthrown, travelled to Washington D.C. to discuss the outcome of Operation Valuable with US officials. They concluded through the CIA that such subversive efforts would in reality have little chance of success. Both the US and the UK along with both Greece and Italy wanted to overthrow the Hoxha regime, put a stop to Soviet influence in the Mediterranean and stop it spreading through southern Europe. But Hoxha was clearly far stronger than anyone had ever anticipated, a fifteen thousand strong security force accompanied by sixty-five thousand regular army troops. In addition to this were fifteen hundred Soviets who were employed officially in an advisory role helping to train the soldiers.

And the communists had an ally. Advance warning of the raids including restricted information on the location of the landings, their strengths and objectives were leaked to the USSR by as ever, the MI6 intelligence chief, Kim Philby.

His controller Yuri Modin commented on Philby's duplicity at this sensitive time:

"He gave us vital information about the number of men involved, the day and the time of the landing, the weapons they were bringing and the precise programme of action... The Soviets duly passed on Philby's information to Albanians who set up ambushes."

Mistakenly the west thought that Albania was a weak link in the eastern bloc and would fall away quite easily with other puppet nations under the Soviet umbrella soon following suit. But both the British and Americans had grossly underestimated the stubbornness of the communist regime and of Hoxha himself. And of course they could not have foreseen the treachery of one of their own. Philby's security breach ultimately would cause the deaths of as many as 300 fighters but he justified the action by saying:

"I do not say that people were happy under the regime but the CIA underestimated the degree of control that the authorities had over the country."

And he was not touched by the conscience and guilt accompanied by the consequence of his actions. Certainly not displaying and not feeling any sense of betrayal against his friends he later chillingly declared:

"The agents we sent into Albania were armed men intent on murder, sabotage and assassination. They knew the risks they were running. I was serving the interests of the Soviet Union and those interests required that these men were defeated. To the extent that I helped defeat them, even if it caused their deaths, I have no regrets."

While Kim Philby was playing his part in the debacle of

Operation Valuable which was still continuing and would do so until 1951, the other side of his life was quite different. The marriage to Aileen Philby was under some strain. Suffering from psychological issues virtually all her life, by the time the family were living the Istanbul her mental state had degraded, spiralling into the pit of depression by 1948. Heavy drinking numbed the situation but did not stop her from suffering from episodes of self-harm by involving herself in accidents and injecting both insulin and urine to infect her wounds. Making her incredibly ill, her harming were nothing more than cries for attention due to her husband's work commitments and frequent disappearing whenever he went off to secretly meet his handler. What did not help matters for Kim was that Aileen for all her faults was fiercely patriotic and actually suspected her husband at various times of spying for more than just MI6. Another thing that also put strain on the marriage was the arrival of Guy Burgess in the Philby household. Aileen disliked her husband's old Cambridge friend and the two were soon sharing heavy drinking sessions together. Burgess's homosexual debauchery made him an incredibly volatile fellow as he always was but following her self-inflicted wounds she was sent off to Switzerland to recuperate. Upon her return however in late 1948 her depressive episodes began again in the Turkish city, this time involved in a second incident, burning herself with a charcoal stove. After this she went back to Switzerland, preventing unwanted interference toward Guy Burgess's antics and Kim Philby's spying actions. The most suspicious of all his acquaintances was for the time being out of the picture.

By 1949 she had returned, but the Philby's were on the move again. While the guerrillas in Albania were being betrayed, arrested and killed based on information provided by Kim Philby's actions, the man himself was undergoing a career rise. He had just been offered one of MI6's most prestigious posts, a considerable promotion to boot. Kim Philby was to become the chief SIS liaison in the United States based in Washington D.C.

This brand new promotion marked the height of his intelligence career. It would start by crossing the Atlantic in a luxurious cruise ship. Little did he know that this was to be the climax of a long and glittery rise to respect and prominence in the intelligence community. It would eventually trigger the start of a long and painful decent into suspicion and denial. For Kim Philby, Washington would mark the end of the beginning and the beginning of the end.

CHAPTER TEN

STANLEY AND HOMER

On the 9 October 1949, the Cunard liner named the Caronia docked at New York. On board was Kim Philby the new SIS liaison officer to both the CIA and the FBI. The Americans arranged a motor launch to meet their new VIP, whisking him through customs without any of the usual formalities the other guests and tourists had to endure. Philby was swept into the United States with the efficiency and hospitality of that given to a head of state, finding himself that night in a high rise hotel with a view overlooking the famous Central Park.

The next day he travelled south to his posting in the US capital, Washington D.C. It was not long, a few days to be exact when Philby was given his first task; to joint head up the body responsible for overseeing Albanian operations under Operation Valuable/Fiend called the Anglo-American Joint Policy Committee alongside James McCargar. The United States had emerged from the catastrophe of the Second World War youthful, virile and an emerging, affluent superpower. It was one that would take on the role as the world's policeman and chief banker to the new world order. The 19th Century was Britain's prosperous era. The 20th Century would be America's. The chief threat to this emerging dominance was the spread of communism particularly in Eastern Europe. In the past the Soviet Union had been a military ally in the struggle against Nazism but had always been a political opponent; one riddled with suspicion and animosity. Now clearly to the US and the west, the Soviet Union was the main threat to global stability in its advocating and facilitating in the spread of world communism. The United States agreed to the British request to finance the whole Albanian operation as well as other efforts throughout the Soviet bloc including Poland where the Americans would end up sending both funds and arms to groups in the country to stir up anti-communist revolutions. But there was double crossing at play as these groups the US were unwittingly supplying were nothing more than a front for the communists in Poland itself.

Washington was the hub of the fight against Soviet influence throughout the world. A capital flushed with the affluence and confidence of king maker and financier through Lend-Lease, the American plan to bankroll the European war against Hitler. Also the subsequent Marshall Plan to aid in the recuperation and rebuilding of the shattered nations involved in the conflict. Philby's appointment to Washington was engineered by the old boys network, facilitated by an old wartime friend who had recommend him for promotion. That man was one of the senior members of the CIA, James Jesus Angleton. Officially his title was First Secretary to the British embassy, but as was a routine certainty in this game it was just a cover for his real intelligence work as the senior liaison officer between the US and the UK.

Officially he was to promote more aggressive policies regarding joint intelligence operations which put him into close contact with Angleton who remained still slightly suspicious of his old friend. Despite this the two reunited men still got on rather well just like in old times lunching every week at a rather upmarket restaurant called Harvey's. The establishment was one of exclusivity; it was where Presidents had dined and held a preference for the very highest of society. Amongst the drinks and lobsters that were served the atmosphere provided the perfect one to share and exchange joint secrets between what Angleton naturally assumed was an ally. Their weekly meetings became a bit of a ritual and the restaurant became the forum where Philby could wave the magic wand of his charm to gain both trust and influence to squeeze the CIA man to innocently reveal secrets not only to his friend, but unknowingly to Moscow.

Due to the obvious aristocratic nature of Harvey's this was where many influential figures from across many careers preferred to be seen including and old acquaintance of Kim's. An Austrian Jew, who was an agent of the Israeli intelligence service Mossad called Teddy Kollek was also the mayor of Jerusalem and fellow diner in the restaurant. He knew Philby from in the days before the war, since he came across him in Vienna. Kollek was well aware of the Englishman's communist past and his real political allegiance. Observing him with Angleton, a man he knew to be in the CIA, he somewhat naively just assumed the American was aware of Philby's double agent spying and managed to turn him into a triple agent. Kollek had the means to destroy Kim Philby here and now, and prevent any more secrets to leak and deaths to occur, but he did not. Philby did not know it but he had cheated exposure again.

Away from the secret sharing (and leaking) sessions at Harvey's, Philby role in his post was to handle both incoming and outgoing communications directly between the British Prime Minister Clement Atlee, and the US President Harry S. Truman. A privilege bestowed upon him thanks to the advocating of James Angleton to the job. Philby did not mind this at all for now he was right in the heart of western Cold War intelligence and where he could do even more damage in his service to Moscow:

"At one stroke it would take me right back into the middle of intelligence policy making and it would give me a close-up view of the American intelligence organisations."

It certainly would. His position would expose him to one of the closely guarded secrets the Unites States had in the early Cold

War, and something that would eventually knock him off the proverbial pedestal he had spent the last decade building up in the business. It was a top secret project bearing the codename 'Venona'.

Venona which was based at Arlington Hall, a former girl's school and headquarters of the Unities States Signal Intelligence Service at Arlington in Virginia gave America the ability to decipher top secret communications and allow them to read whatever was being passed. It was akin to the British Enigma deciphering at Bletchley Park during the war, but geared for Cold War clandestine operations. The threat to Philby's position was already well established and had been since 1945 when a grave error was conducted by the Soviets. A one-time pad is used to transmit encrypted traffic and is impossible to crack or decipher if used correctly and is intended to be used only once per message. But in the summer of 1945 a Soviet cipher clerk had mistakenly reused one when sending a message making the normally secure code vulnerable to breaking by the west. What that message contained was shocking; information confirming that documents had been leaked to Moscow via Washington, with the source coming specifically from the British embassy there. Interception of the message by Venona and the resulting decryption eventually revealed messages that there was indeed a spy in the British embassy operating under the codename 'Homer'. The Americans did not know to who 'Homer' referred to, only that they travelled to New York to meet with his Soviet contact twice a week. Perhaps it was a junior member of staff or even a janitor who could gain secret access to sensitive material. Either way the source of the leak was certainly coming from the embassy and whoever they was, were delivering top level secrets to Moscow.

The investigation began to deduce the identity of 'Homer'. Meredith Gardner a talented linguist and even more talented codebreaker were based with his team at Arlington Hall as part of the Venona project. He discovered numerous messages passed from the New York based Soviet consulate-general to Moscow Centre where upon further study the team deduced that the spy had been operating since 1944. Evidence seemed to point to a massage for which Homer claimed to have decrypted himself between the former Prime Minister Winston Churchill and the former President Roosevelt. Referring to the Allied operation to invade southern France codenamed Operation Anvil (later changed to Operation Dragoon) in August that year, Churchill put forward an alternative idea. He proposed to the President abandoning plans to assault the Germans through southern France in favour of a flanking move further east through Venice and then Trieste before striking into Austria. However the intelligence Homer gathered showed that this strategy was rejected by both the British and the Americans and Dragoon went ahead as planned.

Investigations into 'Homer' continued until a breakthrough came in 1946. Gardner managed to identify that specifically the ciphers that were employed were for the English language and by May the next year he knew through reading decryptions that the Soviets were obtaining information from inside a specific department. The leaks appeared to be coming from the General Staff of the US Army Air Force Corps, Major William Ludwig Ullmann in the War Department. It was sure confirmation and evidence that large scale and deep cover Soviet espionage was occurring within the United States itself.

It took another two years for Gardner to make the definitive breakthrough in tracking down 'Homer'. Deciphering a Soviet message from a telegram originally sent in 1945 between Churchill and Roosevelt's successor the current President Trumann, the team at Arlington compared the secret message to a complete copy provided by the British embassy. From studying the two, they confirmed that the Soviet Union did have a spy which had access to top secret communiques at the highest political level. Thanks to their spy, Moscow was reading everything discussed between the Prime Minister of the United Kingdom and the President of the United States.

Upon his arrival in Washington, Kim Philby was privy to the secret Venona project. The Americans were about to let their most vital secret slip to the USSR. The FBI informed Philby of the ongoing investigation into discovering just who the agent cryptonymed 'Homer' actually was and it would be something that would greatly interest and worry him upon his discovery. Travelling to Arlington Hall himself, Philby would take a rather unusual interest in the Venona decrypts, no doubt gathering as much as possible to pass onto the Soviets as the FBI told him that they were made aware of 'Homer' from a message sent to Moscow back in 1945 from New York that had been cracked. The message originated in the British embassy in Washington. Philby using his uncanny knack for intuitiveness had all the prices in place to correctly (and secretly) deduce just who the spy really was. The Soviet agent known as 'Homer' was his old university friend and fellow Cambridge Spy, Donald Maclean.

Naturally Philby said nothing of this, but it concerned him that both a friend and fellow ideological cohort was now being investigated albeit the Americans did not know who he was just yet, it would only be a matter of time before Donald was identified. And if he was exposed, that there was a chance that his past association with Philby would eventually come to light even though they had not seen each other for many years.

Meanwhile as his secret concerns were fermenting deep in his mind, his home life portrayed a bourgeoisie celebrity that only the quaintness of upper class Englishness could achieve. The Philby family settled into a spacious home at 4100 Nebraska Avenue which became the definitive meeting place for his peers where secrets flowed as much as the drink. Kim was earning a reputation for being a bit of a socialite in intelligence circles. Members of his regular soirees included James Angleton, William K. Harvey of CIA counter-intelligence, his superior, the Director of the CIA, Walter Bedell Smith along with his subordinate Allen Dulles who was the Deputy Director. Robert Lamphere of the Soviet Section of the FBI made up the contingent.

The choice was strategic. These were the men who knew all the high level and intimate secrets of US and western operations. Information that would be highly valuable in the hands of Moscow and Philby knew how to ingratiate with them, dropping in on the offices of Americans late in the afternoon knowing that they would suggest meeting for talking shop. Intelligence officers dealt only in secrets and could not talk to members of their own families about work. This created a bond, a kindred atmosphere between fellow officers on the same side where secrets were shared openly and trustfully to each other, the only people who intelligence officers could truthfully open up to was themselves. It was a goldmine for Philby, the charming and suave Englishman and secret Soviet agent was neglectfully allowed to hear more that he really should have. In the surroundings of exclusivity lay misplaced trust in its most damaging form.

The secret sharing continued every week at Harvey's where Philby and Angleton courted each other in friendship. Kim noticed that his friend had a vice for gluttony despite his thin frame, something which the Englishman found rather envious in a friendly way since he did not appear to put on weight, something which could not be said for Philby now in his thirties and his expanding waistline was showing. His weight was the biggest casualty of these blowouts measuring at thirteen stone and only dropping back down to eleven in twelve weeks on the dietary advice of an elderly friend. Despite the friendliness and comfortable, boozy lunches both men it was clear had ulterior motives in regards to their work. Angleton wanted to place as much pressure in MI6 as possible while minimising pressure on his own department. He did this by placing the responsibility of information exchange between the CIA and MI6 on their office in London which was considerably larger than the one Philby ran here in Washington. He knew what his American friend was doing. He was too wise to overlook it and played ball making him think that he had Philby on a lead when in reality it was Philby himself that was controlling the purse strings.

He knew that the greater the level of trust built up between them the less likely he would suspect him of any illegal action under unwanted attention. Philby strung his friend along all the way, letting him think that he knew what he was doing in MI6 and vice versa, but Kim knew that James Angleton really had no clue what his real activities were. And that is how Philby preferred to keep it.

A new decade dawned but the same old game was still being played. In January 1950 a long brewing scandal finally broke with a storm. The vitally important and fruitful Venona intercepts now finally exposed and led to the arrest of a British born Soviet spy, not Maclean but Klaus Fuchs the atomic scientist who had been divulging atomic secrets to the Russians and was inevitably instrumental in ensuring the Soviet Union becoming the second nation after the United States to develop the atom bomb and become nuclear capable. The arrest of the scientist in Britain opened up an entire network of associates who were also detained including the courier David Greenglass as well as Julius and Ethel Rosenberg putting an end to his spying activities. Back in Washington Philby became aware of Fuchs' impending arrest thanks to his access to Venona but was unable to save him as his warning to Moscow came just too late. Even though he was unable to save fellow spy Fuchs, the rest of the year was to be marked for Philby by the arrival of two very important persons to join him on his assignment. One was a man that would ensure his spying activities in the US would continue, the other would undoubtedly enforce its collapse.

It began in March. On the 5th the 'Batory' a ship freshly arrived from Gdynia in Poland docks in New York. The ship had a full contingent of passengers and amongst them was a 32 year old young man, an American citizen of Polish origin called Ivan Kovalik. The whole thing was a lie, Kovalik did not exist; the real man's identity was Valeri Mikhailovich Makayev, a Russian intelligence officer who had been dispatched by Moscow to become Philby's new controller as a way for him to establish a secure link between himself and the Soviets.

This was the man who had been put in place to ensure the information Philby was passing got to Moscow. However Makayev made Philby distinctly unimpressed with his professionalism. Yuri Modin was a much more efficient case officer to handle the intelligence going out. Nonetheless Philby continued to provide information for Moscow on anything he could get his hands on. That was until October 1950 when another person arrived, his old friend, the raucous Guy Burgess.

Prior to his move to the United States he had been stationed in the Far Eastern section of the Foreign Office but just before his move across the Atlantic he got into trouble at the Royal Automobile Club located on Pall Mall in central London. A regular establishment for the old boys there were plenty of privileged types both young and old. Burgess with his intoxicated rudeness managed to offend one colleague to the extent that he got into a fight. Falling down some marble stairs in the melee and injuring himself he suffered multiple skull fractures for which he never fully recovered from for the rest of his life.

Following this embarrassment he had newly arrived in Washington after being appointed the First Secretary at the British embassy in the city. Knowing his old friend and how volatile he was, Kim suggested to Aileen that Guy stay with them at their house, in the basement. The idea horrified his wife for she did not like Burgess at all she already knew what he was like and what he was capable of during his drunken, homosexual orgies. Burgess had stayed with the family before when they were based in Istanbul and had contributed to the stress Aileen felt when she became unstable. It was absolutely vital that she resisted her husband. However Philby was insistent for he needed Burgess there to keep an eye on him, a fact unknown to Aileen. In the end she gave in to his wishes as usual and Guy Burgess moved into the basement of 4100 Nebraska Avenue.

Immediately he started causing offence to anyone who was not prepared to tolerate him. It only made Aileen resent him even more despite the fact that at this time she was giving birth to the family's fifth child Harry George who was born that same year. The elite gatherings in the Philby household were marred by Burgess' presence and his attitude offended the welcoming Americans who noted that he showed utter contempt for their values and way of life. He even used official vehicles for personal use such as employing them to cruise Washington in his search for endless encounters with other homosexuals. Even J. Edgar Hoover the Director of the FBI noted the diplomat's conduct complaining about his behaviour saying that the use of embassy cars was a way to evade arrest when he was out looking for others.

The effect upon Philby, the necessity and stress of looking after him like he was some kind of special case was taking a particular toll upon his family and the marriage to Aileen was beginning to take the strain. On the 19 January 1951 Kim Philby decided to host another dinner party, one of his many socialite events despite the fact he had his unstable friend dashing around the city causing shock and offence and another who was under investigation which could lead to himself. It would turn out more fateful than he ever expected.

As usual the guests formed the cream of the intelligence community in the United States, James Angleton and his wife

Cicerly, Robert Lamphere and the CIA counter intelligence chief Robert Harvey with his wife Libby were just some of the guests amongst several others. The evening began amicable enough with martinis amongst a cloud of nicotine as everybody but Lamphere was smoking. The drinking continued with Libby Harvey being especially fond of the alcohol just like her husband who at their last gathering at the Philby's ended up slumped at the table. Next there came the meal, the centrepiece of any social gathering and the forum for continued and polite discussion and after the food more drink to move the evening on, this time whisky to ensure it moved smoothly.

It was at this point Guy Burgess barged in on the gathering abruptly and very obviously drunk. His dishevelled appearance and inebriated ranting made it plainly obvious he was being more than anti-social he was being downright aggressive and was positively looking for a fight. Libby, despite the amount she had to drink got up to try and diffuse the situation. Forcing him into a corner she asked him to draw a cartoon of her desperately trying to calm the situation by playing upon his talent for drawing. Burgess was a talented caricaturist and his art had become admired on the Washington social scene despite the near intolerable nature of man who drew them. Libby kept protesting until Burgess finally gave in, picked up a pad and pencil and duly proceeded to draw her. The drawing was anything but flattering, it showed a woman whose distorted likeness was undoubtedly Libby, the body wearing a dress, lifted up around her waist, her legs spread open and exposing her genitalia. The deeply offensive drawing caused Libby to shriek, burst into tears and for her husband Harvey to swipe a punch.

Chaos followed, the whole dinner party disintegrated into a farce that ended with the Harvey's storming out. Philby was incensed with what had happened:

"How could you? How could you?" He shouted at a laughter-

crippled Burgess who found the whole situation quite hilarious. Aileen retired to the kitchen in floods of tears as Philby slumped upon the sofa, the party over, the guests now gone. James Angleton now outside the family home loitered for a while, reflecting on about what just happened in what was undoubtedly an unmitigated social disaster. Philby had to re-build the bridge with the Harvey's that Burgess so selfishly knocked down. Humbly and using all his English charm he personally apologised to the CIA counter intelligence man:

"Forget it." He reassured Philby. Obviously it was not his fault. Still the American was seething inside at how his wife was treated. He did not forget it, and his resentment would soon come to sting Philby himself.

The fall out between the old Cambridge friends did not last even though his conduct troubled Kim, they were too well bonded for that, in more ways that others knew. Both men travelled to the embassy but were still feeling the effects of intoxication were unable to work so had returned to Nebraska Avenue and ended up drinking champagne in the bedroom. A guest from the previous night's debacle the next day came to the family home to collect his car and heard voices upstairs as he did so only to find both men there like nothing had ever happened.

The social scene was just one aspect of a spy's life in Washington in the early 1950's. Work was the most important factor and Burgess had an extremely important role in the service, being privy to sensitive secrets surrounding negotiations for the Marshall Plan, the US programme to give financial and economic aid to Europe in the wake of the Second World War. Burgess alongside his compatriot Maclean in back London both provided Moscow with information on the nature of both the agreements and the implications of what was discussed. Time however was not on their side. The Venona investigations were still continuing in the background and the net was beginning to close on Donald

Maclean.

The man himself was going off the rails at fantastic speed. He told his Soviet handler that he no longer wished to be a spy, but he was mistaken for this was something that he could not resign from. Maclean was effectively trapped both in the Foreign Office and the Soviet intelligence services. Once while stationed in Cairo he smashed up the flat in the grip of a drunken rage of two secretaries within the US embassy in the city. Unashamedly for an upper-class Englishman he ripped up the underwear of the ladies, smashed a bath in two and threw a mirror off the wall. This outrageous act actually got him sent back home to be tested by a psychiatrist in the medical facilities of the infamous Harley Street. Incredibly after a short spell of treatment he was declared fit, returned back into the Foreign Office and was actually promoted to head the American desk within the government department.

But across the Atlantic the authorities were starting to close in Venona decrypts were shared by Arlington Hall with Britain at Eastcote in London, something which had been occurring since 1945. The information received related to the investigation into intercepted coded messages which Soviet clerks re-used one-time pads running between Moscow, London and Washington. Given the information already decoded, the FBI narrowed down possible suspects for the Soviet spy to be down to six thousand people preferring at first to concentrate their efforts on non-diplomatic employees of the embassy. Junior members and non-essential staff such as janitors were ruled out as the Venona cryptanalysts did their work. They discovered a total of twelve coded messages had been transmitted to Moscow; six of these had been sent between June and September 1944 from New York City with the other six sent in April 1945 from Washington D.C. itself. It appeared that the messages were sent by an agent known as 'Gomer' (Gomer is the Russian word for Maclean's codename 'Homer').

By April 1951 the first message that was sent was finally

decoded. It described Homer's meeting on the 25 June 1944 with a man named 'Sergei' as well as a planned trip to New York to visit his wife and mother in law. The spy was also expecting to become a father. This was significant breakthrough; now the Americans knew that 'Homer' travelled regularly to New York, was married and had a pregnant wife for which he used as an excuse to meet his Soviet contact there twice a week. From this profile the list of probable culprits narrowed extremely from a possible six thousand people to just nine. From here it was easy to deduce just exactly who 'Homer' really was. Philby was now in a real dilemma, because of his official role he had to help to uncover the activities of his friend but at the same time wanted to protect him from exposure. He was not so sure he could.

He was right. Before long the Venona decrypts enabled them to formally identify the spy at the centre of the embassy leak. Only one man had served in the British embassy in Washington from 1944 onwards during the time of the messages. Only that same man had a pregnant wife called Melinda, that woman lived in New York and only one man travelled to the city twice a week to meet her (and likely his contact.) That man's name and the identity of 'Homer' as the investigators found out was the British diplomat, the 37 year old Donald Duart Maclean. The first link in the Cambridge Spy Ring had been broken.

Maclean's exposure as a Soviet spy was told to the MI6 liaison Kim Philby. Although privately concerned he took the news calmly on the outside since there was nothing as of yet to link himself to Maclean. He knew that it would only be a matter of time before somebody would connect the dots, everything would be just circumstantial, yes the two were together at Cambridge but both men had not met for several years. For the moment there was no immediate threat to Philby. Moreover MI5 who had been made aware of the breakthrough did not want to arrest Maclean just yet, preferring instead to place him under surveillance since the

Venona intelligence was still too secret to be used in a court of law in any kind of criminal trial for treason. Surveillance would give MI5 the chance to watch their man and try to catch him in direct contact with his Soviet handler.

Back in Washington Philby now knew that Maclean was under immediate threat and that MI5 were watching him. Reporting the news to Moscow through Makayev, he argued that his friend be removed from the UK as soon as possible before he was arrested. If he was and interrogated by the sharp toothed wolfs of MI5, there was a very real chance that he would break therefore jeopardising the entire Cambridge network. And that would implicate Philby placing him in extreme danger. It was vital that Maclean be extracted and spirited back to the USSR.

To compound matters the continued presence and supervision of Guy Burgess was another deep worry in the tense atmosphere of Washington. There seemed to Philby only one ideal course of action, one that would benefit both his friend and his personal life; to get Guy Burgess back to London to warn Maclean who was still based at the Foreign Office's American Desk that he was under intense surveillance by MI5. The priority for the two men was that Guy must be sent back to London to warn Donald to flee to Moscow as soon as possible. A local Chinese restaurant provided the perfect venue to formulate the plan. Secluded, individual booths amidst a serenade of soft music piped across the establishment provided ideal cover against anyone potentially listening in. Confident they would not be heard Burgess agreed that he would return to London to receive details of the escape plan through their old friend and fellow Cambridge spy Anthony Blunt. But Philby was a little more astute about the whole situation than his friend. He knew that if Burgess (who was not under suspicion at all) warned Maclean and fled to Russia alongside him then it would become clear that they were tipped off. Public knowledge of Guy living in the Philby household would undoubtedly put the

STANLEY AND HOMER

spotlight of suspicion upon him. The bond of friendship only required the word of a gentleman to cement it and upon this Philby made Burgess swear that for his sake as well as the rest of the Cambridge network, he would not follow Donald to the east:

"Don't go with him when he goes. If you do, that'll be the end of me. Swear that you won't."

Worryingly, he hoped that his unstably flamboyant chum would heed the warning.

Philby had a great deal to lose. Up until now his rise through the intelligence services had been virtually flawless thus allowing him access to more and more sensitive material to pass onto Moscow. Philby was a master spy and now he was being considered for the job he really wanted and that the Soviets always dreamed he would get, to succeed Sir Stewart Menzies as the Director General of MI6 in the role as 'C'. Both Menzies and the military officer John Sinclair entertained the possibility of Kim Philby being appointed the next head of the service but had to conduct background checks first. For this they approached Dick White, former member of the elite drinking club called 'The Group' back in the early days of the war and now a senior figure in MI5. Asking him to conduct a background check and produce a report on Philby, White then delegated the task to two of his best people, Arthur Martin and the former interrogator of the defector Walter Krivitsky, Jane Archer.

Investigating Kim's past it quickly became apparent he had a communist affiliation, but was concerned at his sudden shift from the far left to the far right in the 1930's. Why would a communist sympathiser radically change course and become a supporter of pro-fascists? But thinks were to get even more alarming. Philby's pre-intelligence career as a journalist for The Times in Spain during the civil war there came to light and the description of his record proved uncannily familiar to the intelligence provided by Soviet defectors such as Krivitsky.

Could it be that Kim Philby was in reality a double agent? This was a man who had gained both the respect and admiration of so many of his peers, exuberating in the process a confidence and charm which lubricated his rise up the career ladder. It hardly seemed possible yet this cast doubt upon him. The spectre of the Soviet shadow was enough for his superiors to think again about bestowing upon him the privilege of heading the intelligence service but not enough to recall him from his Washington post.

Burgess, knowing that his antics were not seen as favourable in American society proceeded to apply his plan early in May. Careering around Washington while driving a grey Lincoln convertible certainly attracted the attention of the police who stopped him three times and issuing speeding tickets, one for each time he was apprehended. The final straw for the State Governor came when he assaulted a traffic cop in Virginia and then audaciously claimed diplomatic immunity. This outrageous act prompted him to lodge a complaint to the British Ambassador regarding the utter contempt of the diplomat Burgess. In light of this the consulate decided it was better if Burgess was removed and promptly sent him back to London albeit in disgrace from the US capital. Secretly this was exactly what Burgess wanted.

Things were best coordinated through Anthony Blunt whom Burgess contacted immediately before his arrival. Travelling back to Britain on board the Queen Mary, Blunt met him at Southampton Docks on the 7 May before making their way back to London. He was now in a position to get to and warn Donald Maclean of his detection and impending exposure, proceeding to inform him personally upon their meeting at the gentleman's club. Blunt, who was still in contact with Yuri Modin by now the controller of the entire Cambridge network notified him of Maclean's precarious situation:

"There's serious trouble, Guy Burgess has just arrived back in London. Homer's about to be arrested…It's only a question of days now, maybe hours…Donald's now in such a state that I'm

convinced he'll break down the moment they arrest him."

Modin required immediate instructions from Moscow on the situation. Time was now against them as orders came through; Donald Maclean was to be extracted from the west and brought to safety inside the Soviet Union. They were desperate for the compromised agent to flee given his current mental state and it was obvious that he would never withstand the rigors of interrogation by MI5. Melinda, Donald's wife was included in the deception agreed telling them to not waste a single moment and to get out as soon as possible. MI5 wanted to arrest Maclean on the 28 May and subject him to interview about his Soviet activities by Herbert Morrison the Foreign Secretary and his ultimate superior. Critically Yuri Modin was told about the date of the arrest but it was not clear who from. Perhaps a senior figure within the security service with access to that type of information or even someone close to Morrison himself who was present at one of his meetings heard about it and managed to warn the Soviet controller.

Meanwhile over in Washington an increasingly anxious Kim Philby contacted Burgess in a wired telegram on the 23 May that can only be described as a masterful showpiece of ulterior meaning. The message was about his Lincoln convertible, the one he had used to cruise the streets and attracted the attention of the law and had now been abandoned in the embassy car park:

"If he did not act at once it would be too late."

To an individual not aware of the conversation in the Chinese restaurant between the two men (and that included everybody) then this seemed like a harmless enquiry into an abandoned vehicle. But it wasn't, Philby was in fact referring to Maclean. It was an urgent warning and instruction to Burgess to tell him, and in many respects Moscow, to hurry up and get him out fast. He also added that he would send his car to the scrapheap saying:

"There was nothing more that I could do."

He was inferring to Burgess that if he did not act then the whole network would be compromised (probably using the metaphor 'scrapheap' as a way to describe this) and now the responsibility for Donald's safe passage was down to him, not Philby. Maclean was by now under sustained surveillance by MI5's specialist department called 'A4'. The men and women of this outfit, most former police officers were known as the 'watchers' a loose term given the way they operated their craft. Selected for their average height, and good hearing and eyesight, incredibly the watchers only operated during daylight hours, not evenings of weekends and even then only rarely left London itself. It was not so difficult to spot them when they were around in their raincoats and trilby hats, the very people whose profession absolutely depended on blending into inconspicuousness actually stood out like a sore thumb. These 'spies' actually looked like spies.

It was partly fuelled by the old boy network. The core of the upper ruling class where trust was based on friendship and a man's word was a concrete bond. With these supposed failsafe assurances that every chap knew and could vouch for each other, there simply was no need for more robust surveillance operations. MI5's inner circle practice of keeping an eye on a rogue official was nothing more than, in the case of Maclean and his class, just a token effort.

It would prove to be a fatal flaw in the class system. Two days later on the evening of the 25th Guy Burgess appeared at the home of Donald Maclean in the Surrey village of Tatsfield just south of London. That day he was working as usual and came home by train shortly before even though it was his thirty-eighth birthday but Guy was not bearing gifts. The rented car he acquired remained parked outside containing two packed bags and two travel tickets, falsely named and booked for a pleasure boat leaving for France that same evening called the Falaise. The ship was bound for St Malo in Brittany and was well known as a vessel where couples would take regular jaunts across the Channel to commit adultery. Few questions were asked and even less documents were required, perfect for two defectors wanting to slip into the vastness of the European continent. It seemed perfect but there was a shock, not only for Maclean, but for Philby back in Washington pretending that nothing had happened; Guy Burgess was also going to defect to the Soviet Union with him. Even though he was under no suspicion at all, Moscow had concluded that *both* Burgess and Maclean had outlived their usefulness and therefore must be pulled out. Moscow cynically justified their decision by saying the value of intelligence that Burgess would be able to provide could never be of the same quality again and so therefore not useful at all. Yuri Modin insisted that Burgess was finished and that he coming east weather he wanted to or not.

Melinda provided them both with a final supper, a treat for Donald's birthday. Shortly after which he then bid both his wife and children farewell before departing the family home in Burgess's rented car. Their destination was southwest, toward Southampton where the booked evening ferry was due to depart. Once there they hastily left the vehicle to which a curious official inquired about the parking for which Burgess hastily but cheerfully replied:

"Back on Monday!"

And with that they were gone.

Upon their arrival in France at 11:45 am the next morning they abandoned their luggage on board, walked down the gangplank and disappeared into the crowds. The objective now was to get east as fast as possible before the authorities had any idea what was happening. They took a taxi to the station at Rennes they then took a train to get to Berne in Switzerland, switching at Paris beforehand. A curious twist in the tale was that at the same time that the two diplomats were defecting to the Soviet Union, Philby's friend Nicholas Elliott was in the same city as Burgess and Maclean as station chief in Switzerland. Both traitors were only a short distance away from the MI6 man, in the Soviet consulate after arriving by taxi, picking up fake passports complete with new identities before continuing on to Zurich. Now was the critical part of the plan, from here they would make the final jump into the eastern bloc by boarding a plane bound for Stockholm but with a crucial stopover in Prague. Once the plane landed in the Czech capital, Burgess and Maclean hastily left and made their way through the airport. Finally they were both safely behind the Iron Curtain and in the hands of the communists. From here the journey was relatively straightforward; bungled into a car they were taken through Eastern Europe and toward the western border of the USSR, bound for Moscow.

Three days later on the following Monday the Foreign Office received a telephone call from Maclean's wife Melinda who asked quite calmly if her husband was there. Even though she was well aware of the truth, her act was so convincing that officials at the government department was utterly duped. MI5 had planned to interview her in relation to Donald but instead delayed the procedure for almost the next week. Negligently even the Maclean household was never searched for clues or evidence, somewhat bolstered by the fact that Melinda was seen as being completely unaware of the real facts and that she was heavily pregnant at the time. Within three weeks she would eventually give birth to a baby daughter called Francis Marling for which her father would eventually travel from New York to help cater for his grandchild. He would eventually leave with the firm conviction that no serious efforts were being made to track down Maclean and bring him in for interrogation. It was as if the Foreign Office could not care less that a Soviet spy had been leaking secrets and had now fled out of their hands.

Donald Maclean had been one of the most damaging spies the Soviets had in the west. He was instrumental in disclosing nuclear material to Moscow but he tried to justify his treachery in a statement which can only be said to display a myriad of misplaced patriotism:

"I am haunted and burdened by what I know of official secrets, especially by the content of high-level Anglo-American conversations. The British Government, whom I have served, have betrayed the realm to the Americans. I wish to enable my beloved country to escape from the snare which faithless politicians have set. I have decided that I can discharge my duty to my country only through prompt disclosure of the material to Stalin."

He really believed he was acting in the best interests of his country. Of course he may have been lying, after all Maclean had taken the decision to spy for Moscow, recruited by Arnold Deutsch all those years ago. But there may have been a part of him that really believed in what he was saying. Perhaps a part that may have convinced his soul that his actions and the consequences of them were of a justifiable cause, one of patriotic intentions rather than treasonous ones.

In all Donald Maclean did not really take to spying. He was different from Kim Philby and Guy Burgess who fed off the thrill of knowing that they were part of an elite group with an extremely secret knowledge with access to high level information. Maclean was different, he preferred to be more practical in how he spied, relying upon how he perceived to be the way he could best do it himself rather than being dictated by whatever secrets he was allowed to see.

Donald Maclean. The first man in the Cambridge Spy Ring. Identified as 'Homer' In 1951

Guy Burgess. The second man and the man who accompanied Maclean in 1951.

Anthony Blunt, the fourth man. Detected in 1964 and exposed as a traitor in 1979.

Kim Philby in 1955 during the press conference Where he denied being the 'Third Man'.

CHAPTER ELEVEN

THE THIRD OF FIVE

Kim Philby had only facilitated Guy Burgess' expulsion back to London in the belief that he would only aid in the defection of Donald Maclean back to the Soviet Union. He knew that if his volatile friend participated in the decampment then it would put himself in a difficult position. It was the reason for the desperate appeal in the Chinese restaurant but apparently had fallen upon deaf ears. The complicity of Burgess in Maclean's spying was a surprise and he may have thought that even though he was to accompany his friend behind the Iron Curtain, Moscow would permit him to eventually return to the west.

But Moscow intended nothing of the sort. In Britain, Special Branch police issued a general alert for the two men once they had found the car Burgess had hired to pick up Maclean in Tatsfield which took them to Southampton Docks. The awful nightmarish truth that had been feared was now beginning to turn in sober reality in the various government departments. Had Burgess and Maclean fled? Were they in the Soviet Union? The Foreign Office put out an urgent telegram to all their embassies instructing them to be on the lookout for both diplomats describing the missing men in unflattering detail:

"MACLEAN, 6'3" normal build, short hair, brushed back, part in the left side, slight stoop, thin tight lips, long thin legs, sloppy

dressed, chain smoker, heavy drinker.

BURGESS, 5'9'' slender build, dark complexion, dark curly hair, tinged with grey, chubby face, clean shaven, slightly pigeon-toed."

It was clear that the authorities wanted both men arrested on sight. In Switzerland where Nicholas Elliott was stationed and had been totally unaware that the fugitives were on his patch just a few days ago loyally assigned his own set of 'watchers' to conduct surveillance on the Soviet embassy in Berne. He even prepared a bottle of poisoned scotch just in case the two men ever turned up and needed to be incapacitated. It was no good. He was totally oblivious to the fact that he and his men were just too late. Burgess and Maclean had already been, picked up false papers and subsequently fled the evening Elliott was in the Schweizerhof Hotel enjoying foie gras, something he considered the finest in all of Europe and his tradition for a Saturday evening.

On the other side of the world the reverberations surrounding the suspected defections were beginning to reach Washington. There a top secret telegram was received by the British embassy marked for the attention of Geoffrey Paterson, the MI5 representative in the US capital and Philby's counterpart. The message unsurprisingly was encrypted as per usual and Paterson needed help in deciphering it. Telephoning his colleague Kim Philby he asked if he could borrow Edith Whitfield, the secretary in his office for her help in unlocking the message. Philby obliged knowing secretly perhaps what the telegram might contain. Maclean must have fled and successfully got out. It seemed like Guy Burgess had stuck to his word.

Philby arrived at the embassy office a few hours later to find Paterson there. Looking rather serious after decoding the secret message, he approached his MI6 opposite number and whispered:

"Kim, the bird has flown."

Philby knew exactly what he meant. Donald Maclean had managed to successfully get out and now he had to play the actor to appear as surprised and dismayed as Geoffrey was:

"What bird? Not Maclean." Said Kim, feigning surprise in the manner he had so well crafted. But there was more. Philby was about to get a bigger shock than those in London who had discovered his flight. Paterson broke the news:

"Yes but there's worse than that. Guy Burgess has gone with him."

Philby could not believe what he had just heard. Alarmed at this he tried to comprehend the revelation. Guy knew what could happen if he went as well and Kim had made him swear that he would not go. Had he forgotten their conversation in the Chinese restaurant? Did the safety and integrity of his old friend to conduct espionage mean nothing to him? They were supposed to be on the same side, what was Burgess thinking? Philby, although worried, tried not to show it for he knew all too well what would happen now. The fact that Guy lived in the Philby household while in Washington would inevitably cast the spotlight of suspicion upon him. If the authorities concluded that if Maclean was tipped off, as Kim thought they would, then he could expect unwanted interest from MI5 and others.

If he was to break cover and suddenly defect, now was the time. But he did not. The FBI at the moment did not suspect him so there was a good chance that MI5 had not connected the dots either. But the clues were there: agent 'Stanley' was not known to the west but the past looked bad for Philby, Burgess' association with himself particularly as he helped to recruit him in 1940 as well as his marriage to Litzi Friedmann in the 1930's was known. Even though Colonel Vivian Valentine was aware of Kim's first marriage to a known communist, Guy Liddell knew that Philby was thoroughly disgusted by his friend's behaviour in the matter. If they were both Soviet agents why would they be doing something so obvious as to be living in the same house together? He knew it would not escape the attention of MI5 and sooner rather than later they would conduct invasive and detailed investigations into his past. The fact that all three were friends at Cambridge University as well as the connection with Burgess in Washington would make him suspicious and he knew it. A Soviet contingency plan to get Philby out via the Caribbean or Mexico was in place complete with Makayev providing false papers and money, two thousand pounds from a dead letter drop to be exact if MI5 closed in. However audaciously he decided that when the call came, he would stay, play the innocent victim and fight it out. While the whole British embassy was in a mixture of anger and disbelief at the prospect that two of its staff had disappeared and were probably Soviet agents, Philby carefully laid low and watched the behaviour of his American friends. He wanted to see the reaction particularly from his former dinner party guest Robert Lamphere of the FBI. There seemed to be no reaction from the authorities just yet for as of this time he was not under suspicion. It was something that could change any day now.

Secretly panicking, he needed to cover his back just in case anybody came snooping around. He had to act fast. Telling Paterson that lunchtime that he was going home for a stiff drink, something which everybody could do with concerning the events of the last few days, he raced home to Nebraska Avenue where, to the puzzlement of his wife and children as to why he had come home, he headed for the potting shed to pick up a trowel. He bypassed the drinks cabinet and made his way downstairs to Guy Burgess' former basement residence to pick up a few secret items; a camera, tripod and film that Makayev had furnished him with at one of their earlier meetings. Sealing them in a waterproof container he made his way out of the house leaving his family wondering why he had come home unexpectedly, locked himself in the basement and then left just as swiftly. Philby didn't care about not saying a word about it, he just had to do this task, it was vitally important he do this. Driving north he headed to Great

Falls in Fairfax County, Virginia just to the north of Washington D.C. on the Potomac River. He knew the areas well since James Angleton had already taken Kim fishing here in the past were they were more than acquainted with a traditional English style public house called the Old Angler's Inn. The road he chose was wise for his task, largely rural and lined with the river on one side and thick woodland on the other where he found a suitably deserted stretch, parked and removed the container and trowel. Setting off in to the dense woods he proceeded in a panicky state to dig a hole and bury the equipment that would certainly incriminate him. Emerging a few minutes later pretending to do up his fly zip for the benefit of any passers buy who would think he simply answered an urgent call of nature. With this act at one fell swoop he at least had disposed of what would be the most damming piece of evidence of his treachery.

He was still rather paranoid about what the authorities would know but despite this Philby had one very powerful weapon in his armoury to counter the suspicions of his past; his powerful friendships in both MI6 and the CIA in the form of Nicholas Elliott and James Angleton.

By now the furore surrounding the flight of Burgess and Maclean became inevitably, public attention causing the scandal to rumble on and was referred to as the 'affair of the missing diplomats' before they would finally resurface in Moscow. What fuelled the public interest was that it was now becoming obvious that somebody must have tipped off Maclean that he was being investigated since evidence against him was uncovered through the Venona intercepts. Intelligence of that nature was only available to only the very highest of officers and only one person fit the bill, had associations with both missing diplomats and access to the relevant Venona material; Kim Philby. This senior officer, the perfect charming gentleman, darling of the intelligence community and once groomed for the MI6 Director General position suddenly became the prime suspect in what was now being termed the 'Third Man' who tipped them off about the investigation. It caused clouds of suspicion on both sides of the Atlantic, setting off mistrust and infighting between and within the western intelligence agencies. The activation of Makayev's contingency plan to get Philby out via the Caribbean or Mexico could be made but Philby was too cunning to just cut and run. He knew exactly what MI5 would have to prove if anything. And the very act of remaining in his post would publicly display a clear conscience and that he had nothing at all to fear or hide from the authorities. He knew that any prosecution that would be brought on him would have to link him directly to the intelligence provided by the defections of both Volkov and Krivitsky. He knew that MI5 would question him on his time as a reporter during the Spanish Civil War and in addition will have to prove that he saw the source books on the Soviet Union he procured back in St Albans from William Woodfield back in 1940 when Moscow wanted information on British spies. Sensing that MI5 would interrogate and cajole him into a confession in order to gain hard evidence that was not circumstantial, Philby was all too aware that the burden of proof lay squarely upon their shoulders. Keeping cool under pressure and not giving anything away, he knew that they would have to work hard to get anything out of him. In effect he believed they had nothing, nothing at all to link him to Soviet espionage and the main lynchpin was his association with Burgess, Maclean and perhaps his university past. He was confident that he could and would indeed get past the storm that seemed to be heading his way.

That same storm that was brewing around the scandal would eventually touch the head of MI6, Stewart Menzies in the form of political pressure from the Foreign Secretary Herbert Morrison and the Prime Minister Clement Attlee. Their insistence was clear about what should happen next regarding the status of their man in Washington.

In his office in early June Kim Philby received a polite sounding note from his own superior in the embassy, Jack Easton. It was exactly what he had been expecting to arrive, an informal message notifying him that he was going to get a formal telegram from London saying he was to be recalled to answer questions regarding the Burgess and Maclean disappearance. The stigma attached to the scandal would eventually poison the relationships he had in the US, something very clear with the attitude of his colleagues in both the CIA and the FBI who found them very suspicious of him now the allegations were swirling.

At least James Angleton was still on his side and their lunches along with their secret sharing still occurred on a weekly basis. On the 11 June, the night before his flight to London Angleton decided to probe in a friendly way about his friend's departure:

"How long will you be away for?" He asks,

"Oh about a week." Philby replied. Casually he was trying to shrug off any inkling of worry which may be interpreted as suspicious. It was at this point that the American passed over a letter, asking Philby if he would not mind forwarding it on to the head of MI6. He would have done it earlier but he had missed the diplomatic bag that week and since Kim was heading to London, would he mind playing the postman and deliver it? The grip of paranoia had never left him since he heard about Burgess' flight so this may be a trap of some sort. Did James Angleton suspect him as well? Was he being played in a game that as of yet he could not fathom? If he refused however would that not look highly suspicious? His ideas as it turned out were simply paranoid. It was just a harmless note Angleton wanted Philby to forward onto Manzies since he was going back across the Atlantic. He fully expected his friend to return in a week where the two would resume their ritual launch at Harvey's as usual. That evening Kim Philby, with bags packed boarded the evening flight bound for London. It was the last time in his life he would see either the

United States or James Angleton ever again.

He arrived in London the next day. Jet lagged and exhausted by the afternoon he arrived at Leconfield House, the home of MI5 on Curzon Street just off Park Lane in the Mayfair district of the capital. Here he was to receive his first and embarrassingly polite meeting with Dick White, Philby's old friend from Section V during the war. White was now a senior figure in the organisation, destined to head first MI5 and then MI6, this mild mannered but direct man was the head of counter-intelligence and responsible for rooting out spies planted in society. Spies just like Kim Philby.

White like many others in the old department were pleased when the MI6 man achieved promotion over Felix Cowgill and did his very best to keep the atmosphere friendly. Jack Easton, Kim's Washington superior had also accompanied him and was present at the interview for moral support. Over next few hours amidst the teacups and tobacco smoke Philby was subjected to a friendly conversation that was an intense interrogation in disguise. White needed Kim's help in clearing up the Burgess and Maclean business for which Philby duly helped his interviewer in a way that would only serve his own protection but not appear to do so. It was a stern test of his duplicity. He disclosed information on Burgess concerning his past and how his personality came across to others. Philby stressed that someone like Guy who courted notoriety and indiscretion would be totally unsuitable for espionage work, especially a Soviet agent. Knowing that that was not going to make a convincing argument, he used it to assert the fact that he was defending himself and that he was ultimately fooled by Burgess just like everyone else. It was a clever ruse to throw White off his scent, or at least plant a seed of doubt in his mind. Moving onto Donald Maclean he just said that he was not aware of any recent knowledge concerning him or his activities, arguing that he had only met him twice since 1937 and for no longer than thirty minutes at that. That of course was a lie, but it was one that Philby felt he could comfortably get away with.

The whole interview was extremely convivial if not a little tense. Menzies had only agreed for White to question Philby on the pretext that he was only there to aid in the investigation and provide any clues as to shed light on what was an awful and scandalous situation concerning the missing diplomats. Jack Easton was convinced that he could see that his colleague Philby had nothing to hide. He had not run away, he had stayed and helped in the investigation. Yes he had an association with Burgess which at the most be interpreted as indiscretion but not treason and it was not a crime. If it was then half the intelligence case officers in the world would be guilty. Philby it was assured was a gentleman, one who acted with the social graces one expects from his class. Everything about him, his accent, his connections, his club, everything pointed to his complete innocence. Somebody as high-flying and distinguished as Kim Philby could not possibly be a Soviet spy.

This was the view shared by his colleagues throughout MI6 and it was clear to White and the rest of the internal security service that they were determined to shield their man from further accusations. This was despite the fact that Philby simply refused to publically renounce his friendship with Burgess later remarking:

"There are fair-weather friends and foul-weather friends, and I prefer to belong to the second category."

White conferred with another one of the old boys, the musically talented Guy Liddell admitting to him that he was not wholly convinced by Philby's explanations. Liddell could see that the MI5 counter-espionage man was worried with what he had seen and heard as was he. Guy personally had known Burgess for many years since the old days of the heavy drinking sessions at the home of Tomas Harris way back in the blurry days of the war and was totally shocked to hear of his defection. Was it possible their mutual friend Philby really was a Soviet agent? And if Burgess was then why not Kim? Thinking on Liddell also began to entertain the astonishing fact that another old friend Anthony Blunt could also be part of some kind of espionage network in league with the others. Blunt was loosely connected to the Royal Family, surely the communists could not have penetrated this far in to the establishment? Although he was never an obvious collaborator with Burgess, they were known to each other and it may just be possible that his activities may have been on behalf of communist sympathies. The key to this was Kim Philby himself, and during the investigations they issued him, somewhat mockingly with their own codename. It was an apt choice, one that reflected his personality; an exotic fruit that was ripe for plucking. The codename he was to be referred to was called 'Peach'.

The suspicion that 'Peach' generated cut through the intelligence services splitting the two main branches. If anything both MI5 and MI6/SIS were now at odds with each other, one the attacker, and the other, the defender. Their approaches to the investigation showed attitudes revealing their intimate nature and the split caused by Philby was a large crack between the organisations. MI5 was the working class service full of ex-soldiers and policemen. These were men who had patriotically guarded the colonies of the Empire abroad and the safety of the realm at home. They were all trilby hats, woolly scarfs and mackintosh raincoats. MI6 in contrast was the upper class service full of privately educated public individuals who had privileged positions. Their attire was the old school tie, Savile Row suits and posh umbrellas. These clubbed together old boys went into government, intelligence or diplomacy, administering the height of the British Empire in the old days from Auckland to Bombay, from Cairo to the Caribbean. Beyond they ensured sustained influence in the changing world as the colonies steadily pushed for independence.

The divisions both social and in approach was stark and the Philby investigation was creating a wider gulf than was comfortable. Yet this was not the end, certainly not for MI5. Like a bulldog with razor sharp teeth MI5 kept picking at little pieces of evidence to prove Philby's complicity in spying. The evidence White had was sketchy at best and would take, as Philby believed a more astute officer than him to uncover damming evidence. MI5's source of information came not from their own investigations, but from the other side of the Atlantic.

In the wake of the Burgess and Maclean disappearance the CIA in Washington were conducting their own investigation and had their own reasons to suspect Kim Philby as a possible Soviet spy. A damaging revelation regarding the case of Ismail Akhmedov came to light to implicate Philby even more. Akhmedov was a former Soviet GRU officer who had originally defected in 1942 whose evidence seemed to point to espionage activities in the west. However by 1945 his intelligence was ultimately dismissed, fuelled chiefly by a report at the time compiled by Philby himself denouncing his information as not being important and effectively stifling a potential exposer. But the report was not the end of the affair as the defector gave evidence to the US Senate Internal Security Subcommittee under the alias Ismail Ege in 1948. The evidence he provided pointed to a potential identification of Kim Philby as a Soviet mole.

The evidence at least in American eyes was mounting and yet the Philby affair was beginning to polarize the US intelligence services the same way it was doing to their British counterparts. The CIA Chief Walter Bedell Smith approached his two best officers James Angleton and William K. Harvey to compile and submit reports concentrating solely on what they knew about Philby specifically. Other officers were ordered to write up any generalised knowledge on the association between him and Guy Burgess. The CIA was determined to find out what Philby knew and what exactly if anything he could have leaked. Harvey was the one with the axe to grind against Kim; the debacle with Guy Burgess as the disastrous dinner party which offended him and humiliated his wife was something he did not forget and strove to implicate the suspect on anything he could pin him on. His five page report was as scandalous as it could be argued defamatory. Harvey had studied Philby's career in meticulous detail, surgically picking up on every piece of evidence he could find, his involvement in Volkov's defection, the part he playing in the failed Albanian operations, his knowledge of the investigation into the search for 'Homer' as well as his association with Burgess. Piece by piece he sought revenge for the dinner party by building up a comprehensive case to prove that Kim Philby was in reality a traitor, coming to the conclusion that he was indeed working for the Russians.

Harvey's report was a scathing denunciation of their former colleague. James Angleton's report was a robust defence of his friend and former mentor. He argued that Philby, far from being traitorous was in fact an honest man who had simply been fooled by the duplicity of Burgess. Convinced of his innocence Angleton absolutely believed that Philby would be cleared by the British investigation, stressing that he was severely embarrassed by the actions of his friend. Angleton warned that if the CIA started making unsubstantiated allegations of treachery, Anglo-American relations would invariably suffer as a consequence since Philby was still held in high regard by many colleagues in London.

The Angletons, the Elliotts and the Philby's were all close knit in the social circle and hosted many guests such as fellow intelligence officers, journalists and artistic types. The very intimacy of their friendship convinced James that he knew Philby, a man whom taught him everything he knew and acquainted with both professionally and socially. There was no possibility his good friend was guilty of any espionage. At most he could be found guilty of improper association with a conspicuous character but no complicity in anything which may suggest illegal or subversive activities.

The two reports submitted by both men painted Kim Philby as a disreputable traitor and the innocent victim of an awful intelligence storm. When Harvey, who by now was convinced that their man was a Soviet spy read Angleton's report with some disbelief. His response was anger for which he manifested in the form of an angry scrawl at the bottom. It read:

"What is the rest of this story?"

By now the upset was beginning to cause fractures within the CIA itself. One fellow officer was beginning to accuse another over the Philby question of ignoring the facts and being totally blind to the truth.

Harvey's report was the more clinical whereas Angleton's was more personal and Beddell Smith was totally convinced by the former's account. It was only now the Americans acted writing directly to Sir Stewart Menzies at MI6 to angrily assert the fact that Kim Philby under no circumstances whatsoever was permitted to return to Washington D.C. The Americans believed (save Jim Angleton) that he was really a Soviet mole, even though the British were still suffering from infighting over the situation. Furthermore Beddell Smith urged the Whitehall officials in the British government to *"clean house regardless of whom may be hurt."* To add a little insult to injury perhaps reflecting the anger they felt over allowing a probable enemy agent into its camp, the CIA stated that such a breech would never have happened in the US, therefore undermining their UK counterparts. In time that would change with the case of John Walker in what would come to be known as the Walker Spy Ring, the American version of the Cambridge Spies. History would come to record that not even the United States was impervious to the duplicity of Cold War spying.

It did not matter who blamed who, the damage had and was still being done. The message from Washington and the rhetoric they used was sheer bluntness disguised as a threat:

"Fire Philby or we break off the intelligence relationship."

Pressure regarding Kim's status in the service was growing and two days after his initial meeting with Dick White, Philby was back again in his office for a second meeting. The atmosphere this time was certainly more formal and distinctly cooler than before thanks to the aggressive tone of the CIA response. The obvious strain on the UK-US special relationship creaked like never before and the Foreign Office was still deeply shaken by the disappearance of two of its officials. The Americans correctly deduced that MI6 was not taking kindly to one of its officers being treated this way. Even Dick White, already vying for a confrontation with both Philby and SIS himself, also wrote to Menzies urging the service to take action immediately. It all made the backdrop to this second interview invariably more serious as the dossier on Philby ('Peach') was growing all the time. Investigations into his past revealed his communist flirtations at Cambridge, his first marriage to Litzi, the Volkov case, Operation Valuable, Walter Krivitsky, and Spain. Everything seemed to point to the fact that Kim was working for the Soviet Union.

Armed with the new information White now wanted Philby to explain in more detail exactly what he knew about Burgess:

"I'm in no particular hurry." White impatiently informed his opponent as he tried to squeeze the information out of him. Feeling that this time he could trap him he wanted much more than what the MI6 officer had disclosed previously. The allegations and growing file on 'Peach' labelled Philby as a suspect not a helper in the investigation. Little did he know that getting the truth out of Philby was like getting blood out of a stone. Nonetheless he tried. When did they meet? How did their friendship begin? And what did Kim know about his friend's left-wing politics? When questioned about his relationships he confirmed his first wife had been a communist but stressed that he had managed turn her away from it and that he was never tempted by it at all.

White then moved on to ask how Donald Maclean came to be

aware that he was going to be arrested. Philby defended himself by denying in a long answer that seemed to go on and on that he had ever discussed the topic of Maclean with Burgess.

It was at this point that Dick White realised that Kim Philby was lying. His rambling and demeanour had given him away.

Carrying on, White then moved onto the topic of his time in Spain beginning in 1936 as The Times correspondent covering the war there. Cutting in Philby corrected him by saying that he had originally gone to the country as freelance and was actually recruited by the newspaper while on assignment. If caused some anger on White's part as the reddening of his skin showed. Philby was supposed to be rather destitute at the time given his time in Austria, how on earth could he afford a trip to Spain? Deep down he suspected what Philby already knew; the trip was purely financed by Soviet Intelligence, the NKVD on orders to go. Kim blatantly lied to his interrogator, saying that he had paid for it simply by selling old gramophone records and books for which White just marked this down as yet another lie. He had missed the chance to put Philby under real pressure, enough to oust him perhaps with just a few more questions; how many books and records did he sell? Was he paid in cash? Did he remember the people he sold them to? Are there any financial statements to corroborate Kim's story? It was an incalculable mistake by an experienced counter intelligence officer.

The whole interview lasted longer than the first, several hours, after which White rose to his feet to signal the end of the session. Philby was not stupid, he could read the signs, their failure to shake hands like gentlemen at the end and the way the whole thing had gone told him that far from convincing Dick White, he was now his prime suspect.

CHAPTER TWELVE

FIGHT LIKE HELL!

By now Philby's very presence in the secret service was becoming toxic. The Americans who had effectively expelled him from Washington called for his head under the threat of dissolving the intelligence relationship and MI5 was now baying for his blood. He still had friends, Jim Angleton in the CIA and Nicholas Elliott, newly arrived in London after a three year stint in Switzerland. Elliott simply refused to believe that his friend was a Soviet spy. Here was his good friend and mentor, a relationship he cherished and revered and he was being virtually harassed by the vicious allegations swirling around the government. Elliott knew Kim intimately; they had drunk in the same clubs together, played and appreciated cricket together and socialised with one another. Never at one time in all their years of companionship had he even heard of Kim talk about politics, promote any sort of left wing ideas and certainly not advocate communist ones.

Elliott could see that at worst Philby was guilty of making a simple mistake concerning his friendship with Guy Burgess. Yes he may have flirted with radical left wing politics at university but that did not automatically make him a communist. He may have even married one a long time ago but even that did not make him guilty. Elliott knew and firmly believed that at most his friend was guilty of error, but nothing criminal at all. Even the fact that he refused to disown his friendship with Burgess was seen in MI6 circles as an example of his decency.

Most of the evidence MI5 and the CIA had gathered was circumstantial and was in effect feeding off the populist anti-communist agenda perpetuated by Senator Joe McCarthy in the US. Nicholas knew the men of MI5 were using the anti-communist McCarthyite stance to conduct a witch hunt against his old friend and he was determined to stand by him and not let him be destroyed by this persecution.

Philby by this time was living temporarily in the flat of his mother in Drayton Gardens while the investigation continued. MI6 was still resolutely defending him in the face of the vicious accusations and echoing his innocence. The head of this was Elliott who considered it an affront to the very values of the bond they had both forged during wartime and carried forward. In his mind the defence of Philby was also a defence of both his club and his class.

By September 1951 it was clear the rally behind Philby propped him up but even the robust defence of his colleagues and friends could not in the end quell the jeopardising of his job. His position rapidly untenable and under pressure from both the Americans and MI5, Stewart Menzies was faced with little choice. Philby could see what going to happen as he received the summons to face his boss. The protégé was about to be reluctantly cast off into the cold.

"I'm no good to you now. I think you'd better let me go." Philby offered, knowing that what he really meant by that was that he could never be allowed into a position where he could obtain such valuable intelligence to pass to Moscow ever again.

Menzies formally offered to ask for resignation under some considerable distress. He had been backed into a corner on this and the pressure over the last few months had been too great for the service to bear. Regrettably he was forced to release what he saw as a loyal and capable officer who was being unfairly treated as many in MI6 saw that Philby was a scapegoat for the international storm in the wake of the Burgess and Maclean disappearance. None more so than Nick Elliott who continued to vehemently argue in defence of his friend stating at the time that he was a:

"Dedicated, loyal officer had been treated abominably on the basis of evidence that there was no more than paranoid conspiracy theory."

Menzies himself supported his, believing he was entirely innocent, agreeing to give him a generous payoff upon his exit from the service. Kim Philby left his high flying MI6 career with a sum of four thousand pounds a considerable fortune, one half as a down payment with the other half being paid in six month instalments of five hundred pounds each. The gesture was obvious; by signing Philby off with compensation MI6 was defiantly bowing to pressure from outside and showing a continuing vote of confidence in their ex-employee. It was to be the start of a deeply troubling time. Once courted as the future head of British Intelligence, now he found himself out of work, suspected of being a traitor and undoubtedly under surveillance from MI5.

He was correct about that. Upon his dismissal the family that consisted of his wife and their five children moved out of London to Hertfordshire and into a rather small rented gatehouse in the village of Heronsgate. Now out of touch with the intelligence world and with a large family to support, he started looking for employment but also spent much time in the village pub. It was not the exclusive posh London clubs or fashionable bars he was used to but it served liquor all the same. He knew the authorities were watching him, making no attempt at incognito. They kept tabs on his communications by bugging his telephone, every week or so a policeman would appear to patrol around the area and his mail was regularly intercepted and checked before forwarding it on. Philby did not dare attempt to make contact with any sort of Soviet liaison while under this kind of surveillance, something which was picked up by the authorities. No matter how long they watched, they could find nothing at all to link Philby to any sort of espionage despite evidence to the contrary.

He continued to portray himself as a man that was forced out of a job but showed no bitter recriminations toward the service. Nicholas Elliott visited the family often, trying to cheer his friend up by joking that if his own telephone was bugged then at least it would be repaired rather quickly. The conversations between friends were carefully logged by MI5 for anything incriminating but nothing was found until August 1952 when they picked up on Nicholas and Elliott talking about Kim going on a sailing trip with a friend from the City who had a yacht moored in Chichester on the south coast. Alarm bells began ringing out as the authorities concluded that this was only a short trip to France, just like Burgess and Maclean had done. Further evidence compounded matters when it was revealed that Aileen asked Elliott if her husband had done a 'dis', meaning she was wondering if he can done a disappearing act. Elliott laughingly reassured her saying that Kim would never disappear. There was no danger of him ever defecting at all because he was entirely innocent.

Guy Liddell wondered if a general alert be sent out to the French warning them of Philby's flight or even sending ships out to intercept them while out at sea. However MI5 decided to wait nervously to see what would unfold. Perhaps Aileen was not serious about what she said and perhaps their man had not flown after all. Sure enough Kim Philby returned from his jaunt that evening totally unaware of the panic he had caused the authorities. It only served to reinforce their convictions that they were dealing with a traitor. By December MI5 were ready to strike again and this time they were determined to force a confession out of him.

Philby received a summons from 'C' to a meeting regarding the ongoing inquiry. This time he was to be interviewed again, but not by the malleable Dick White, but by an abrasive critic who did not mince his words. His name was Helenus Milmo who possessed the nickname 'Buster'. Buster was a lawyer by profession, pompous, ruthless, very traditional and breathed legal authoritarianism. He was MI5's legal advisor, a decisive cross-examiner, a stinging accuser and Kim's old colleague in the intelligence service. As Philby travelled to his meeting he wondered if MI5 had gathered some new evidence against him and realised that the next few hours were going to be tricky at best.

The whole thing was in fact engineered by the Prime Minister. Winston Churchill, newly elected once more after succeeding Clement Attlee, the head of government for the second occasion and first in peacetime approved the decision personally to bring Philby in for more questioning. Buster Milmo was known for being extremely intimidating; a loud booming voice throwing over a barrage of accusations to batter the defendant into submission in a condescending old school type of way. Once Philby arrived he had no idea who he was going to face. The fifth floor room of Leconfield House where he was ushered into soon provided him with an answer:

"Hello Buster." He said.

It suddenly dawned on him what he was about to go through. Philby had witnessed Buster's savage attacks before during the war where he destroyed suspect German spies as they were caught and interred in a secret camp in Richmond. Now armed with the Philby dossier containing all the evidence MI5 had, Buster intended to break his suspect and force a confession out of him using sheer brutality and utter accusatory derision.

The meeting began with Philby sitting down, taking out a pipe, something he always smoked and proceeded to light it. Buster promptly told him to put it out arguing that this was a formal judicial enquiry bound by law. Philby obeyed, extinguishing it and putting it back in his pocket. What he did not know was that Milmo was himself lying, the meeting had no legal status; it was a tactic to impress pressure upon his intended victim.

Buster then set to work. Instantly he accused Philby of actively spying for the Soviet Union, being complicit in the betrayal of Konstantin Volkov, tipping of Burgess and Maclean and betraying information leading to the deaths of hundreds of western agents. Philby counter argued each point until Buster moved onto what seemed to be a damming piece of evidence. Going back to the Volkov affair, he concentrated on the monitoring of radio traffic the British had picked up during the defection. He pointed out the volume of traffic between London and Moscow and then from Moscow to Istanbul had increased once the defection became known and before Philby travelled out to Turkey. It suggested a tipoff to Moscow so how would Philby account for such activity?

"How would I know?" Kim replied.

The interrogation moved toward Walter Krivitsky and his claims that an agent had been sent to Spain during the civil war there with a mission to assassinate General Franco. Milmo then asked the direct question:

"Who was that young journalist? Was it you?"

Of course it was him, but Philby already had a parrying answer, why would Moscow send, as Buster was alluding to, a Cambridge student who had never handled a firearm before over an experienced contract killer. Surely the Russians would send a professional to carry out such an act, not a novice.

Milmo the expert cross-examiner was now frustrated for certain accusing him directly of handing secret information to Burgess before his flight. Philby in truth had done no such thing so was easy to refute such claims, so Buster moved onto Kim's first marriage to Litzi Friedmann a known communist. He accused him of smuggling her out of Austria and into Britain, trying to connect him to communist sympathies. Philby though cunningly told him that she was Jewish; if he had allowed his wife to stay in the country at that time she would inevitably had been arrested and ended up in a Nazi concentration camp:

"How could I not help her?" He declared to which Milmo instantly snorted.

Now the interrogation was beginning to turn increasingly heated by deteriorating into something of a shouting match between the two men. Buster was now getting ever louder and animated along with it, thrashing and banging on the table with each of Philby's deflections. The lawyer was angrily running out of options as his face became ever redder with each of Kim's cunning circumventions.

Throughout the entire four hours of the interrogation the whole spectacle was being monitored from the next room where a gathering of senior intelligence officers were listening in. Philby's former boss Stewart Menzies, the man who suspected him, Dick White along with Guy Liddell was keeping tabs on the duel that was being played out only a few feet away. A stenographer was taking down every word that was being recorded. The battle concluded in a complete stalemate, Milmo had not managed to get a confession out of him something which Philby knew would be needed to secure a confession. He had not pointed to any protest of innocence which might indicate something to hide. Buster knew he was guilty, Kim also aware that he knew but without a confession, the facts were groundless.

He was allowed to leave but not before being asked to surrender his passport. He complied for if he did not, it may be another indicator of suspicion. If he were to defect suddenly then he would not need them anyway, his Soviet controllers would provide all the false documentation needed to travel abroad. Meanwhile Milmo summed up the confrontation in his report to Dick White saying:

"There's no hope of a confession, but he's as guilty as hell."

White believed it even though he could not prove it.

MI5 knew Philby had the upper hand here. Doubt started creeping into the internal security service. If Philby, as they believed were guilty, then what about Anthony Blunt? Was he involved in the Burgess Maclean affair? And what about Tomas Harris the former host of the officers in such opulent surroundings and was also suspected as being a Soviet spy?

Philby on the other hand expressed abject fury over how he had been treated, something which Nicholas Elliott picked up and shared all too well. Outraged at how his friend had been treated, he was determined to force an apology out of MI5 for the way the interview had been handled. MI6 was counter attacking and to do this Elliott contacted a senior officer called Malcolm Cumming the one person in MI5 that actually attended Eton just like himself. He complained bitterly that Philby was furious at the Milmo interrogation saying that he did not mind such an investigation being carried out but objected to being lured to MI5 under false pretences into what essentially was a formal judicial enquiry. Elliott went onto to explain that it came as a complete shock especially after the more cordial conversations with Dick White beforehand.

MI6 was indeed standing by and fighting the corner of its former employee, but MI5 were still determined to prove his guilt and extract a confession. They turned in a very different direction for their next tactic employing the services of William Skardon to obtain the admission of guilt from Philby. Skardon, known as 'Jim' was a former detective inspector in the metropolitan police and head of the A4 section, the 'Watchers'. He possessed a mild demeanour, a skilful trick to coax confessions out of suspects, a master of the subtlety of interrogation and the complete opposite of the forcefulness of Buster Milmo. Whereas the latter relied on intimidation, the former wormed his way into the consciousness of his victim, helped by his soft whispery voice and lack of eye contact asking the same question over and over again, each time slightly varied until his victim made a fatal mistake. His large moustache, trilby hat and mackintosh raincoat made him the epitome of the private detective, appearing as weak as wounded pray, but could never be underestimated in guile. Jim Skardon had actually dealt with this type of suspect before, in January 1950 using the tactic he had successfully interrogated and obtained a confession out of the fellow Soviet spy Klaus Fuchs following his arrest which led to his conviction. Now the police officer was about to do the same to Kim Philby.

Knocking on the door of Hersonsgate, the former MI6 man knew what this unassuming, almost apologetic little was after. He already knew a great deal about Skardon. Both men chatted away while puffing on their pipes, Jim vaguely approaching different subjects but making nothing obvious. Philby concentrated hard to evade any little traps the former policeman was subtly tying to lay but he could never be sure if he ever managed to dodge them all. He knew all too well Skardon's method of operation. The charade of their cosy little interrogations disguised as friendly chats between confidents were to carry on several times over the next few months. Despite Skardon's probing though, he remained open minded about Philby's guilt such was his opponent's skill at evading questioning.

In January 1952 Skardon's visits ceased causing him to wonder if his adversary had detected something; why else would he just leave him so abruptly?

He needn't have worried. Jim Skardon the veteran investigator had become yet another victim to fall for the charm of Kim Philby. In fact his final report left him with a favourable impression of the man who concluded that the charges against him were totally unproven. Philby's passport was subsequently returned to him.

MI5 wholly refused to perceive he was innocent preferring to firmly believe he was guilty and working for Soviet intelligence while employed by the SIS but was unable to prove it. MI6 however were staunch in their conviction that Kim Philby was entirely innocent and incapable of committing such treachery on a scale their counterparts were suggesting. Throughout all this infighting between Britain's security services Philby was left in a state of perpetual confusion on exactly where he stood in all this. Was he cleared or were MI5 gathering more damming evidence on him? Guy Liddell privately thought and hoped the whole matter would be an unremitting mistake on the part of MI5 while some within MI6 equally privately wondered if Philby was really guilty after all. It got to a point where even though closest to him were beginning now to doubt his innocence. Chief amongst the sceptics was his wife Aileen.

By 1952 she was now convinced that her husband was a Soviet spy. She knew him intimately and realised that he had lied to her all throughout their relationship. She was already unstable but the realisation of her spouse's duplicity sent her spinning into a psychological black hole from which her mind would never return from. Arguments between the two were becoming ever more frequent; she confronted him about his spying, he subsequently denied it. All it did was strengthen her solid belief that Kim was a liar to her and a traitor to their country. Her psychiatric issues only intensified as their subsequent poverty especially following Kim's dismissal after the Burges Maclean affair. One such manic episode occurred in an interaction with Elliott who continuingly laughed off her accusations whenever they spoke about it. Philby had gone out of the house something he did regularly which only heightened her suspicions that he would defect to Moscow to join the disgusting Guy Burgess at any time. The continuous heavy drinking and depression caused her to lose all grip upon reality as she telephoned Elliott to inform him of what he had done.

"Kim's gone." Aileen cried,
"Where?" Enquired Elliott,

"I think to Russia."
"How do you know?"
"I got a telegram from Kim."
Elliott hesitated before stammering on:
"What does the telegram say?"
"It says: Farewell forever. Love to the children."
Elliott cold not believe it. Surely his friend had not defected? He could not have. The risk of it being true was too great to ignore, immediately he put a call into the duty officer at MI5 who subsequently put out an alert to all ports and airports instructing that Kim Philby be apprehended should he attempt to flee the country. Elliott himself decided to make his own enquiries; when asked, Aileen could not produce such a physical telegram instead saying it had been read to her over the telephone. Nicholas approached the Post Office who could find no trace of such a telegram being sent. By now it was late evening as he phoned the Philby household once more. The phone ringing, it was picked up and Kim's familiar voice spoke out on the other end:
"Thank God it's you at last." Said Elliott overcome with relief,
"Who were you expecting it to be?" Philby replied,
"I'm glad you're home."
"Where else would I be at night." Kim asked,
Light-heartedly Elliott replied:
"The next time I see you I'll tell you where else you could have been tonight." He laughed before putting the phone down.
Things were now tough for Philby. Out of contact with both British and Soviet intelligence (for he would not even dare to attempt to make contact anytime soon), his life was now a mess. He had an unstable, alcoholic wife and five children to support, his own drinking habits were also heavy, and no means of employment. His friends rallied around him, Elliott propped him up with money, paid his children's school fees as well as relying upon Aileen's mother's funds form whatever she could provide.

He needed a job fast, Kim Philby the master double agent was now officially in the job market. Sending off a few discreet enquiries to local newspapers with the thought of resuming his old journalistic career brought nothing. An old friend from the old Section V, Jack Ivens, found him a small office job in London as the family moved house again, a large Edwardian cottage in Crowborough, East Sussex. The job was with an import-export firm dealing in the fascinating world of Spanish oranges and castor oil and paid an annual salary of six hundred pounds. The job, the commute everything about it he hated. His heart lay in the intelligence world, not some menial job in a small-time firm and rapidly his attitude began to suffer. Philby was now an alcoholic himself but always a high society one not the ill-tempered lower middle-class one he had become. MI5, still convinced of his guilt continued to monitor him and his awful temper, bugging his telephone and listening in to his conversations noting his tendency to become totally inebriated as he was utterly rude to his friends.

Moscow however had not forgotten about their star agent and were worried. They knew Philby was being watched and they knew he dare not re-establish contact for fear of being caught by MI5. They knew he was out in the cold.

Nicholas Elliott though knew the value of his friendship with Kim. Through all of the drunken berating and abuse he continued to stand by him, he knew what his friend must be going through at the moment. The marriage to Aileen was by this point collapsing under the strain and still he stood by his friend in this time of need, continuing to funnel money to him by paying his bar bills and indulging in their shared passion: to watch cricket at Lord's.

Desperately trying to salvage his friend's flagging spirts he advised him to go on the offensive against his accusers:

"You must fight like hell! If I was accused of spying, I would go to the Prime Minister and complain."

Philby smiled at the suggestion and the hope that Elliott gave him that soon he would be cleared and allowed to resume his career with MI6 where it left off before these accusations took hold.

He certainly hoped it would, and so would Moscow.

CHAPTER THIRTEEN

THE INNOCENCE OF A GUILTY MAN

By the 1 April 1952 Elliott, while at the Travellers Club, offered to ask for an advance on the allowance Philby had received upon him leaving the service. He was sure he would eventually be cleared and return to his rightful place within the intelligence world. It was a view that was shared by his other good friend on the other side of the Atlantic, James Angleton who was convinced that he would return and eventually become head of British Intelligence. However Philby knew he would never be allowed to return to such a powerful position again. Out of touch with his Soviet masters and fearful that MI5 could pounce at any moment to him it seemed that his whole life had already crashed all around him.

But the battle between both MI5 and MI6 over his culpability had effectively degraded to a stalemate. MI5 themselves were irritated at the way the SIS were still standing by him, even the outgoing Sir Stewart Menzies concluded that he was innocent. By June he retired and the role of 'C' was assumed by Sir John Sinclair. Known by his nickname of 'Sinbad' he, like his predecessor also stood by Kim Philby and believed in his expected exoneration felling that he could not let one of his own chaps down. However he discouraged the officers from actually associating with him, which as it turned out, completely ignored both by Elliott and the majority of MI6 personnel.

MI5 were still watching, waiting, listening. They continued to bug Philby's telephone and intercept his mail, waiting for the slightest slip up that would point to his perceived guilt. Their records eventually filled thirty-three volumes of collected information, all of which contained absolutely no incriminating evidence whatsoever. Instead they found out that Philby was actually engaged in an affair with a female Civil Servant in London, often disappearing for days at a time and seldom returning home. He and Aileen often argued quite strongly usually resulting in her resorting to sleep outside in a tent. The two were now experiencing intense friction between each other and he often accused her of denouncing him to the Foreign Office to their friends, effectively blaming her for ruining his career. Aileen herself knew that Philby had a mentally abusive hold over her and claimed that he had done his best to make her commit suicide. She was eventually reduced to working in the in the kitchen of a large house in Eton Square just to earn enough to pay the bills; her husband Kim was now estranged and very little money was coming into the family. Elliott and his own family, ever faithful, helped out financially and also offered moral support to the woman. It was deeply depressing times.

For Kim, his fortunes were not about to get any better anytime soon. The import-export firm he had been compelled to join eighteen months ago went bust and Philby suddenly found himself unemployed once more. He scraped some sort of living doing odd jobs such as freelance journalism but nothing sustainable ever came of it. Here was the lowest point of his life. He was now almost totally dependent upon friends and family who were supporting him financially such as with school fees, continuing to be paid for by Elliott and his father now in Saudi Arabia as an adviser to Ibn Saud sent whatever he could spare to help his son. Tomas Harris, Philby's old intelligence friend arranged for him to write a book about the Spanish Civil War, securing a contract with a local publisher with a six hundred pound advance. It appeared however just to be a way for him to pass much needed funds to his desperate friend as such a book nor a deal never materialised.

Philby was still in contact with many of his old intelligence friends, attending dinners hosted by Harris and meeting figures that were involved in the investigation such as Guy Liddell who treated him with civility rather than suspicion. But still MI5 were out to get him, the bugging of his telephone continued despite evidence to the contrary, even Liddell himself noted nothing unusual in Kim's demeanour beyond what his present situation was. It all meant that should Philby wish to activate his escape plan, as he sometimes did, then there was no way he could contact the Soviets since the British were still monitoring him.

By 1953 massive changes were happening inside the Soviet Union. The period of absolute power abruptly came to an end on the 5 March when Joseph Stalin died of a suspected stroke aged 74. The dictatorship had run its course and so did the total grip on power he held over the state. His offices of responsibility were divided and delegated to his subordinates: the top job in the USSR the General Secretary of the Communist Party fell to his main successor Nikita Khrushchev who assumed power in Moscow. The Chairman of the Council of Ministers fell to Georgy Malenkov and the People's Commissar for Defence went to Nikolai Bulganin. For the first time in less than thirty one years the Soviet Union was finally free of the terror of Stalinism while retaining its status as the world's largest socialist state.

Even now, with all the power shifts happening in the wake of the dictator's death, Kim Philby was still not out of danger. The threat of exposure persisted once more, this time arriving in the form of yet another Soviet defector called Vladimir Petrov.

Petrov was born in Siberia into a peasant family who throughout the 1930's managed to survive the purges Stalin had wrought upon the USSR to make his way up through the ranks of the Soviet intelligence services. By the early 1950's he was a colonel and the local rezident based in the capital of Australia, Canberra. He was well aware of the crimes the dictator in Moscow had perpetrated through policies of collectivisation within the Soviet Union which saw his village destroyed by famine. Working as a cipher clerk revealed all about the regime which he served but by August 1954 had decided to defect to the west in Australia. His wife had planned to join him but she would almost become one of the first victims of the new and reorganised secret service, the Committee for State Security of the Soviet Union, better known by its abbreviation, the KGB.

The KGB had been established on the 13 March that year and replaced the Ministry of Internal Affairs and the Ministry of State Security to supersede the NKVD as the main state police and internal security in the USSR. The KGB would go on to be one of the most efficient and brutal security services in the eastern bloc comparable only to the Stasi, the secret police operating in East Germany. The heavy hand of the KGB would be felt by Petrov when a snatch squad kidnapped his wife Evdokia while she was planning to join him. She was however rescued aboard a plane in the northern city of Darwin when the Soviet agents tried to manhandle her.

Petrov was a high ranking official, just like the former Konstantin Volkov and had access to extremely sensitive material on ciphers and major espionage networks including six hundred KGB agents working in diplomatic roles worldwide. But there was one piece of intelligence he did bring to the attention of the west, knowledge of agents who were located within the Soviet Union, in Kuibyshev, a city on the banks of the Volga and Samara Rivers. The identities of these agents would prove to be of some interest to the British and the Americans; they were called Donald Maclean and Guy Burgess. This was the first piece of evidence that the two missing diplomats were actually behind the Iron Curtain even though Khrushchev had not officially acknowledged their existence in the USSR. But Petrov's revelations also contained something which would blow open the whole scandal; confirmation that a third man had indeed tipped off the two before their defection, something which the CIA had believed and MI6 had been pressing Philby on for some time. It was explosive stuff, all throughout the government, the media and the diplomatic services in both London and abroad speculation and rumour began to spread on just who this mysterious 'Third Man' really was. The media frenzy about the defection tolled upon Kim as he became privately anxious; what did he know? What if he was publically named? He expected a visit from the cunning Jim Skardon any day now with police officers and a warrant for his arrest. But it did not happen. Hours turned to days which tuned to weeks, then months. With the passing of time it was becoming ever clearer that Petrov did not know the identity of the man who tipped off Burgess and Maclean but Kim was still worried. What if he divulged something that he did not know about himself? Something that MI5 knew and could be used to trap him into a confession and incriminate him.

Meanwhile over in Washington, Kim's friend James Angleton was now the head of CIA counterintelligence reporting directly to Allen Dulles, the Director of Central Intelligence. Angleton was one of only two staff to gain the acute attention of Dulles when giving advice, usually administered during late night meetings. Angleton over the years through his air of slight snobbishness had developed an additional sense, one that could sniff out the falsehoods in those around him. He was only ever really comfortable around Englishmen and friends in the Israeli intelligence service. It was these slightly awkward but surgical qualities that gained the respect of Dulles. Their meetings which were always focused on intelligence matters were destined to turn toward the focus on the intense suspicion surrounding Jim's old tutor and very good friend Kim Philby.

Angleton recalled that day back in 1946 in London when they were off to Buckingham Palace to collect awards from the King for their wartime services. Angleton explained that Kim was rather disappointed to receive an OBE when he would much rather, as he believed he was entitled to, receive a full knighthood. He recalled that infamous remark he had made outside when Kim turned to him and uttered the words:

"You know what this country needs is a good dose of socialism."

Those words still haunted him after all these years. He told Dulles,

"From that moment on, I've been wary of the fellow. You know, he sounded like a Commie. I have a feeling in my bones about him."

Even though Jim Angleton still refused to believe that Kim Philby was really a Soviet spy, his thoughts and instincts reflected what the CIA really suspected.

The wake of the Petrov defection and the speculation of the identity of the confirmed third man galvanised MI5 once more in trying to pin the guilt upon Philby. Dick White was now the Director General of MI5 having beat Guy Liddell to the role. Liddell's friendships were seen as being rather dubious, even to the extent that some may have even speculated he was a Soviet agent himself. However upon White's appointment he congratulated his fellow officer before resigning his position from the organisation. Now the head of the internal security service, Dick White was going to exploit the Petrov issue to finally flush out Kim Philby once and for all. The plan was to use the perceived uncertainty that must be in the suspect's mind by calling him in for yet another interview, convincing him that the authorities must have damming new evidence. He approached the Deputy Prime Minister, Anthony Eden about releasing the revelation of a 'Third Man' to the public in order to frighten Philby as a precursor to this and once he would get the summons, he would be convinced he was now found out. But the head of MI6, Sir John Sinclair was convinced that White was pursuing a vendetta against Philby as the divisions between both branches of the secret service grew increasingly bitter. Eden subsequently refused permission for MI5 to apply undue pressure by releasing the fact that there was a third man in the affair.

Watching all of this was the Soviets. Moscow quite rightly had reason to be worried about their master spy and his financial plight. Yuri Modin was all too aware that MI5 were watching Philby, for the KGB had their own counter-surveillance teams watching them. They reported the presence of several British agents within the vicinity of their suspect. By now he was totally dependent upon handouts from friends and family. The Russians had to do something, a drunken spy like Philby could not be left to confess or demand to be extracted without attracting attention. Modin argued that Philby had rendered valuable service to Moscow and therefore a large sum of money should be given to him to keep him stable since they may need him in the future. The funds that would be issued would instil confidence in Philby and assure him the Soviet Union would stand by him.

There was a problem with something like this. The simple transfer of money would not be possible since Moscow was aware that Philby continued to be under watch from MI5. Modin was told under no circumstances could he ever make direct contact with Kim himself and that would lead to exposure. The only way was to do it through a third party.

On the 16 June 1954 Yuri Modin moved to make contact with Sir Anthony Blunt the former MI5 agent and fourth man in the Cambridge Spy ring. He had already been interrogated by his old employers in 1952 and Jim Skardon eleven times since 1951 in the wake of the Burgess Maclean scandal. By now he had largely scaled down his Soviet espionage activities and was now a distinguished art historian at the Courtauld Institute of Art. After giving a lecture on the Arch of Gallienus to a group of students comprising of members of the public and classical architecture students one individual, blond haired and broad shouldered who was sitting in the front row, a Norwegian calling himself Greenglass stayed behind. As students gathered around the academic, the man pushed his way into the crowd and placed a postcard emblazoned with a renaissance painting into his hand:

"Excuse me. Do you know where I can find this picture?" He asked as Blunt turned over the card to find the message: 'Tomorrow 8 p.m. Angel.' The handwriting was unmistakable; the message was from Guy Burgess. Staring at the messenger, Blunt immediately knew the man who had given him the card. Greenglass was in fact the Cambridge network controller Yuri Modin:

"Yes, Yes." Blunt said enthusiastically. He knew exactly what this meant.

The next evening at 8 p.m. Anthony Blunt met Yuri Modin in the Angel pub in the London borough of Islington, an established watering hole used for clandestine meetings in the past. After a quick catch up where the traitorous academic revealed how he was interrogated but admitted nothing, Blunt reported that Philby was in a bad way. Unemployed, virtually bankrupt and battered by a barrage of hostile interrogations at the hands of MI5, Kim was holding out but for how long? Modin asked if he would be able to pass cash onto Philby and Blunt duly agreed.

Philby himself drove from his home in Crowborough to Tonbridge a few days later. There he bought a first class train ticket to London. It was an almost certainty that MI5 were watching him. However he used the old trick, the one he used when he was in Section V to deliver copied documents to his old handlers during the war; he waited until everyone else had got on the train and he boarded at the last minute. At Vauxhall he departed and took the Underground to Tottenham Court Road, stopping to purchase a large coat and hat while using the shop windows to check around him for MI5 tails. He then stopped for a drink before going to the local cinema. Inside he took a seat in the back row but only stayed for around half the performance before getting up and slipping out. The whole thing was a trick; if he was being followed by MI5 then his watcher would inevitably show himself by getting up to leave at the same time as Philby. By one single act he had effectively thrown off any potential tail the authorities would send to keep an eye on him. But even this was not enough, walking around for the next two hours before catching a bus and getting off again later down the route. By evening he found himself in North London certain that he was no longer being followed.

A small square off the Caledonian Road in Islington, not far from the Angel pub was where Kim Philby, Anthony Blunt accompanied by Yuri Modin found themselves but not together. Philby kept his distance as the exchange took place when Modin, true to his orders from Moscow, passed Blunt the package containing £5000 in cash while Kim, virtually unrecognisable in his new overcoat walked behind along the tree lined path. That night he returned home to Crowborough like a man reborn. Here he had funds, the £5000 and re-established contact with Soviet intelligence. He was at least half back in from the cold.

He was however still under suspicion no matter what his financial situation. It would be another thirteen months until the wheels would begin to turn to lift Philby out of the stale wilderness he had spent the last few years enduring.

By the 20 July 1955 the Director General of MI6 Sir John Sinclair wrote to the Director General of MI5 Dick White regarding the scandalous interview Helenus 'Buster' Milmo had put Philby through. Still displaying loyalty to the former employee of the service, he complained saying that the whole conduct was bias, arguing that Kim had been the unfortunate victim of a momentous miscarriage of justice.

Sinclair wrote to the Permanent Under-Secretary of State for

Foreign Affairs, Sir Ivone Kirkpatrick to argue once and for all the case for Kim Philby's defence. He said that the Milmo interrogation produced no direct evidence to prove he was a Soviet spy or the so-called 'Third Man'. This would make evidence inadmissible within a court of law and therefore invalid. Accusations Sinclair argued were circumstantial at best and dressed up to look worse than what it was for the case for the prosecution, emphasising the fact that a perpetual finger of suspicion was being pointed at Philby. Sinclair further pointed out that he had been convicted of nothing at all in the last four years and was totally against tradition for a man to be forced to prove his own innocence. He concluded that this was a case that relied on nothing at all but suspicion.

To his opposite number in MI5, Sinclair argued that for the last four years Philby had been subjected to surveillance and interrogation under the perceived assumption that he was already guilty. Yet there was not definitive evidence of his complicity in spying or his involvement in the Burgess Maclean affair. Mail intercepts and volume upon volume of telephone logs had revealed nothing suspicious and both the smoothness of Jim Skardon and the abrasiveness of Buster Milmo failed to extract any sort of confession. The allegations against him were purely circumstantial, at best based upon his association with Guy Burgess, and nothing that could be used against him in a prosecution in a trial for treason. He went on to tell White in no uncertain terms:

"Produce the evidence, and there'll be no further dispute."

Sinclair knew he had backed White into a corner. He knew he could not produce any sort of damming evidence to conclusively prove Kim Philby was a Soviet spy. Reluctantly he agreed to invite his suspect in for another, final interview.

But things were about to get a little more complicated. News broke of Petrov's defection to the general public on the 18

September including a barrage of scandalous revelations; the evidence that Guy Burgess and Donald Maclean were Soviet spies recruited while at Cambridge and Maclean's defection just before he was going to be arrested. It only served to accuse the authorities of a massive cover up since it had now come to light that they were more like fugitives on the run rather than missing diplomats.

The speculation of the 'Third Man' was not going away and Philby's name was still being mentioned with some trepidation by many. Even his wife was beginning to denounce him as a traitor even going so far as to drunkenly shout during one dinner party:

"I know you are the Third Man!"

By now the scandal was not only public, but beginning to turn political. The new Foreign Secretary, Harold Macmillan, a man destined to be a future Prime Minister, issued a White Paper explaining the Burgess Maclean affair. Full of political spin it mentioned no role of Kim Philby even though he was still the central figure in the middle of this storm. It was a hastily prepared government cover up since just five days earlier Macmillan realised he would have to act by saying:

"We are going to have to say something."

It was clear the document intended to quash any speculation. It did nothing of the sort. Officials in the United States were not convinced at all. J. Edgar Hoover, the chief of the FBI, was as certain of Philby's guilt as MI5 was in Britain. Incredulous that the authorities had failed to apprehend him, he planned a little attack of his own. The conduct of the intelligence services on the other side of the Atlantic would fuel his haste as Philby was summoned once more on the 7 October. Expecting to be grilled again about perhaps some kind of new evidence that had come to light, he arrived at an MI5 safe house in London close to Sloane Square. The whole thing was a setup. The room marked for the interview was bugged with a microphone hidden in a telephone placed on top of a sideboard. A sofa and chairs arranged around a small table filled the middle of the space complete with an amplifier to the hidden listening device placed strategically under the chair Philby was going to sit.

Everything was subsequently relayed back to MI5 headquarters at Leconfield House where recordings were made before being transcribed by typists. The man himself was quickly ushered into this little trap as soon as he arrived. This was his fourth interview and he was now getting nervous, although he never wanted to show it, their suspicions may be aroused. Why else would they want to talk again? He was sure the Petrov defection had indeed thrown something up to incriminate him yet he stated openly that he welcomed the chance to clear his name in all of this. He braced himself for yet another exhausting barrage of awkward questions.

But this time things were strangely different. This time he would not be questioned by MI5 officers, but by two of his old friends in MI6, the very people who were standing by him. Harold Macmillan had set up an inquiry to rule on this decision and the interview therefore sounded and felt more like an informal chat than a formal interrogation. Throughout the interview, as the tapes rolled the travesty began. Gentle questioning, a poke and a prod here and there it was nothing too strenuous as Philby was subjected to nothing more than a chat rather than an interrogation. His communist past, his association with Burgess and more, Philby stuttered over everything but the officers in the room were always there to hold his hand. It was clear they were guiding him toward particular answers, offering explanations as to why this and that happened to which Philby would agree before moving on to the next topic.

The listening MI5 officers at Leconfield House were filled with outrage, declaring the interview as nothing more than a travesty.

At the end of the session Philby and the MI6 officers all shook hands as they told him something that he thought he would never hear:

"You may be pleased to know that we have come to a unanimous decision about your innocence."

Naturally Philby was totally overjoyed. Finally after all these years, amidst all the allegations, accusations and subversion he was finally relieved to be in the clear. He put the decision by the authorities squarely on the fact that he had made no attempt to flee during the investigation. He knew that there was literally nothing MI5, nor the CIA for that matter could do to prove his guilt. But J. Edgar Hoover was waiting for something like this for now he launched his planned assault on the man he was convinced was a traitor. Furious over the MI6 decision to exonerate their former employee and determined to force the British into launching a judicial investigation, he leaked a story to a journalist. He cynically told him that Kim Philby was a Soviet agent and the real 'Third Man' who had aided in the escape of both Burgess and Maclean in 1951. That journalist hungrily lapped up the story, a major scoop for the press and published the revelation in the New York Sunday Times on the 23 October 1955.

In Britain Philby's name had been known to journalists but had been kept out of the papers for the last four years for security. But on this Sunday the crowd of journalists were laying siege to the Philby household in full voice typical of a media scrum. Elliott advised his friend to hold them off as much as possible. It was easier said than done. With everyone talking about the so-called 'Third Man' and his name in the American papers, he was now subjected to the probing intrusion of the British media. The hunt for answers was on. It was a hunt that would reach the very corridors of power.

Two days after the Philby allegation broke his name was still not printed in the British newspapers, for that would be libellous. But on the 25 October, a Tuesday, events in the Houses of Parliament were move the scandal on tremendously; all thanks to one particular politician called Marcus Lipton.

Lipton was aligned to the Labour Party and a Member of Parliament for the constituency of Brixton in South London. He was a politician moulded from the ways of the old school; he hated modern pop music thinking it would destroy the monarchy and intensely distrusted government. Lipton was an agitator, a privileged trouble maker of the ministerial and parliamentary offices. He was well known for being blunt and asking questions others may find embarrassing. Awkwardness was not in the vocabulary of this politician who was well acquainted with the procedures of parliament. Often, and on this day in the House of Commons during the twice weekly clash of Prime Minister's Questions he invoked the right to make statements in the house without fear of prosecution; the 'parliamentary privilege'. He wanted to ask the Prime Minister, Churchill's deputy and eventual successor Anthony Eden about the whole Philby affair:

"Has the Prime Minister made up his mind to cover up at all costs the dubious third man activities of Mr Harold Philby who was first secretary at the Washington embassy a little time ago, and is he determined to stifle all discussions on the very great matters which were evaded in the White Paper, which is an insult to the intelligence of the country?"

Prime Minister Eden refused to reply to Lipton's question but it certainly caught the attention of the press.

That very same afternoon Kim Philby was travelling home on the London Underground like any other commuter when his eyes idly wandered across to the newspaper the person next to him was reading, a copy of the Evening Standard and noticed with abject horror what was written: 'MP talks of "Dubious Third Man Activities of Mr Harold Philby".'

The paper went on to quote Lipton word for word. Philby now realised that his secret was virtually out. After staying under the radar for over twenty years and evading detection from the security services, the press of all people, his old trade, managed to flush him out into the open. He was virtually sure that MI5 would come knocking once again. Arriving home he immediately telephoned one of his staunchest friends, Nicholas Elliott:

"*My name is in the newspapers. I have to do something.*"

"*I agree with you.*" Elliott replied in a calming tone: "*Certainly, but let's think about it for a day or two, at least. Don't do anything for a day, all right? I'll call you tomorrow.*"

Kim accepted this. If Marcus Lipton MP did have access to information, would he not have passed it onto the security services by now? All the politician was doing was simply repeating what was already known, nothing new by any standard. Elliot's advice was to simply stand firm on this and let his old friends in the service do the work. MI5 lacked the evidence to prosecute Philby and MI6 along with Harold Macmillan would either have to publically support or criticise him. True to his word, Elliott telephoned Kim the next day:

"*We've decided that naturally you must respond. But it should be done only done when the parliamentary debates begin. Please bear up for two weeks.*"

Those two weeks resulted in Philby being stalked by crowds of journalists who had overtaken Crowbridge, laying siege to the house. They followed him wherever he went even to the local pub. Politely he declined every question put to him. He even declined an offer of one hundred pounds put up by the Sunday Express if he agreed to participate in a debate with Lipton himself. The telephone rang almost non-stop, it was tantamount to torture. Elliott, looking on concerned arranged for Aileen and the children to be moved away to a relative while Philby moved out to stay with his mother in her Drayton Gardens flat in South Kensington.

The Government had promised to issue a statement and hold a debate on the issue on the 7 November. Elliott in the meantime employed the services of their mutual old intelligence friend

Richard Brooman-White to draw up for Macmillan a brief on the situation which was supposed to be impartial but in reality leaned in Philby's favour, arguing rather subtly the case for Kim innocence and total exoneration. Brooman-White had left the intelligence services in 1951 for a political career and was now Conservative MP for Rutherglen so held some influence over the Foreign Secretary. In the draft, he stated that no hard evidence had been laid against Philby and that he had lost his job due to a flirtation with communism in his youth accompanied by a poor choice friendship with Guy Burgess. Macmillan, the aristocratic Etonian regarded intelligence work as dirty work and did not want the clash between MI5 and MI6 to continue. A public trial would be embarrassing in his mind and he himself really just wanted to consign the whole façade to the past.

On the 7 November 1955 the day parliament was due to debate the Philby affair, Foreign Secretary Harold Macmillan rose to his feet in the House of Commons and issued the following statement:

"Mr Philby had been a friend of Burgess from the time when they were fellow undergraduates at Trinity College, Cambridge. Burgess had been accommodated with Philby and his family at the latter's home in Washington from August 1950 to April 1951 . . . and, of course, it will be remembered that at no time before he fled was Burgess under suspicion. It is now known that Mr Philby had Communist associates during and after his university days. In view of the circumstances, he was asked in July 1951 to resign from the Foreign Service. Since that date his case has been the subject of close investigation. No evidence has been found ... to show that he was responsible for warning Burgess or Maclean. While in government service he carried out his duties ably and conscientiously, and I have no reason to conclude that Mr Philby has at any time betrayed the interests of his country, or to identify him with the so-called "Third Man', if indeed there was one."

With this endorsement there was nothing anyone could do

without hard new evidence. Harold Macmillan had officially cleared Kim Philby of spying. The debate now ensued and Richard Brooman-White viciously attacked Lipton on the opposition benches accusing him of being rather McCarthyite:

"He is in favour of acting on suspicion, of smearing on suspicion, by directing public suspicion on to an individual against whom nothing at all has been proved. We must leave it to his own conscience to straighten out what that may cost in personal suffering to the wife, children and friends of the person involved. The only thing that has been proved against Mr Philby is that he had Burgess staying with him and he had certain Communist friends. He may not have been very wise in his choice of friends, but what honourable member of the House could say that all his friends were people against whom no shadow of suspicion could ever be cast?"

Labour claimed yet another cover up in the Philby matter with Frank Tomney MP replying in blunt tones:

"Whoever is covering whom and on what pretext, whether because of the membership of a circle or a club, or because of good fellowship or whatever it may be, they must think again and think quickly."

Lipton's accusations were quickly flagging in the intense debate. He tried to go on the offensive by declaring:

"I will not be gagged by anybody in this House or outside in the performance of my duty."

The response from the Conservative benches was to challenge him to repeat the allegations outside without the protection of parliamentary privilege. Lipton had no intention to do such a thing. He fought back:

"Even Mr Philby had not asked for it to be repeated outside."

For Kim himself he knew that he would be exonerated by Macmillan but he needed to clear his name fully by removing all doubt. He could only do that if he could force Marcus Lipton to publically retract his allegation. Prompted by a telephone conversation with Nick Elliott, Philby informed his mother that the very next morning he would he hosting a press conference held here in her flat in Drayton Gardens.

Just before 11 a.m. on the 8 November 1955 the 43 year old Kim Philby opened the door of his mother's flat and let the waiting journalists from around the world in:

"Jesus Christ! Do come in!" He said as the stairwell was packed with the press, all eager to grab a piece of the story from this new found celebrity. What followed was an extraordinary display of duplicity on a scale worthy of a corrupt politician. Here was Kim Philby, clean shaven wearing a pinstripe suit, similar patterned shirt with a professional looking checked tie. Looking and sounding confident, devoid of any nervousness and stammer, he prepared to look the press the eye with a steady unfazed gaze and completely dupe the world in his version of events. He sat down in a chair to face the cameras next to Edwin Newman, an American journalist with NBC, the man delegated to put the questions to Philby. Newman began with a short question as soon as the cameras began to roll:

"Mr Philby, Mr Macmillan the Foreign Secretary said there was no evidence that you were the so-called 'Third Man' who allegedly tipped off Burgess and Maclean, are you satisfied with that clearance he gave you?"

Philby replied with a straight answer: *"Yes…I am."*

"Well if there was a Third Man, were you in fact the Third Man?" Newman asked,

"No, I was not." Philby said while biting his tongue with a wry smile:

"Do you think there was one?"

"No comment."

Newman continued: *"Now Mr Philby the disappearance of Burgess and Maclean is almost as much of a mystery today as it was when they went away about four years ago or more. Can you shed any light on it at all?"*

"No I can't." Philby lied: *"In the first place I am debarred by the Official Secrets Act from saying anything that might disclose to unauthorised persons information derived from my position as a former government official. In the second place, the Burgess Maclean affair had raised issues of great...delicacy in the sphere of international affairs. I left the service some four years ago and I haven't any means of knowing whether words of mind perhaps slipped it from context perhaps even garbled as they sometimes have been, wouldn't severely prejudice or damage the government in its conduct of international affairs."*

With this statement over, Newman then posed the next question:

"Erm, Mr Philby you were asked yourself to resign from the Foreign Office a few months after Burgess and Maclean disappeared and Mr Macmillan had said that you had had communist associations, is that why you were asked to resign?"

"I was asked to resign from the Foreign Office because of an imprudent association with Burgess, and as a result of his disappearance. Beyond that I'm afraid I got no further comment to make."

"Can you say when your communist associations ended, I assume they did?" Newman then asked. Philby replied with a bare-faced lie:

"The last time I spoke to a communist knowing that he was a communist was sometime in 1934." He looked his questioner directly in the eye with the slightest of smiles. Duplicity disguised as pleasantry. Newman then repeated his question but in a slightly different way:

"My Philby you were asked to resign yourself from the Foreign Office a few months after Burgess and Maclean disappeared and the Foreign Secretary has said that in the past you had communist associations. Is that why you were asked to resign?"

Philby repeated his answer: *"I was asked to resign because of an imprudent association."*

"That was your association with Burgess?"

"Correct."

"What about these alleged communist associations, can you say anything about them?"

Leaning back and away, a typical defensive posture, Philby appeared to repeat his carefully prepared answer: *"Err the last time I spoke to a communist knowing him to be a communist was sometime in err 1934."*

But Newman was waiting with a typical journalistic entrapment: *"That rather implies that you have also spoken to communists unknowingly and you now know about it."*

Philby smiled, perhaps in admiration of the cunningness of the question, worthy of his own ability:

"Well I spoke to Burgess last in April or May 1951." He bit his tongue once more:

"He gave you no idea that he was planning to go."

"Never." Philby said softly:

"Err would you still regard Burgess who lived with you for a while in Washington, would you still regard him as a friend of yours, how do you feel about him now?"

A slight pause form Kim: *"I consider his action deplorable…"* Another pause: *"On the subject of friendship I'd prefer to say as little as possible because it's very complicated."*

Throughout the whole interview he looked uncomfortable. Perspiring, looking down and shifting, his neatly combed back hair just starting to lose its place, his mouth jiggling in a furtive manner. Newman continued:

"Do you have any other reason for keeping silent Mr Philby?"

"I have. The efficiency of our security services can only be impaired if there are organisations and techniques are discussed in public."

"I'd like to ask you one more question Mr Philby, err the Foreign Office asking you to resign because of your imprudent association as you call it with Burgess do you think that was fair?"

Philby, clearly uncomfortable, answered promptly:

"I understood perfectly well their reasons for doing so."

It was there the interview ended. Ever the consummate host the journalists were treated more like guests than inquisitors. Even his mother was paraded before the cameras with her son.

That evening the whole interview was broadcast across the main news under the title 'Philby Talks'. It was watched by Yuri Modin who was still in London and described it as *"breathtaking."* Modin could see the real aspect of his performance worthy of any trained actor. He knew that agent 'Stanley' was playing his cards so close to his chest that he knew that the authorities would have nothing to pin upon him at all.

In the wake of the interview, Marcus Lipton became forced into a corner on the issue. He released a statement where he was forced to withdraw his comments about Philby stating that his evidence had been based upon that which MI5 held. Since MI5 had nothing on him, there was nothing the politician had either. He stated that MI5 officers were strictly prohibited from making contact with politicians so therefore his hands were tied. Not wanting to be embroiled in a libel case he withdrew the allegations upon the advice of his lawyers.

Kim Philby was now formally and politically exonerated of any wrongdoing much to the fury of Dick White and MI5 whose fingers he had slipped through. The way was finally clear to facilitate his return, a spectacular resurgence of his career into the welcoming, extended arms of MI6.

Agent 'Stanley', Kim Philby was after four years, about to come in from the cold.

CHAPTER FOURTEEN

A GENTLEMAN IN FOREIGN LANDS

Harold Macmillan described Kim Philby as a *"hero"* and an *"upstanding citizen"* and Marcus Lipton was forced to retreat humiliatingly. He later put on the record that he deeply regretted the comments. Nicholas Elliott on the other hand was absolutely jubilant that his friend had emerged out of all of this totally victorious. He had defended himself and his class, and Elliott, his faith justified, had stood beside him all the way. He now wanted to facilitate the rehabilitation of Kim back into SIS where he felt he rightly belonged. It would be an opportunity for Philby to leak further information to the Soviet Union once more.

But his re-entry back into the service was not going to happen just yet. William Allen, who had worked previously with Philby while serving as the press councillor at the British embassy in Turkey, offered him a job while he was in the Republic of Ireland. Allen, an Old Etonian who owned a large printing company called David Allen & Sons, asked Philby to write a centenary history of the company. For several months he lived as a guest at the family home in County Waterford even though Allen and Philby were polar opposites politically. Allen was a far right sympathiser who was a close friend of Oswald Mosely and had no idea that his recently cleared house guest and friend was a secret far left communist. Philby duly wrote a long and quite boring work on the history of the family firm before returning to Britain just in time as a political storm was about to break.

Nicholas Elliott was about to be embroiled in Operation Claret, the secret attempt to take advantage of an official visit to the UK of the Soviet premier Nikita Khrushchev by employing the services of a veteran underwater diver named Buster Crabb. Widely seen as one of the best frogmen of the Second World War he was experienced in many exploits of the Mediterranean theatre of operations and was employed again in 1956 during the visit of Khrushchev and his deputy Nikolai Bulganin. Crabb was employed by MI6 to investigate a Soviet naval cruiser, the Ordzhonikidze which was docked in Portsmouth harbour for the duration of the visit and suspected to have a new design of propeller. MI6 wanted to know more about it but the operation ended in mystery when Crabb disappeared, fuelling speculation that he was captured by the Russians and taken to the Soviet Union. Further controversy ensued when it emerged that Anthony Eden had not given his consent for the MI6 operation to commence in the UK, which should have been the responsibility of MI5, the internal security service. With the Prime Minister still outraged over the affair, the whole bungled façade only served to hasten the departure of Sir John Sinclair as the Director General of MI6 making way for his replacement. That would be Sir Dick White, newly arrived from being the head of MI5 with Jack Easton as his deputy. Upon the move across his own replacement in MI5 would be Sir Roger Hollis but despite the changes at the top, Crabb's fate was still unknown. The conspiracy theories continued, from he was shot by a sniper, to being taken to Moscow and brainwashed. It would be less than fourteen months later, when Crabb's body would be found, mysteriously and clearly murdered. It would later be speculated that the Soviets *did* kill Crabb upon a tipoff from a British spy that may have been Philby.

But Nicholas Elliott believed that Crabb tragically died in the water from respiratory trouble. He was a known heavy smoker which could have been a contributing factor. The thought that he may have been betrayed simply did not register in his mind and despite being caught up in the whole affair appeared to be surviving relatively intact. The whole controversy surrounding Buster Crabb was still swirling with himself in the middle of it all, yet he still managed to stick true to his promise to his friend. Through his contacts and influence in the classic Old Boy network he was working tirelessly to secure a position for Kim with the security services once more. The key was his relationship with active journalists and editors of mainstream newspapers with whom Elliott had built up over many years, like a mini network of informers. He would host regular dinners for his editorial friends in White's Bar, a popular haunt for espionage types for years and introduce young journalists to the Director General of MI6. It was a very effective way for SIS to stay in contact with persons deemed useful to their operations. One such influential friend from Naval Intelligence during the war was a certain man called Ian Fleming, the creator of James Bond. He was a man with considerable connections and was willing to share interesting information with the intelligence agencies even though he was based at Goldeneye in Jamaica. Indeed many foreign correspondents were permitted to liaise with MI6 and in turn many operatives took on active journalist roles as cover; the ability to ask the most sensitive and impertinent questions without arousing suspicion. This was the way in for Philby, and Elliott knew just the man to smooth the process, the editor of the Observer, David Astor. Both men knew each other very well; both were of the same elite class since they both attended Eton and were both stationed in The Hague back in 1939 before the outbreak of war. Astor always tried to distance himself from his links with the secret services but now was called upon to do one of their best men and his ex-colleague a very gratuitous favour.

Elliott asked Astor if he would be willing to employ Kim Philby as a freelance correspondent based out in the Middle East, Beirut to be precise. By now the Suez Crisis was building; Israel the Jewish state created in 1948 invaded its Arab neighbour Egypt followed by the colonial powers of Britain and France. The whole thing would end in humiliation as both western countries would eventually be forced to back down and mark the ignominious end to Anthony Eden's tenure as Prime Minister. But for now the whole region was a magnet for journalists all flocking to see how events of the Israeli led invasion would turn out. This was Philby's old trade prior to his intelligence career; covering war zones for newspapers, including the Observer itself. His experience in Spain working for The Times back in the 1930's would stand him in good stead. Kim would also be able to gain access to influential people through his father St John Philby who was now living in the same city, a useful asset for a correspondent. The oily wheels of the Old Boy network turned faster than ever before as Astor proceeded to contact his friend, the editor of the Economist, Donald Tyerman. He too was on the lookout for a man to be stationed in the Lebanese capital.

Nicholas Elliot had worked his tricks to secure his friend Kim Philby employment that would smooth his re-entry back into undercover work for SIS. Both newspapers would employ his services on a freelance basis and pay him a salary of three thousand pounds a year with travel and expenses on top. On the side Kim would conduct espionage work as an agent for MI6. The whole deal was sanctioned and passed by the MI6 Middle East Operational chief George Kennedy Young through negotiations with Elliott. They too would pay him through Godfrey Paulson, the station chief in the city. At last the rehabilitation of his friend was now totally complete.

In July 1956, seven months since Macmillan's exoneration of Kim Philby, Elliott telephoned his friend to ask him to come down to the 'firm', the informal name for the intelligence services. Philby wondered why on earth the authorities wanted him yet again, they must have uncovered new evidence:

"*Something unpleasant again?*" Philby asked expecting a vague answer,

"*Maybe just the opposite.*" Was the reply.

The loyal Nicholas Elliott had managed to bring his friend back into the fold and facilitate Kim Philby's dramatic and surprising return to MI6.

MI5 did not protest since the case against him had now gone very cold and there was no new evidence as Kim happily agreed to undertake the new job offer. Finally he was back in the intelligence business, two publications would secure the services of an experienced journalist and he had a new life away from the dreariness of Crowborough for the sunny and exotic climate of Beirut. The move would also become the final nail in the coffin of his deteriorated marriage to Aileen as she was already convinced he was a traitor and the stress of the accusations, investigation and eventual public acquittal had sent her into the spiral of depression. Now news of her husband leaving for foreign lands was the last straw, she would not join him out in Lebanon, nor did she ever try to prevent him from going as her mental health deteriorated to such a state that alarmed even her psychiatrist. Kim's departure affected Aileen so profoundly that it committed her to an over reliance on alcohol for which ever her friends could not stop her. With the children removed to a boarding school, she was finally sent to a mental institute for a short time for treatment before returning to the dour surroundings of the family home. Shutting herself away for long periods she hoped to reconcile with her wayward husband but to no avail and to the irritation of their old friend, the woman who paired them together, Flora Solomon. Kim did not really care about saving the marriage. All he told her before departing for Lebanon was that he would refund her household bills. Then he left.

In August 1956 Kim Philby arrived in Beirut living initially on his father's estate, Mahalla Jamil, located in the village of Ajaltoun just on the outskirts of the city. It was where his father was initially exiled to after criticising King Saud, Ibn Saud's successor in Saudi Arabia. Immediately he set about cultivating contacts, military personnel, diplomats and politicians, anyone deemed suitable for journalistic as well as for espionage purposes.

It was not long before St John Philby returned to Saudi Arabia with his other children leaving Kim alone on the estate. Looking for somewhere else to live, he took a flat in Beirut itself in the Muslim quarter but found he was rather lonely in the big city. This inner solitary was picked up by Richard Beeston, a fellow journalist and foreign correspondent for his old paper The Times. Both men had met not long after Kim's arrival when he was building up his network of contacts for his papers, but also clandestinely for MI6. His quintessential Englishness coupled with his gentle stammer made him, as it always did, charming and irresistible to everyone, including the women. Beeston sensed this was just a front, a cover to hide and perhaps blunt the stigma of the loneliness of being in a new setting without any real friends or major contacts. But that was about to change.

Another colleague who Kim was acquainted with was Sam Pope Brewer, an American Journalist working for the New York Times and based in the city. He was married to a woman called Eleanor Brewer, born in Seattle and a former Red Cross worker. She was slim, tall and sweet natured and completely different from the personality of Aileen back in Crowborough. Brewer knew Kim from the old days covering the Spanish Civil War and was keen to extend a welcome once he had heard that his old friend was now in Beirut. By September he had to leave to cover an extended story, telling Eleanor to keep an eye out for the forty-four year old Kim and introduce him to their friends. On the 12th she was out socialising with friends in a local bar called the St Georges when a member of the group spotted Philby there having a drink. Instructing the waiter to extend an invitation to Kim to join them he instantly struck the gathering with his indomitable charm, especially with Eleanor herself.

  She noticed quite strongly his reserve which seemed to stick out from the rest of the crowd, feeling his loneliness every bit as he did. She felt an instant attraction to him even though she was married to another she could not help but notice his blue eyes, revelling in the atmospheric ease which he seemed to protrude to all he met. Soon she found herself talking freely to him as if she had known him all her life. Over the course of the next two weeks the two became lovers, acting more like lovesick teenagers than adulterous spouses. They arranged secret meetings in Arab coffee houses while smoking bubble-bubble pipes, cafes, notably one called the 'Shaky Floor', little picnics in the hills and mountains or on the beaches. Anywhere where they could not be spied upon was a suitable rendezvous place for the two to express their love for one another. Philby showered Eleanor with little love notes written on the paper of cigarette packages. She felt safe as she knew that her husband Sam had long since lacked concern for the state of their marriage, he only wanted to talk about politics and often criticised her cooking, the marriage between the two was only held together for the sake of their daughter Annie. She felt neglected but here was Kim making her feel wanted and loved. For Philby he loved the whole thrill of the subversion. The secrecy, the lying and secrets, the old spy in him flowed over into his personal life as they conducted their clandestine affair. Amidst the secrets he was constantly but discreetly checking for any signs of surveillance from Sam, friends or otherwise. Was he aware that there was a real possibility of Eleanor being employed by the CIA to spy on Philby while he was out here? There is certain evidence through letters to suggest that she was an informant of Wilbur

Crane Eveland the CIA station chief in Beirut.

Philby became a close family friend of the Brewers, even though knowledge of the affair was unknown. That first Christmas was spent with the family and it signalled the beginning of a happier time in Philby's life than what was endured over the past few years. He was producing a good amount of articles for his newspapers while at the same time collecting intelligence for MI6 largely by chatting informally to Arab politicians and passing their real thoughts on various situations onto London. MI6 were pleased with what their man in Beirut was producing on various Arabic policies and after one year in the region was evidently satisfied with the quality of information. He was taken to lunch at an expensive restaurant situated on the coast by the head of the Middle East desk and told that his MI6 pay was being increased. Philby sought to reward his paymasters by working as efficiently as possible. But secretly he knew it would only be a matter of time before his activities would come to the attention of his former employers. He knew at some point the Russians would make contact.

The Normandie Hotel, a cheaper watering hole than the St Georges was where Kim began to down his first drink of the day; vodka with V8 before opening his post and read through the newspapers. It was a daily habit that was more like a ritual as one particular afternoon he was approached at his corner table by a young man in his thirties with a stocky build. The man was neither Arabic nor western as he handed him a card that read: 'Petukhov, Soviet Trade Mission.' The individual's comment was one that only a spymaster like Philby could have deciphered:

"I read your articles in the Observer and in the Economist, Mr Philby. I find them very deep. I sought you out to ask you for the favour of your time for a conversation. I am particularly interested in the prospects for a Common Market of the Arab countries."

Philby knew exactly what was happening here. This man Petukhov was no trade delegate he was a representative of Soviet intelligence. The KGB had finally, inevitably come calling.

Here was an opportunity for Kim to end his Soviet spying career, he could have turned down Petukhov's (and the KGB's) offer. His fellow Cambridge spy Anthony Blunt had done it, he distanced himself from espionage activities in favour of concentrating on his art career. Right here, right now Kim Philby had the ample opportunity to go the same way. But the seduction of spying, the thrill of knowing secrets that only himself or a few others knew, the superiority of being privy to sensitive information over his fellow colleagues was too much for him. Here at this moment he lay at a pivotal crossroads in his life. He was already a spy but was given the chance to become a double agent once more. Excited at the thought of being in direct contact with the Soviets yet again instead of dismissing the man and therefore renouncing his spying for Moscow, he invited the young man for tea at his flat. He had let the Soviets back into his life.

He laid the reason for the decision squarely upon ideological allegiance having pledged a total commitment to the Soviet Union way back at Cambridge at the age of twenty-one. Never discussing politics at all with anyone, he sustained his belief that what he had done for the Soviet cause was right without the need for comfort or comradeship from like-minded individuals such as the other members of the Cambridge Spy Ring. In effect Philby was very nearly the perfect spy, always stable, mostly cool under pressure, embraced charm as a defence and never hesitant in the consequences of his actions. Always the professional he adopted a dogmatist attitude, believing he was right whether it be leading to the death of allies or betraying his friends. For Philby the political aspect was the fundamental ideological principle throughout his entire life which actually made him think he was loyal and absolved of all guilt.

But there was another aspect to Philby's deception. The adrenaline rush that made it so addictive was the cause of why he actually enjoyed spying. The retaining of information provided for Philby an exotic brand of superiority over others especially to those people closest to him who thought they knew him, but in reality knew nothing at all. There were two Kim Philby's, Philby the kind lover, the charming host, the good friend the consummate professional. Then there was the other Kim Philby, the real persona of opinionated arrogance, the political man, the liar, the traitor. He could not give up spying even if he wanted to. The addiction had gripped him and it was now too late.

He was a neglectful husband but a gentle and kind lover and the reliance of alcohol helped to maintain the duplicity. The inebriated stupors for which he was becoming so well accustomed were a signpost of his increasing alcoholism for the double life and the burden of the secrets drove it all. The cool smoothness of the bottle, the colour of the liquid in the glass was an expression of his faithlessness to western capitalism in favour of eastern socialism.

At three in the afternoon the very next day Petukhov arrived at Philby's flat in the city. The move was risky for there was a real danger of being seen by unwanted eyes. They could never meet here again. They therefore developed a system for communication involving Kim standing on the balcony holding a newspaper at a pre-arranged time. This would mean Philby required a meeting with his new KGB handler. If it was a matter of urgency, Kim would display a book. Together they agreed to meet regularly, always in a quiet corner of the city and always in the evening once the sun had gone down. The KGB had agents deployed all throughout the volatile area of the Middle East and Philby was to play his part. Moscow asked him to prioritise his spying, reporting first and foremost what the United States and Great Britain intended to achieve in the region before anything else was divulged. Kim Philby was back now in his element, a reporter by trade, MI6 spy under the radar and a KGB agent above all else.

In the autumn of 1956 his private life was about to take a turn as Sam Pope Brewer finally realised that his wife had been having an affair after she informed him of her intention to leave. She temporarily moved back to America and her home city of Seattle to obtain a Mexican Divorce, which was seen as less hassle than a typical American one. The way would be clear for Kim to move in formally on her if it was not for the ruined state of his own marriage, the remains of which were still festering back in Crowborough in the shape of Aileen Philby.

At no time did she go to accompany her husband in Beirut, instead staying at the family home with the children. Flora Solomon was becoming increasingly worried about her friend as her mental state dramatically turned for the worst. Watching Aileen destroy herself, Flora began to hold the firm conviction that her husband had abandoned her in his jaunt to Lebanon. Outraged at what her friend was going through, she wrote to Philby to complain about how he was treating her. This was the man whom she had introduced Aileen to, how could he behave in such a way? His reply was nothing short of sheer single-mindedness and utter contempt for his marriage. He summed up her claims about him in one word: *"hooey"*. He also attacked his wife by referring back to the vague promise he made her before he left regarding the family expenses:

"I had made a clear arrangement with her that she should pay the household bills and forward me the receipts, whereupon I would refund her." He knew full well that Aileen had not sent him one receipt so took the opportunity to fire a sarcastic broadside at his estranged spouse:

"So, no receipts, no money." He went further by saying that if she could afford:

"the luxuries of risking her neck at point-to-points, she can damn well send me the receipts." By the end he claimed that he was:

"fed up with her idleness."

The attack on his wife was totally selfish and essentially blamed her for everything. It was self-validation for him to justify and take forward his relationship with Eleanor Brewer by painting his long suffering wife as the bad person. But there was also a subversive element to the conflict between the two. Aileen was staunchly patriotic and long believed Kim to be a traitor and a liar. Kim knew that if he was to be exposed, the main finger of suspicion would emanate from her. Publically she was a wife and mother. Privately she was more of a liability and therefore more of a threat to him and that also made her the bad person.

By the 12 December 1957 Aileen's torture finally ended when she was discovered dead in the bedroom of her Crowborough home. The whole scene appeared to be a suicide from a lethal cocktail of alcohol and barbiturates which the coroner ruled as death by tuberculosis, myocardial degeneration and heart failure. Aggravating factors was influenza inducing a respiratory infection accompanied by a large intake of alcohol. Some people such as her psychiatrist thought she died not by misadventure but by another hand, namely Kim Philby who wanted to silence her and Flora Solomon blamed him for her fiend's demise. She swore to strike him from her memory and forget all about him.

When Philby himself heard about his wife's death his reaction was a little strange to say the least. Beirut's Bab Idriss square in the central district was busy at Christmas. Richard Beeston was shopping with his wife Moyra in the area when Kim Philby spotted then from the other side of the street. Rushing across the road to greet them he said:

"I have wonderful news darlings, I want you to come and celebrate."

He took them to the nearest bar, his regular haunt the Normandie where he produced a telegram and informed them of his wife's death calling it a *"wonderful escape"* and declaring that he was now clear to go ahead and marry another girl. The Beestons were utterly bemused at his reaction to the news about Aileen. His wife had just died and here he was celebrating. But Philby had very good reason to celebrate; he had now been rid of the one person who could decipher his real personality. Despite endeavouring to maintain his cover, building up a fake persona over many years to fool his friends into thinking those closest to him knew him intimately. Here was Aileen, supposed to be the closest of all was in reality Philby's biggest threat. She suspected quite rightly his lying was deliberate and became his biggest critic. Her death freed him for this fear of exposure from within. He was now free of the one person who could have ousted him once and for all if she had the right information about him.

Despite being in a jovial mood about her demise he was slightly annoyed at the way her death had raised questions regarding his potential involvement complaining:

"She can't even die in an uncomplicated way, it has to be all crumbled up with problems."

Aileen Philby's funeral was arranged and held by the family. Kim failed to attend and the children were not informed of the location of their mother's grave site. It was a rather quiet end to a tormented existence.

Several months passed before Philby was in a position to begin his next marriage since Eleanor (nee Kearns) finally obtained her divorce from Sam Brewer. Immediately upon her new found freedom she sent a telegram to Kim who promptly replied back:

"Clever wonderful you fly back happily song in heart life is miraculous greatest love Kim."

A few hours later that same morning Kim set off to the St Georges to find Brewer. Once he did locate him he declared in typical arrogant fashion:

"I've come to tell you that I've had a cable from Eleanor. She has got her divorce and I want you to be the first person to know

that I'm going to marry her."

Brewer's response was typical of his type. Politicising the situation while removing the emotional element:

"That sounds like the best possible solution. What do you make of the situation in Iraq?"

Just over a year after Aileen died, Kim Philby married Eleanor Kearns in London at Holban registry office on the 24 January 1959. Nicholas Elliott travelled from his station in Vienna to attend the ceremony along with other MI6 colleagues, it was like a reunion of all his old friends once more. Elliott took his friend's new wife to heart even though he never forgot about his previous one as the newlyweds spent their honeymoon in Rome. Philby declared that he will both paint and write in a house they would take in the mountains for this was to be a long-awaited time of peace and stability in his life.

Upon their return to Beirut that 'house in the mountains' was in reality a fifth floor apartment in the city itself on the Rue Kantari.

Like his friends, Eleanor had no idea of the man she had now devoted her life to. He was still spying for the Soviet Union and his marriage had changed nothing. Yuri Modin was still monitoring the progress of agent 'Stanley' and noted that even though he was not privy to high level intelligence, he was still sending via Petukhov excellent quality information to Moscow even though the KGB had plenty of trained Arabic agents of their own. Philby's intelligence was still making waves in the highest echelons in the Lubyanka even though his reports were more poetic than hard facts.

Despite this the Soviets were satisfied with Philby in this time of happiness a period of unflinching journalism, quiet espionage and hard socialising. The apartment in the Rue Kantari was large enough to accommodate the five children when they came to stay from their boarding school, for they adored their loving and attentive father. At other times the place was a venue for social gatherings and the region was ripe for outdoor picnics, despite the fact that at this time Lebanon was embroiled in a civil war. The little bubble in the Arabic turmoil was filled by the abundance of alcohol for which Philby was now drinking quite heavily. Daily routines included visits to the Normandie and the St Georges to associate with fellow journalists. He often appeared then disappeared which did not alarm his new wife for Kim attitude to the profession was more relaxed than that of Sam Brewer. He even vaguely hinted to her that he was connected to the British intelligence services.

The weekly articles he submitted to both newspapers were written in a rapid fashion. It was almost as if he was taking his responsibilities too lightly much to the irk of other writers who considered him lazy in his approach to the profession.

But his intelligence gathering activities were not much greater than his journalist ones. Often he courted the company of businessmen, bankers, consultants and university academics, all not known for their knowledge of Arab politics but more useful for siphoning any useful piece of information. Anything of value was forwarded onto MI6 station chief Paulson while simultaneously being passed onto Petukhov of the KGB as well as anything else that may be helpful. Philby was living not just a double existence but a treble existence; his KGB spying was covered by his MI6 spying and his MI6 work was covered by his journalist work. None except for the KGB was aware of each other and the role each was playing in his life in Beirut.

However this triple duplicity had a price. The quality of the information was beginning to wane. It was a classic intelligence trick, dressing up what was already news to make it look like confidential secrets. Soviet intelligence could tell the difference, their Arabic agents could see past the bluster of Philby's reports and decipher that a lot of it was made up as could his paymasters in MI6. They could tell that everything he was submitting could be read in the newspapers, there was hardly anything solid that could be used since a great deal of the information was either false or inaccurate. Philby was actually letting his intelligence work slide in favour of the bottle. His drinking habits had always played a prominent part in his life, but now it was beginning to interfere with his work in a counterproductive way. He was settling for the soft option, a little journalism now and again, a little spying here and there. This man, once muted as the future head of MI6 was rapidly sliding into becoming a second rate reporter and a third rate spy for both the Soviets and MI6.

But then his life was about to get a shake-up. Godfrey Paulson was replaced as station chief in Beirut. His replacement was none other than a man from Vienna called Nicholas Elliott.

James Angleton. Philby's friend
and supporter in Washington.

Nicholas Elliott. Philby's best friend and supporter.
Defended him against all accusations until
he learnt the awful truth. Confronted Philby in 1963.

Dick White. The man who hunted
Philby for over ten years.

Kim Philby. Official portrait taken in
the Soviet Union in later years.

CHAPTER FIFTEEN

HELLO MR ELLIOTT

Elliott had spent only but a brief time in Vienna. The Buster Crabb controversy had not harmed his career and now he found himself here in the Middle East, an important promotion in this vital area of world affairs. He had not been here since 1942 and eagerly reminisced about dining in the Hotel Lucullus the place where his secretary who was now his wife, had been courted by him then. Immediately he wanted to dine at the same restaurant which they did. Finding a table, they were seated and were ready to begin browsing the menus when Kim Philby happened to be there approached his old friend, giving him a generous hug. In truth the meeting was likely staged since he was the only person he wanted to see first before he took up his official role.

Eleanor joined in the party as bottles of wine were consumed to wash down the feast of bouillabaisse. It was a blowout of upper class proportions as Elliott desperately wanted to catch up on the events in his best friend's life:

"Fill me in old boy." He said. The two old chums were reunited once again. Philby's life was turning ever happier.

The Immeuble Tabet on the Rue Verdun was where the Elliott's set up home, a top floor apartment there on the border between the Muslim and Christian quarters in the city. It was within the earshot of the muezzin's call to evening prayer reminiscent of the mosques of Istanbul. Elliott was as happy as he was when he was in Turkey during the war, in a city where the local customs and espionage were blurred into the sounds and smell of the exotic. The battleground of the Middle East in fighting communist expansionism alongside his most trusted best friend was both enticing and intoxicating in the service of western interests.

Elliott had been rather naïve in eastern politics and needed Kim to educate him in the ways of the Arab world. Coming from a European point of view, he knew relatively little regarding regional affairs, something which Philby's wife Eleanor noticed about their recently arrived friend. The complexities of Lebanese politics would be daunting to say the least. He needed Kim Philby to guide him through it all.

Kim was not the only hack to notice the arrival of the new station chief in the city. The other journalists did too, describing him in a typical tabloid stereotype; a thin man with round glasses. An expression of humour in his glances and the dress sense which gave away his class was described by the journalists as one who came from a smart college but with a touch of ruthlessness. Despite looking like an upper class academic his networking proved popular with the other nationalities especially the Americans who liked his particular penchant for telling slightly indecent stories and their air of authoritarianism that he brought, especially through the image of his wife by his side. It gave one the impression that the intelligence division in the region was being professional, and overseen by a true gentleman.

Elliott's presence had a jolting effect upon Philby. Elliott wasted no time setting Kim to work, sending him on trips, making him write reports which were then scrutinised in conversation. His previous lax attitude to spying suddenly burst into life with fervent activity and the quality of his information gathering jumped considerably.

Philby now travelled widely, covering vast distances in the neighbouring countries, Yemen, Kuwait, Iraq and Jordan were all visited on his espionage trips. Gathering evidence under the guise of a reporter, his destinations were not matching his articles. It appeared that he was travelling to more places than he was writing about. Just six articles were received from Kim Philby by the Observer between January and September 1960, far less than that indicated by his travels. The Economist also noticed the decline in his output, prompting an editor to go out and visit him to investigate why. Kim was asked if he was struggling to serve two masters, a statement that scared him somewhat: how on earth did he know about his espionage. Things calmed down when the editor pointed out that he was referring to his journalism.

The relationship between Elliott and Philby produced a vast wealth of information based upon political development in the Arab countries usually divulged twice weekly in intimate debriefing sessions. The two families would meet up and both Nicholas and Kim would disappear into the next room to discuss the information while their wives chatted. As a reward for the industrial volume that he was providing for MI6 Elliott rewarded his good friend with a generous bonus, a fist full of money which Philby happily returned home with:

"Oh boy, this is going to make our Christmas!" He told his wife as he scattered the notes around the home.

Elliott had no real idea that his friend was still involved with Soviet intelligence. He had no knowledge of Philby's association with Petukhov and accepted him as a productive MI6 agent in the Middle East. Dick White back in London the man who previously chased Philby during the Burgess Maclean investigation also now considered the matter closed. Elliott trusted with complete confidence the actions of his best friend of twenty years.

Philby relished the intelligence life. He seemed rather buoyant in the confidence displayed in him by all his old colleagues. Even his wife noticed the changes, sensing that he was getting rather restless with writing articles for newspapers for it was just not the same as obtaining and sharing secrets with a privileged few. Some of these 'few' Elliott thought was those in MI6, but Philby included the Soviets in his work, passing onto them continuously everything he could find out and anything he could get out of his old friend. The weekly meetings after sunset with Petukhov continued all along the line and unbeknown to Elliott, he was, through Philby, feeding information directly into Moscow's hands.

This increased Kim's status as a Soviet agent since he was able to access confidential information from Nicholas including sensitive material such as the names of sympathetic politicians and MI6 contacts throughout the Arab region. It meant that Philby knew the details of intelligence London really wanted and was able to pass it onto the KGB in secret. His abuse of Elliott in this way only served to increase his own selfish status within Soviet ranks.

But away from the inside-out world of espionage, the two friends, such as Kim saw it, was one of smoke and mirrors. They spied together as intensely as they socialised together and the bond of friendship, two decades old, only got stronger in the humidity of Beirut. Both women, Eleanor and Elizabeth forged their own closeness every bit as strong as their husband's. Weekend rituals were spent at the 'Acapulco', a small cabin on Khalde Beach. Guests included a mutual friend in the region, a war veteran, a one-eyed heavy pipe smoker called Colonel Alec Brodie, the military attaché at the British embassy in the city.

The children played together often with Elliott's teenagers being rather fond of their father's friend, the ever drunken, ever charming Philby. Swimming and walking were common activities during the day in this little idyll amongst the rise in political tensions. The evenings were marked by fancy cocktail parties where the drink was as plentiful as it always was. Nicolas and Elizabeth Elliott played host regularly, something they had done in years gone by in Switzerland. A tidal wave of visitors streamed to the couple's soiree's including the now famous writer Ian Fleming who came to stay in 1960 while on the way to Kuwait to write a story on the country for the state oil company there. Fleming, despite his fame still indulged a little espionage occasionally for his old employers in Naval Intelligence and asked Elliott if he could provide information on the naval defences on the Red Sea port of Basra on the Iraqi coast. Elliott struck a deal with Ian saying he would if he would bring back a box of white truffles which was rare, even so in the desert nation since they had encountered a rare spell of rain.

Philby and Elliott continued their partnership on the formal social circuit as the weeks turned into months. Meeting diplomats and officials in order to gather intelligence as well as the more relaxed social gatherings frequently included Kim becoming ever more intoxicated more of the time. Despite the frequency of the gatherings and the solidness of friendship, Philby's behaviour was starting to become more outrageous under the influence of the drink, quite often interjecting conversations with remarks that would cause silence. It was reminiscent of the antics of Guy Burgess even though Philby would only try to lighten the mood of a party and partly egged on by Elliott himself. But these antics were not always welcome as exhibited at one particularly disastrous dinner party.

Elliott and his wife held a cocktail in their Beirut apartment for forty people including their elderly parents who were there. The British ambassador Sir Moore Crossthwaite was also in attendance as was Kim and Eleanor Philby. At one point during the conversation Kim turned to the ambassador and quite pompously asked as question regarding a lady called Anne who was the wife of one of the embassy staff:

"Don't you think Anne has the finest breasts in Beirut?"

The remark offended Crossthwaite who thought such a subject was not a suitable topic of conversation. Anne herself was annoyed that she was being discussed in public in such a way as did her husband. What followed was more of a farce; the wife of another staff member called Jane was offended because she thought her own breasts were better than Anne's and Jane's husband became agitated because he thought his wife had just been insulted. Eleanor took offence at all this because she was not blessed with large breasts at all, meanwhile the co-host Elizabeth became upset because the whole party was beginning to get out of control.

Just like Guy Burgess had done at that disastrous dinner party in Washington back in 1951 with his offensive drawing of William Harvey's wife, Kim Philby thought the whole episode here totally hilarious. Elliott would use the incident as an anecdote for many years to come but at the same time he was beginning to feel a measure of concern about his friend's consumption of alcohol. He was not getting any younger and the intake would surely start to have an impact upon his health. Kim's mother Dora had dies back in 1957 just two years after that infamous press conference regarding the Lipton allegations. At the time she was consuming a bottle of gin per day and it seemed like Kim's boozing habits were starting to go the same way, even though he had no reservations about getting drunk in front of others.

When socialising and drinking, both men were busy cultivating intelligence relations, especially with the Americans which were more like a healing exercise than active collaboration. Relations between the United Kingdom and the United States were strained in the wake of the Burgess Maclean affair and the whole controversy surrounding Philby himself but by start of the 1960's things were starting to be patched up once more. There were still some who still harboured a measure of lingering suspicion against Philby; his two biggest doubters was William Harvey of the CIA and J. Edgar Hoover of the FBI.

Despite this it was generally accepted that Philby must be innocent given the backing of Harold Macmillan and the trustworthiness of MI6. The whole attitude was orchestrated by

James Angleton who had by now been promoted to head the counter-intelligence staff, making him the main spy catcher in the United States. He displayed an air of authority and fear in his department and was not the most trusting of people but remained in contact with his friend Philby on occasions. Kim used the correspondence to maintain the assurance of his innocence with the Americans; even now he was manipulating his other great champion across the Atlantic. The proof of this manifested itself in the fact that Kim mixed freely with the American spies in the region. If the CIA did suspect him and had placed him under surveillance, surely their operatives would avoid him, but they did not. His 'friendship' served only to cover his own back once more, allowing his Soviet spying to continue unhindered. Just like Nick Elliott, Kim Philby was abusing the trust and faithfulness James Angleton had displayed in him over the years.

There were many American operatives that he associated with. One notable figure was an officer sent by the CIA chief Allan Dulles independently from the official station in the city. His name was Wilbur Crane Eveland. He worked chiefly as a paymaster to bankroll CIA operations to overthrow the Syrian government which was Soviet backed, support the pro-western Lebanese administration and fund the Saud family in Arabia. Eveland and Philby had met each other through their mutual friend Sam Brewer, it was clear to the American that the Englishman had ties to the intelligence community. Philby would prove useful for disseminating information for the CIA during various conversations, something which Kim himself thought about Eveland. But Philby's motivations were less clear he knew the intelligence he could squeeze out of his new American friend would prove very useful to MI6 and more importantly, Petukhov and the KGB. Getting information out of his would be easy; just one single evening between the two and Philby, and the Soviets would know all about CIA operations in the region.

Another American he befriended and tried to exploit for intelligence purposes was Edgar J. Applewhite, the CIA station chief who had been in the country for the last two years. Applewhite initially received Philby in a lukewarm way, but later took to embracing him once their relationship blossomed. The reasoning for this stemmed from the fact that he was aware of the earlier suspicions surrounding the journalist. Philby's indomitable charm always struck through to worm his way into Applewhite's trust who naively concluded that Kim was too sophisticated to identify himself with Marxist-Communism. Both men came to develop a close friendship. The Anglophile Applewhite enjoyed talking about Arab issues with Philby and showed him a more welcoming attitude in the American intelligence community. They seemed friendlier toward him than the British security services.

It all played into Kim's hands. They saw him as principled, a good man and an ally in the Cold War. He got on well with all the Americans in Beirut and it was this trustworthiness encased in friendship that eased them to open up to Philby. It was not hard to get them to talk.

There was one of these talkers who divulged more than most and so provide extremely useful for Philby. His name was Miles Copeland Jr, a former CIA agent originally from Alabama and now a PR executive for the firm Copeland and Eichelberger but continued to dabble in espionage circles. Originally a gambler on the river boats in his formative years, he ended up attending Yale University to study mathematics. He joined the OSS in 1941 shortly after the Japanese assault on Pearl Harbour after a career jazz trumpeting with the Glenn Miller Orchestra and a radio band and was one of the officers sent to London along with James Angleton to learn espionage techniques from the British during the war. Sharing Angleton's world view he believed that the CIA had a duty to guide the course of Middle Eastern politics. He therefore became one of the most effective operatives in the organisation helping to turn Egypt's President Colonel Nasser away from the USSR and had a role in organising a coup against the elected Prime Minister of Iran in 1953.

By 1956 he was in Beirut and privy to all of Applewhite's intelligence cables and he openly flaunted his espionage links as part of his business pitch. Copeland was a prime target for Philby who had known him since 1944 as a former pupil. Nicholas Elliott was also a friend of Copeland and the three men and their families developed a bond of socialising and professionalism. Gatherings usually held at the Copeland mountain top household included the familiar mix of drinking and secret sharing, the husband's prerogative while the children indulged in Skiing or tennis together. Copland was an individual who never took himself too seriously and one of the most loose-lipped officials around. Elliott was captivated by him, so was Philby, but for a totally different reason. Like the others, Miles Copeland provided through Kim valuable intelligence that fell directly onto the eager eyes of Moscow.

However Miles Copeland was not a dummy mouthpiece. Unknown to both Englishmen, he was an active agent under the control of James Angleton back in Washington. The CIA chief of counter intelligence obviously had his own informant network in the region for which Copeland was a part of. Even allies spied on each other in the negative world of Cold War espionage. Copeland could have been instructed to place Kim Philby under surveillance, but despite being James Angleton's eyes and ears in this unique social circle, he did not. The simple reason being that like his boss in Washington, Copeland simply did not believe that Philby was a Soviet spy.

The whole story of Philby against the backdrop of the Cold War was one where black was really white and vice versa. The conspiracy theories were rife; MI6 were trying to trap him, orchestrated by his old hunter Dick White, James Angleton also suspected him and both Nicholas Elliott and Miles Copeland were sent to prove it through spying. But the real truth was that Kim Philby was in fact deceiving them all as the only real spy in this little network of associates. In this covert battle of ideology, allegiance and the procurement of information nobody even suspected him, because he was the one spying on them.

The sheer duplicity of Kim Philby occurred on a Wednesday evening every few weeks where he would stand upon his balcony holding a newspaper, the signal agreed with his handler Petukhov early in their relationship. A few hours later under the cover of darkness he would slip out of his Rue Kantari apartment and make his way to a small discreet back street restaurant called 'Vrej'. Totally under the radar and away from prying eyes, here the real Kim Philby emerged, the Philby nobody knew because this was where Petukhov was waiting to receive his latest information.

This was a time of professional and personal satisfaction for him. No longer under the clouds of suspicion from the British or the Americans he was free to conduct all aspects of his life. Here he was paid a regular salary by the Observer and the Economist, in the pay for his 'official' spying under MI6 and free to gather information on the rounds of the social circuit. His powerful friends stood by, trusted and indulged him. Sometimes Philby would play the perfect house-husband, demonstrating his talent for cooking or reciting German poetry to his wife. Everything at this time could not be as further away from the stressful events of the last few years when he was pressed by those wanting to prosecute him. Philby was at a time of peace, confidence and prosperity. Spying for MI6, spying for the Soviet Union and fooling everybody without hesitation.

The household was completed by the addition of an unusual pet, a baby fox cub christened 'Jackie' who would act more like a domestic dog than a wild animal. It slept on the sofa and was trained by Philby who reared it by hand and quite fittingly, like its master, it too developed a taste for alcohol by regularly lapping up spirits from a saucer. Eleanor noted the sense of satisfaction and tranquillity in her husband's life, noting that these were the happiest years.

But this was the high point. Beyond this the only way forward was down because Kim's life was about not just to go downhill, but fall off a sheer cliff. Everything was content for now, but it was about to fall apart, bringing everything out into the open.

After nearly thirty years, the mask Kim Philby wore so well was about to slip.

CHAPTER SIXTEEN

TRAITORS AND SUSPECTS

Events began their inexorable downturn in 1960. The start of the new decade, one that would signal powerful and elaborate revolutions, political, cultural and sexual began with a tragedy for Kim Philby. That summer his father St John Philby was in Moscow attending a conference on Oriental matters. Following this the ever irascible sixty-five year old then travelled back to Britain where he attended a cricket match in London where England were playing South Africa at Lord's, a match which the home side won convincingly. His plan was to travel back to Saudi Arabia but decided to stop and see his son in Beirut along the way. Upon arrival he checked himself into the Normandie Hotel where he was greeted with the same privilege as that due to a respected Arab diplomat. Nicholas Elliott heard that Kim father was in town and out of respect arranged a launch in his honour. He knew full well the elder Philby's capacity for causing offence and embarrassment in his old ways but was used to it nonetheless. In fact he and his wife was one of few people who were prepared to tolerate the cantankerous nature of the revered diplomat. Surprisingly the whole occasion passed in a rather diplomatic and cordial manner which was attended naturally by Kim and his wife as well as the Copelands and the British ambassador to Iraq. Lebanese wine accompanied the meal and lubricated the event.

Late that afternoon, at around teatime the St John Philby was sleeping the food and wine off but later that evening was wide awake and socialising in a local bar. There he displayed with typical colonial outrageousness, an attempt to make a pass at the wife of another embassy staff member. Suddenly and almost fatally he suffered a heart attack. He was taken to bed with his son keeping a vigil by his side where the old man uttered the innocuous phrase:

"God I'm bored."

They were the last words St John Philby ever said, dying shortly afterward in his bed with his son by his side on the 30 September 1960 and leaving behind a volume of works on the Arab world, as scholarly as they were impassioned. He was buried under his adopted Muslim name of Sheikh Abdullah with full Islamic rites in the Basta district of Beirut. Kim took his father's death quite badly, often disappearing for long periods or consoling himself with the bottle, drinking himself into alcoholic annihilation. His habits began to change him for the worse his mind and his body suffered. The past between the two men had been chequered; in his youth Kim had both admired and feared his father and was the first person he ever spied upon after pledging himself to the Soviet cause. He once reported to Moscow that his father was 'not well in the head' but the truth was that Kim Philby was a chip of the old block of his father, albeit a rather wayward one. It has been suspected that St John the well-known Arabist sabotaged British plans for the creation of a Jewish state and used his influence to help secure oil concessions for the Americans in Saudi Arabia. He was abrasive, intelligent and an old fashioned argumentative thug but he never betrayed his country like Kim. He died without ever knowing who his son really was.

One aspect of Philby life had fallen away. The next would have a profound effect upon him that strangely had nothing at all to do with him directly. Prior to St John's death an agent arrived in

Beirut, a Dutch born thirty-eight year old by the name of George Behar, a former resistance fighter in Nazi occupied Holland during the war. He was captured but managed to escape to London in disguise whereupon he subsequently joined MI6. There he was trained to interrogate prisoners in different languages and he changed his surname from George Behar to George Blake. After the war he was posted to North Korea but was captured by the communists thereafter only emerging after three years where he was welcomed back with open arms and posted to East Germany as a case officer in Berlin. Here he was tasked with turning Soviet intelligence officers to by double agents under Peter Lunn, Nicholas Elliott's old friend. Blake had an Egyptian background on his mother's side and was considered ideal for a posting to the Middle East in 1960. Upon his arrival Blake attended the Middle Eastern Centre for Arabic Studies just outside the city for an eighteen month language course, which was seen more like a spy school since diplomats, intelligence officers and businessmen attended there.

Nicholas Elliott saw him as a credit to the service but what he did not know until a telegram arrived from London informing him, was that he was in fact a Soviet spy. He had been turned during his incarceration in a North Korean prison and the authorities wanted to fool him into returning to Britain where he would be arrested and interrogated. His conversion to communism was triggered by the bombing of small villages by large American bombers during the Korean War but for this they wanted to try him for treason. Never fully accepted by MI6, his resentment was further compounded by the fact that although already married, he fell in love with his secretary but was prevented from marrying her because of the class system. Therefore upon his assignment in Berlin he immediately began passing confidential information onto the Soviets including covert plans and surveillance operations. Unscrupulously copying out Peter Lunn's index cards, he passed to the Russians every MI6 agent within Germany, some four hundred people were caught and likely sent to their deaths all thanks to Blake's deception on a scale close to that of Kim Philby. Now the dashing, handsome young man had arrived in Beirut where upon his arrival he had contacted his KGB handler Pavel Yefimovich Nedosekin who provided him with a telephone number to use in an emergency. However this would not be enough; the way the authorities discovered him was a classic piece of counter-espionage.

In the early months of 1961 a defector called Michael Goleniewski, a Lieutenant-Colonel in the Polish Intelligence Service arrived in Berlin. For years he was leaking Polish secrets to the Soviets but then in 1959 he turned and started passing on Polish and Soviet secrets to the CIA. The Americans subsequently forwarded intelligence onto MI6 which included proof of an agent codenamed 'Lambda' within British Intelligence. Goleniewski provided evidence of this by showing documents that the spy leaked to Moscow giving MI6 the chance to work out only ten individuals could be in the frame. One of those was George Blake. MI6 was sure that 'Lambda' was George Blake by the spring and planned to lure him to London under the ruse of discussing another posting for him whereupon they would immediately arrest him for interrogation. Dick White sent a telegram to Nicholas Elliott informing him of the plan and crucially he in turn kept secret about it, telling nobody not even Kim Philby. If Philby had been told even in a casual way, then work would have got back to Blake and events would have been very different. Instead there was nothing Kim could do. He did not know Blake but nonetheless both were ideological allies.

On Saturday 25 March Elliott's secretary called Blake family and told then she had a spare ticket for a theatre production of the play Charley's Aunt. George's wife Gillian Blake was busy babysitting for their sick child and the secretary wondered if he would like to accompany her instead. Blake agreed and went along where during the half time interval they retried to the bar only to meet up with Elliott and his wife there. The trap was now set, Nicholas pulled him to one side and mentioned that his appearance saved him a trip to see him at his home. He had received a note from headquarters asking Blake if he would like to go to London for a few days to discuss a new appointment. It recommended that he travel on the Easter Monday so that he be ready for the consultation on the Tuesday, the perfect cover as to not arouse suspicion; a request by letter not an order by urgent telegram.

But Blake was suspicious at this for he was in the middle of his language course and would by returning to London that July so what was the rush? Concerned he telephoned Nedosekin to arrange a meeting that evening on a nearby beach. The KGB handler told George that he would consult Moscow on the proposal and the next day he contacted Blake to tell him that they saw no cause for concern at the offer. The KGB had failed to detect Goleniewski's information and fatally told Blake that he was free to go to London as required.

Before he left Elliott asked him if he would like to be booked into St Ermin's hotel next to MI6 headquarters. Blake declined saying he was staying with his mother in Radlett just to the north of London.

Blake arrived in London on the Monday where he was immediately taken to Carlton Gardens, and the MI6 safe house there. Dick White was determined to catch this traitor and not let him slip like who he still believed to be guilty, Kim Philby. As standard practice he was ushered into an upstairs room that was bugged where the three interrogating officers began asking questions about his time in Berlin. Blake was not ready for this but he now began to realise with flinching certainty that he was now in serious trouble. Over the course of the next few days the three MI6 officers first challenged his explanations then showed him evidence of his espionage. Blake's defence began to waver as it now dawned on him that they must know that he is guilty of spying. By the third day the breakthrough came; MI6 said they knew he was a spy and that he must have been tortured by the North Koreans to get him to confess before being blackmailed into working for the communists. It was a clever tactic to gain a confession and unlike Philby, in the case of Blake it worked:

"No, nobody tortured me! No, nobody blackmailed me! I myself approached the Soviets and offered my services to them of my own accord."

By playing on his own ego and pride, MI6 finally had their confession that George Blake. Previously Behar was a KGB spy. He was charged under the Official Secrets Act and remanded in prison awaiting trial. MI6 urgently flashed a telegram to all its stations and embassies around the world in two parts; the first stating: 'The following name is a traitor.' The second part which was encrypted would read: 'GEORGE BLAKE.'

When news of the Blake scandal broke it alarmed many people both within and outside the intelligence community. When Kim Philby heard of the news in Beirut he was genuinely alarmed. How could he have been caught? Was there an MI6 mole inside the KGB? If there was, then if Blake could have been exposed, there was every chance he could be next. It must have seemed to Kim that he was living on borrowed time.

A few weeks later George Blake stood trial at the Central Criminal Court the Old Baily in central London. He stood to serve a maximum of fourteen years for his crime but the prosecutors brought separate cases against him, five in all for each of the different time periods he was spying. An expected guilty verdict was delivered at the end and the judge did not hold back in his leniency, fourteen years as expected for each of the five charges with three of these terms to run consecutively. The final verdict was that George Blake was sentenced to a total of forty-two years in prison, a sensation that made headlines around the world.

When Kim Philby heard of the sentence handed down to Blake he was notably shaken. He had been spying for longer and at a higher level and that made him a more damaging spy than Blake ever was. For the first time in his life the glamour of espionage had gone and he knew that if he was ever caught and convicted he could expect a life sentence or worse the death penalty by hanging. It suddenly dawned upon him just how much trouble he was really in.

Richard Beeston went to see Kim about the whole Blake affair in the wake of his conviction at his apartment to find both him and his residence a complete mess. The whole residence was strewn with empty bottles and glasses where Kim was nursing a large hangover and still drunkenly incoherent. Looking notably ragged and deteriorated he mumbled that he had never even heard of George Blake until news of his arrest was made public. The strain showed during a dinner party when Kim's drinking began to get out of control, arguing publically with Eleanor. The whole evening ended with both drunkenly hurling ornaments at each other. As time went on Philby deteriorated into alcoholism, usually spending dinner parties and social gatherings to drink himself senseless often ending up slumped at the table or on the sofa. He had always drunk copious amounts throughout his life and had never let it interfere with his spying, rather using it as a way to build ties and strengthen his position. But now it was starting to overtake his life, brought on by the stress and fear of expected exposure.

Now for the first time his meticulous standards, rigorously self-imposed, began to slide. Consistency was the path to detection in the spying game but a friend remarked to him that he noticed Kim's Wednesday night trips, teasing him by saying:

"I know all about your Wednesday nights."

The remark frightened Philby. So much so that a few nights later at another Beirut drinking establishment called Joe's Bar Richard Beeston's wife Moyra decided to ask Kim in a joking manner if he really was the 'Third Man'. Grabbing her wrist in a forceful manner he replied rather cryptically:

"You know Moyra, I always believe that loyalty to your friends is more important than anything else."

Such a back-handed statement from someone who had betrayed all his friends in the past in favour of an overriding ideology he had pledged his allegiance to in his youth. Yet this was not strictly a lie, Philby did value friendship, but did not respect it in the face of political choices. He was always prepared to betray for what deemed a noble cause.

The sensation and fright the Blake affair which was the worst since the Burgess Maclean scandal brought was just the latest part to fall away from Kim Philby's life to become unstuck. His fears about a mole in the KGB were not totally unfounded as the old danger of a defector began to rear its head again. This time another would escape to the west in 1961 with damming evidence that would renew the investigation into Philby and finally break the remains of the Cambridge Spy Ring. His name was Anatoliy Golitsyn.

Golitsyn was a high ranking official in the First Chief Directorate of the KGB with the rank of major. In December 1961 he arrived at the door of the United States embassy in Helsinki asking for asylum in exchange for high level information. The secrets he was willing to share would be like striking gold to the west. The defector was prepared to reveal scores of KGB agents operating within both the United States and the United Kingdom and was subsequently spirited away to America for a debriefing. The Soviets were shocked at the defection and was prepared for the leaking of sensitive secrets by placing no less than fifty KGB stations around the world on alert. They were instructed to relay any information back to Moscow Centre on what they knew about the traitor, meetings suspended, appointments cancelled it was as if an earthquake had hit the organisation. The KGB found itself in a position where it was prepared to authorise the assassination of Golitsyn at the earliest opportunity.

Meanwhile he told the CIA all about the work of a Soviet mole that had operated up until 1949, the description sounding a little like Kim Philby. After obtaining secret information themselves the Americans referred Golitsyn onto MI6 to reveal what he knew about British operations. Under interview with SIS he confirmed the existence of an espionage ring operating within British Intelligence, a network of five members all of whom knew one another. Golitsyn went further to disclose that this spy ring, known in the USSR as the 'Ring of Five' were all members at the same university and had been recruited by the Soviet Union since the 1930's. He confirmed two members were already in Russia; the first man was Donald Maclean along with the second man Guy Burgess. The description of the third man strongly resembled Kim Philby while the fourth man was confirmed to be an art historian who had conducted spying for the USSR in the past and called Anthony Blunt. MI5 had suspected Blunt for some time but the indication that Philby was involved in the network put a spark back into the cold investigation into his involvement as being the 'Third Man'. Dick White always suspected Philby as being involved in the affair and here was new evidence from a fresh defector at a high enough level to at least put some life back into the investigation. The defector had already told the Americans about the members of the network, now he also indicated the presence of a fifth man in the spy ring (John Carincross) but his identity at the moment was unknown.

Golitsyn's accounts were viewed with suspicion by certain members in the intelligence community and actually divided opinion on the quality of his information. However there were some individuals who were convinced of the revelations, partly because they were so startling. The first was James Angleton who upon hearing the intelligence regarding his friend and revered colleague could not believe what was hearing. He knew Kim, he knew him so well so how could it be that the man who had taught him the business of catching spies was really a Soviet one himself? How could Kim have fooled him and others for all these years? The news changed him for the worst. The realisation that for over twenty years had had been duped by one of his most intimate friends induced and in many respects exacerbated paranoia inside him. He began to think, quite irrationally, that the CIA must be infested with Soviet moles, concluding that Philby was orchestrating some kind of great subversive plan within the organisation. It was a task that would unhealthily consume him and the entire US security services for at least the next decade, frantically searching though old files muttering:

"This is Kim's work."

Apart from the fanatical and simmering mistrust and betrayal that had poisoned Angleton's mind the other person to be convinced of Philby's complicity was MI5's senior counter-intelligence officer Peter Wright. Like so many others in his class, Philby came from the same mould as him, who had been born in 1916. He had followed his father's footsteps into the intelligence field since he had been involved in signals in the First World War. Wright was hired into MI5 as a scientific officer in 1954 with a mandate to modernise code-breaking and eavesdropping techniques but by 1962 had launched an internal investigation in the wake of Golitsyn's intelligence. He poured through the files, checking, double checking and then re-checking every detail, every profile, even that of the Director General of MI5 Roger Hollis and his deputy Graham Mitchell. It was clear there had been leaks and it was clear there had been a spy. But the identity of the traitor had to be confirmed even though Wright at one point incorrectly wondered if Hollis himself may be a KGB agent.

He based his assumption on the analysis of the differences between Hollis and Mitchell noting that the deputy was more secretive than his boss tinged with shyness that made him avoid eye contact with others. For some time he even suspected Mitchell as the source of the leaks. Each evening Wright placed his files on the investigation into a safe using an old intelligence trick, on top of two pencil marks so he could tell if they had ever been moved during the night. Only two men within the organisation knew of the safe's combination, Graham Mitchell and Roger Hollis and one day Wright returned to find the documents had indeed been moved from their original position. By now paranoia was beginning to grip the departments, who was the fifth man in the network? Mitchell's office was watched with a camera placed discreetly behind a two-way mirror so Wright could scrutinise his every movement. There was nothing untoward in his behaviour. Next he moved to actively searching through his wastepaper basket, desperately looking for clues, torn paper was painstakingly reconstituted to see if there was anything incriminating but again nothing.

Wright now turned his attention to Hollis. The bases of his suspicion rested upon his boss' refusal to allow any kind of penetration of the organisation, why was this? Wright set about finding out, travelling to his former university at Oxford to scour his old undergraduate records only to discover that Hollis left after only five terms and never actually received his degree. It only fuelled Wright's suspicion, why was this? Where did he go? Increasingly he became convinced of Hollis's treachery.

The seeds of mistrust and suspicion between friends and colleagues were the product of the fallout from the Golitsyn defection and indicative of the havoc Philby and the other Cambridge spies were causing in the intelligence services. In the

United States, Jim Angleton was single-handedly driving the paranoia in the CIA. In the United Kingdom the mistrust and infighting between the services was being orchestrated the conspiracy theories of Peter Wright. He was also asked at some point about Kim Philby and replied somewhat sketchily that he knew his people. This was typical of the influence Kim had on individuals, everybody thought they knew him, knew his class, his type. The negative-positive attitude projected by Philby across the services created divisions and suspicion with actually tarred people with the wrong brush, labelling loyal officers as traitors. It is believed Wright's conspiracy theories particularly that aimed at Hollis were rather ludicrous and had no real chance at exposing any sort of spy operating within the security services.

Whatever the truth or misinformation appeared to be stoking the fire of suspicion and division between the British and American security services, the authorities needed something else to pin on the Cambridge spies and in particular to Kim Philby.

In Beirut the tension was beginning to get to him personally. He started suffering bouts of severe depression flooded by heavy bouts of drinking, something which his wife Eleanor could not help but notice her husband's spiralling downfall. Given the crisis surrounding the Golitsyn defection Yuri Modin who had left Britain in 1958 travelled to the Middle East in August 1962 to warn Philby about the secrets that was being spilled but the Philby's were at this moment on a sight-seeing trip to neighbouring Jordan, something which Kim returned back to Beirut early, possibly to meet up with Modin who warned Philby not to return to Britain for the danger of arrest. Modin advised him that he should prepare to escape. By now it was clear to see to the veteran KGB handler that their prized agent 'Stanley' was by now nothing but a shell of his former self. Knowing nothing of this, Eleanor returned home at the end of the trip a few days later to find Kim, who was by now extremely drunk and gripped by pure fear over the revelations sitting in the dark. Tears were rolling down his face as he sat upon the balcony:

"Jackie's dead." He slurred, pointing out that their pet fox had fallen from the terrace.

Perhaps Philby knew now he was in the endgame. He must have known now that it would only be a matter of time before a definite link between him and the Soviets would be found. His greatest fear, exposure from a defector it appeared, was coming true. But he was wrong; that final piece of information, crucial evidence would not come from a defector but from an old acquaintance who had a grudge against him. Here was the final and damming blow to Philby's secret life and along with Golitsyn's account, would finally expose him for what he was.

CHAPTER SEVENTEEN

TEA IN BEIRUT

Flora Solomon, the retail executive who had known Philby for many years and had introduced him to his second wife, her friend Aileen Furse. Deeply resentful of Philby at the way he treated her during their tempestuous marriage and the circumstances of her death she was now further offended by his newspaper articles. Despite his spying he was still writing pieces even though his output had fallen to just a trickle. These articles, given his travels across the Middle East took on a distinctly Arab flavour almost to a point where it could be considered bias and even degrading toward Jewish interests. This was certainly what Solomon thought since she had fallen in love with Israel and embraced Zionism; time and again she found herself being repeatedly offended at the pro-Arab, anti-Jewish or anti-Israel stance exhibited in Philby's journalism.

Flora's approach was typical of Cold War attitudes. Israel was backed by the United States whereas the Soviet Union was typically more pro-Arab and according to Flora all Kim Philby was doing was producing propaganda for Moscow. By late August 1962 she was in Israel attending a conference in Rehovot at the Chaim Weizmann Institute, a science research centre endorsed by the chairman of Marks & Spencer Baron Sieff, and Flora's boss. During a reception for the guests she approached the former intelligence officer Victor Rothschild an old friend of hers for almost thirty years. Rothschild, a George Medal recipient headed the sabotage and explosives section of MI5 during the war. He was an associate of Guy Burgess and Anthony Blunt as well as the Israeli security service, Mossad and was a regular face at the parties held by fellow officer Tomas Harris. During their conversation the subject inevitably turned toward Kim Philby whom was a mutual acquaintance:

"How is it that the Observer uses a man like Kim? Don't they know he's a communist?"

The comment surprised Rothschild since he knew Kim as well as Flora did. Surely he was not one of them. But Flora went on to describe an incident which she had never forgotten; back in the 1930's around the time when he was a Times journalist covering Spain when Kim approached her under the pretext that he was doing a very important job for peace. She revealed that he actively tried to recruit her into being a communist spy. By now she definitely had the full attention of her friend. Rothschild listened intently as she revealed all; he had followed the Philby controversy as it unfolded and was aware of the vast amount of evidence, none of which was directly linked to Kim himself but more circumstantial. Now here was a fresh allegation directly linking Philby to the Soviets as Flora continued to say that she had further suspected their other old friend Tomas Harris to be a KGB spy as well:

"Those two were so close as to give me an intuitive feeling that Harris was more than a friend."

Her resentment of Kim regarding his politically damaging views in his newspaper articles coupled with the fact that she had never forgotten his treatment of Aileen was the primary motivation for publically exposing Philby as a Soviet spy:

"You must do something." She implored,

"I will think about it." Rothschild replied.

He certainly did do something about it. Upon his return to London he reported the whole conversation to MI5. As expected the officers there were jubilant that at last something could be pinned upon the man they had always suspected of spying. At last this was the major breakthrough they had been waiting for, and their allegations would be vindicated.

Rothschild used his connections to arrange for Flora Solomon to be interviewed in his London apartment by an MI5 agent called Arthur Martin, and efficient officer who had followed the Philby case like no other. Also involved was Peter Wright, already knowledgeable regarding the Golitsyn defection. Wright made sure the whole interview was taped for evidence and was monitoring it back at Leconfield House.

It was clear this woman held a grudge but nonetheless proceeded to tell Martin her version of events. She said that she had already known Kim since before the war and had initially been rather fond of him and his charming nature. This was around the time he was out in Spain together during the civil war in the country at the time when he was working for The Times covering events there from the Nationalist side. She confessed to MI5 the incident in question; during one of his trips back to London they had met up and he took her out to lunch. During the meal he made his move, telling her that he was doing a very dangerous job for peace and that he needs help in this task. Recalling it in amazing detail, Flora said that he asked if she would help him in the task. She then said that Philby confessed to her that he was working for the Russians as part of the wider Comintern and it would be a great thing if she would agree to join the cause. Flora insisted that she refused Kim's offer but extended a hand of friendship to him if he was ever desperate.

This indirect confession that MI5 had gotten from Philby through Solomon was almost as good as a personal one, but the details were passed over by Martin. He failed to quiz her on some of them and now she was starting to get a little scared, fearing that if she openly testified against Philby in court she could become the target for a KGB assassination. The justification for this came from the fact that Tomas Harris whom she suspected as a fellow Soviet agent was mysteriously killed in a motor accident while on the island of Majorca. The circumstances were suspicious; he had been driving his new car, a Citroen along a stretch of road he knew well with his wife as a passenger when suddenly the vehicle veered off to the side, hitting a tree and killing him in the process. No speeding or drink-driving was involved and the police could find nothing mechanically wrong with the car. It was suspected that the 'accident' was really the work of the KGB who wanted him silenced before he could talk to the authorities.

Because of this she became increasingly anxious about her own safety and the repercussion of her actions:

"I will never give public evidence. There is too much risk. You see what has happened to Tomas since I spoke to Victor. It will leak, I know it will leak, and then what will my family do?"

The evidence Flora Solomon provided as well as the intelligence from Anatoliy Golitsyn proved that Kim Philby was indeed a Soviet KGB agent. He had been spying for almost thirty years, had leaked high level information to Moscow, had deceived all those around him and had repeatedly lied under interrogation. When Dick White heard of the revelation he queried:

"Why didn't she tell us ten years ago?"

Knowing such a question would undoubtedly arise, Solomon replied with a ready-made answer:

"I had not volunteered information as every public statement had pointed to his innocence."

That information was in fact crucial. Buster Milmo had failed to extract it during his cross examination and Philby's supporters thought it did not exist. But now things were finally out in the open. No longer protected by the Old Boy network within MI6, the officers of MI5 was now ready to corner Philby and bring the traitor to long overdue justice.

By now the debate began on how to do just that. Philby himself once approached would continue to deny everything just like he had done before and without a confession a conviction could not be secured. Solomon simply did not want to reveal her evidence in open court for fear of her life and it simply would not be enough in a legal framework, even with the corroborative evidence brought by the Golitsyn defection to secure a guilty verdict. In any case a public trial would be deeply embarrassing not only for the security services who was still paying Kim a salary, but also for the government as well. Harold Macmillan had publically cleared Philby of spying so a revelation like this would be incredibly damaging politically and personally. This could finish his career or bring the government down altogether.

The possibility of using the old entrapment trick of luring Philby back to Britain through a summons, in this case by his newspaper editors was doubted. Kim was too cunning to fall for that and he had seen the way George Blake had fallen for the same trick. He was not expected to bite at that bait at all. Other possibilities were entertained; abduction from Beirut and even contract assassination was considered but such actions might provoke a reaction from Moscow in response to the murder or kidnap being taken against one of their spies. Given the tensions of the Cold War neither of these approaches was advised.

Dick White informed Harold Macmillan of the revelations surrounding Philby saying:

"We need to know what damage he caused." He commented, *"A full damage report with all the details of how the Russians had operated and who else was working with Philby is of great importance."* Both agreed that even though their man was a criminal he was still a gentleman and should be treated as such.

White subsequently devised a plan to catch Philby in a way that would cause the least amount of embarrassment and diplomatic tension for everyone involved. Kim was to be confronted with the irrefutable evidence in Beirut and Arthur Martin was the man chosen to do it. Once the proof of his treachery was laid out before him, Philby was to be offered a way out; immunity from prosecution. The conditions were that he had to cooperate fully with the authorities and offer a full confession in the process.

The Under-Secretary at the Foreign Office and the Attorney-General approved of the plan as did Harold Macmillan but he insisted it had to be kept quiet, instructing his MI6 chief to

"Keep a lid on things."

The whole operation was to be conducted in absolute secrecy. Nothing was to be officially documented even though MI5 created for Arthur Martin a brief full of the evidence so he could prepare for the coming showdown. The evidence was studied over and over again, Martin was determined to break down Kim Philby this time and expose him for good. The way was almost clear for the authorities to snare the trap. Now they just had to convince Nicholas Elliott, one of his best friends and staunchest supporter.

By October 1962 Elliott had been promoted to head MI6 African operations, a considerable step up the career ladder. The role was based in London so he left Beirut as head of station there to take up his new post. He had been in London just a few days when he was summoned to the office of 'C', Sir Dick White. Once there the Director General informed the new head of Africa about the recent events concerning Kim. Elliott was told that new and incontrovertible evidence had come to light regarding Philby. Accounts from his old friend Flora Solomon about how he tried to recruit her into the cause nearly three decades ago proved beyond all doubt that he was undeniably a Soviet spy. White laid bare the awful truth to a stunned Elliott. Philby had been cheating and lying to everyone, MI5, his colleagues in MI6, the Americans in both the FBI and the CIA. James Angleton, his family, his friends the ones who stood by and believed in him. Everyone had fallen for the duplicitous charm of Kim Philby, and worst of all he had been lying to Elliott himself. All those years of friendship, comradeship, respect and admiration; all lies and built on utter fabrication. All those secrets he shared with the man he thought were his confident and trusted friend, all the lies he was told back.

It hit him like a bombshell.

Elliott started to wonder just how many people from the information Philby obtained were actually condemned to death. The hundreds of agents sent into Albania along with their families, the defectors who would have proved so valuable to the west such as Walter Krivitsky and especially Konstantin Volkov. The Catholics in Germany identified by the Vermehrens, all betrayed, all died at the hands of the occupying Russians in the aftermath of the war. Through these betrayals, Philby helped to ensure that half of Europe would fall under the thumb of Stalinist brutality and the influence of global communism would ensure. Scores more agents in the Middle East, all betrayed and all killed along with their families, it started to become clear just how much damage Kim Philby had really done. All those details over decades of association suddenly came to light; the conversations at the cricket, the drinking sessions at the clubs, the dinner parties and social gatherings. Everything about the man who Elliott considered close was just a ghost, a phantom to gleam intelligence. Philby had made him feel used, betrayed and a complete fool.

Enraged, humiliated and bitter about the betrayal and driven by the ongoing thought at how somebody so similar to him could have actually turned out so differently, he demanded to White that it would not be Arthur Martin to confront Kim but himself. It seemed like a logical choice, the two men had known each other for years and this personal attachment might be enough to coerce their man into divulging other Soviet agents embedded in the security services. White knew that Elliott had been Philby's greatest advocator during the Burgess Maclean investigation in 1951 and the anger he now displayed might be enough to convince the traitor that MI6 had more proof than they really did. The deal was struck, it was to be Nicholas Elliott and not Arthur Martin who would confront, break and extract a confession from Kim Philby. White told him that they had specific evidence from Golitsyn even though the intelligence was not as direct as he made out. But the logic was to smooth it out as much as possible by making Philby think MI5 had a stronger hand then what they actually did.

On a broader front the CIA was not to be involved in the case. The proof about Kim was inescapable but the British wanted to keep this strictly in-house. If the Americans knew the full extent of Philby's betrayal they would undoubtedly demand extradition to face trial, bringing the whole affair out into the open no matter how damaging or embarrassing. The chaos generated by the defection of both Burgess and Maclean eleven years previously had certainly hurt Anglo-American relations, something like this could destroy the western intelligence ties altogether. By only getting Philby to admit to spying up to 1949, the point where he went to Washington, there would be nothing the CIA could officially pin upon him and allow London to deal with him personally.

Meanwhile in Beirut Philby was rapidly becoming a burnt out drunken wreck. Sensing MI5 were closing in on him, he was frightened, one could tell; consoling himself in alcohol, hiding in his apartment and seeking solace in both. On the odd occasion he went out to social events he would drink himself into oblivion, his wife could only watch as her husband frantically deteriorated from a respected journalist into an alcoholic mess. The remote and distant attitude he took caused Eleanor to appeal about what was going wrong in his life:

"What is the matter? Why don't you tell me?" She repeatedly asked Kim to which he would only reply:

"Oh nothing, nothing." The fear of exposure and possible abduction tolled upon him.

By the 31 December, the eve of Kim's fifty-first birthday, Beirut was full of New Year's Eve parties, but Philby was not in the jovial mood preferring instead to drink champagne on the balcony with Eleanor in silence as the sounds of the city echoed all around them. The next day his wife had prepared a small drinks party over lunch but by 2:30 pm all the guests of this intimate gathering had left leaving the Philby's to spend the rest of his birthday in peace. The tranquillity was shattered by Miles Copeland who vehemently insisted that they join an all-day New Year's party being thrown by some of the local Americans. Philby was already pretty drunk after the lunchtime party but they attended anyway. It was not until late that evening when the couple finally staggered home, worse for wear to the apartment on the Rue Kantari. The evening should have ended there as the couple prepared to go straight to bed when Eleanor suddenly heard a crashing sound coming from the bathroom where Philby was located. Hearing him cry out in pain, another loud crashing sound immediately followed where she found her husband on the floor covered in blood from two nasty gashes to his head. Philby had slipped over, smacked his head on the radiator, got up and fell over once again, causing the nasty injuries. Eleanor wrapped Kim's head with a towel and telephoned the medical services where a Lebanese doctor arrived at the scene. He insisted Kim should get to hospital but still drunken he refused to leave the home as the doctor issued a stark warning:

"If we don't get your husband to the hospital I will not be responsible for his life."

It was clear he needed urgent medical attention as he was persuaded, somewhat cautiously to go to the hospital at the

American University. During treatment a doctor quietly took Eleanor to one side and gave her an astonishing fact:

"One more ounce of alcohol in his blood, he would have been dead." This was how bad Kim's alcoholism had become and an indication of the intense stress he was under. That night they returned home, Kim with two black eyes and bandaged around his head he reflected on the night's sobering events in his blood stained dressing gown:

"I've been a bloody fool. I'm going on the wagon...forever." Right here, right now he vowed to swear off the drink.

One week later the final showdown loomed, Nicholas Elliott was ready to travel back to Beirut to face and confront his former friend. Elliott had already steeled himself up for the task but there was no room for error here, he knew exactly how Kim worked under interrogation, he was determined to pin him down and come out on top. But he needed reassurance, a way of letting off steam and getting the awful task in hand off his chest. So on the way he stopped off in Athens to see an old friend whom he met while in Istanbul back in the war, Halsey Colchester the MI6 station chief in the city and like Elliott, fellow supporter of Philby during his ordeal:

"I've got an awful task." He told Halsey and his wife Rozanne. Like everyone outside of MI5, who always believed Kim was guilty, they too were shocked at the revelation that he was this *"Awful spy"*, noting that he had always seemed outwardly intelligent and amenable.

Both guests noted a change in Nicholas's attitude at dinner that evening. Normally he was so jokey, a likable way of hiding his insecurities, but now he was changed; he was hard and serious, almost anxious about what he was about to do. He felt so aggrieved at Kim that he remarked that he wanted to go as far as to shoot him yet he kept on talking obsessively about him as if he was trying to comprehend who this man really was, or convince himself of who he wasn't. There was no order from his superiors in MI6 that he had to go through with the confrontation, but after all the years and the secrets, he felt he had to.

Elliott arrived in Beirut once more on the 10 January 1963. He checked into a quiet hotel away from the journalists and spies. It was all very sombre and inconspicuous as only a few people knew of his presence there. One of those was Peter Lunn, Nicholas's replacement as station chief in the city once he took up his new post in London. By the next day the bait for the trap had now to be set; a small apartment in the Christian quarter close to the coast would be the setting for one of the Cold War's most dramatic episodes. The room was bugged, a microphone carefully placed under the sofa with a wire running to the next room where Lunn and a fellow operative, a stenographer would listen in on a tape recorder and transcribe every word.

Everything was set to lure Philby in. Elliott brought in a bottle of brandy just before the station chief finally made contact. A few minutes later Philby received a telephone call at his apartment from Peter Lunn who asked him in a casual voice if he would like to attend a meeting between the two to discuss future plans tomorrow afternoon. Philby agreed since there seemed no cause for alarm. Lunn, knowing that Kim had stressed the need for security, given his own anxieties, suggested that they meet at his secretary's flat where they could chat in private. Again Kim agreed, setting up the meeting at the address given. As soon as the phone hung up, privately Kim knew something was going on.

The afternoon of the 12 January was a fair one in the city. Everything was ready in the small apartment as Elliott waited, Lunn and the stenographer in the adjacent room wearing headphones, the microphone in place and the tape recorders ready. All that was required now was the arrival of the traitor. However it was now, of all times that Nicholas Elliott made a huge mistake; because of the weather he decided to open the windows while he was waiting. The vibrant sounds of the city life outside flowed into the room causing problems for the recording. An annoying mixture of Arab voices, cars and combustion engines. But it was too late now, for Kim Philby, still bandaged from his accident was in the building and climbing the stairs. At four o' clock Elliott, waiting anxiously heard the knock on the door. His guest had arrived and the drama was about to begin.

He opened the door as the two men stared at each other. Philby seemed strangely unsurprised to see his friend standing there offering a rather strange quote that only served up paranoia amongst his peers:

"I thought it would be you." He said

That remark sparked a belief in the security services that Philby must have been tipped off about Elliott's visit. It would spark an obsessive root and branch search for another possible Soviet spy, one that would last for at least the next twenty years.

Shaking hands Philby entered the room and sat down along with Elliott. This was to a be a very English confrontation, a battle of wits and ideology, a fight fought with tea and china cups rather than fists under a mask of stiff politeness. The secretary poured tea for the two men then left them alone to play out the drama. It began with Elliott asking about Philby's health:

"Perfectly tolerable." Said Kim, remarking he was recovering from a bout of bronchitis and flu, adding that:

"They were both against me."

Kim then returned the favour, asking about his friend's family to which Elliott replied that they were well and that his own son Mark was beginning a term at Eton, following in his father's footsteps. The customary pleasantries over, now was the time for business:

"Wonderful tea." Elliott said before a slight pause. Perhaps steeling himself for what was to come before Philby interrupted:

"Don't tell me you flew all the way here to see me?"

Taking out his pen, Elliott did not reply straight away, instead placing it on the table before rolling back and forth underneath his hand. It was meant as a distraction, perhaps a self-comforting trick before replying:

"Sorry for getting right on with it Kim, I don't have time to postpone this. And we've known each other for ever, so, if you don't mind, I'll get right to the point." He then paused before continuing again:

"Unfortunately it's not very pleasant. I came to tell you that your past has caught up with you."

Instantly Philby reacted:

"Have you gone mad once again? You want to start all that? After all these years? You've lost your sense of humour. You'll be a laughing stock!" But Elliott was ready:

"No, we haven't lost anything. On the contrary we've found additional information about you. It puts everything in place."

This was the very thing Philby had been dreading. Now it was coming true. He attacked:

"What information? And what is there to put in place?" He said desperately trying to deflect the impending truth. At this point Elliott stood up and walked over to the window, staring into the street below:

"Listen Kim, you know I was on your side all the time from the moment there were suspicions about you. But now there is new information. They've shown it to me. And now even I am convinced, absolutely convinced that you worked for the Soviet intelligence services. You worked for them right up until 49."

Slightly baffled as to why Elliott would mention that year, the British needed Philby to only admit to spying up to that date for the purposes of the plan set out by Dick White in London. If Kim admitted to spying after that date, James Angleton and the Americans would want to get involved and demand Philby face charges in the US. For the purposes of secrecy, London absolutely preferred to keep Washington out of this for now. However it hung on getting a confession and Philby was not going to admit anything:

"*Who told you that nonsense? It's totally absurd. You know yourself it's absurd.*" But Elliott was not going to fall for yet more lies. He had come too far for that. He pressed:

"*We have new information that you were indeed working with the Soviet intelligence service.*"

"*Do you want me to go into all this again?*" Philby interrupted before Elliott hit back:

"*Kim, the game's up. We know what you did. We've penetrated the KGB, Kim. There's no doubt in my mind any more that you were a KGB agent.*"

By now the atmosphere was getting a little tense but remained cordial. Their friendship though was beginning to sink. More tea was poured and the Mont Blanc pen was rolled again in the awkward silence which Philby broke:

"*Look how stupid this seems. Astonishing! A man is suspected for a long time of mortal sin, they can't prove a thing, they're embarrassed in front of the whole world. They apologise. Then ten years later, some chief is struck by the old idea again. They decide to send on old friend, a wise and decent man, with only one goal, to persuade an innocent man to confess that he's a Russian spy. Is that why you're here?*" Even now he was still trying to manipulate his old friend:

"*Kim, if you were in my place, if you knew what I know…*" Elliott replied before being interrupted again:

"*I wouldn't talk to you the way you're talking to me.*"

"*And how would you talk to me?*"

"*I would offer you a drink instead of this lousy tea.*" Elliott did not find the quip remotely funny. The bottle of brandy he brought in yesterday was not opened:

TEA IN BEIRUT

"Do you want me to give you my version of your work for the Russians? Do you want me to tell you what you were thinking?"

Philby fired back: *"Nicholas, are you serious?"*

"I am." Was the straight reply. He now proceeded to lecture his former friend on his version of events and set the conditions for the deal in a way Philby would have no answer:

"I understand you. I've been in love with two women at the same time. I'm certain that you were in the same situation in politics: you loved England and the Soviet Union long enough, you've helped it enough. Now you must help us. You stopped working for them in 1949, I'm absolutely certain of that. Now it's January 1963. Fourteen years have gone by. In that time your ideas and views have changed. They had to change. I can understand people who worked for the Soviet Union, say, before or during the war. But by 1949, a man of your intellect and spirit had to see that all the rumours about Stalin's monstrous behaviour were not rumours, they were the truth. You decided to break with the USSR."

He calculated right, Philby could not reply. All he could do was shrug his shoulders and shake his head. Still he did not admit anything, instead probed their friendship once more:

"You came here to interrogate me. And I keep thinking I'm talking to a friend."

Elliott suddenly had enough of the games and the lies. He snapped:

"You took me in for years. Now I'll get the truth out of you even if I have to drag it out. You had to choose between Marxism and your family, and you chose Marxism. I once looked up to you, Kim. My God, how I despise you now. I hope you've enough decency left to understand why."

Neither spoke or flinched for the next few seconds after the outburst, the first time ever between the two men. Elliott slowly began to regain his composure:

"*I'm sure we can work something out.*" He said, hinting at a deal. He then proceeded to lay out the terms of such an agreement. Philby would have to confess to everything either here or in London. In return he would not be prosecuted but only if he revealed every contact he had with the Soviets, every KGB mole in Britain and every secret he had leaked to Moscow over the years. Elliott summed everything up:

"*I can give you my word, and that of Dick White, that you will get full immunity, you will be pardoned, but only if you tell it yourself. We need your collaboration, your help.*"

Kim did not reply but the circumstances could not be made clearer in Elliott's now cold voice. If he did not cooperate, the consequences were total and complete isolation; his passport withdrawn, residence permit taken away, eligibility for even a bank account shut off. His employment with any British newspaper and of course the intelligence services would be immediately terminated and his children removed from their private schools. His family effectively would be shamed and he would be forced to live the rest of his life virtually broke and bankrupt. He had a choice to make; full cooperation in return for full immunity on the word of a gentleman, or he could stand by his morals and live the rest of his life as an outcast from any civilised society. It would be the ultimate humiliation and an epic fall from grace.

By now Philby was on his feet and heading for the door as Elliott still protested:

"*If you cooperate, we will give you immunity from prosecution. Nothing will be published.*" He said as Kim opened the door:

"*You've been a lucky chap so far, Kim.*" He continued in a last desperate attempt: "*You have exactly twenty-four hours. Be back here at precisely 4 p.m. tomorrow. If you're as intelligent as I think you are, you'll accept.*" Still he continued: "*I'm offering you a lifeline, Kim...*"

Philby shut the door behind him. He was gone.

Afterwards Elliott approached Peter Lunn who was listening to every word:

"Kim's broken. Everything's OK." That evening he sent a cable to Dick White in London informing him of the outcome. After more than ten years hunting Philby, at last, through his former best friend, he finally cornered him. Time would tell if Kim would stick to his word or flee as both men thought was a possibility during their showdown.

At four o' clock the next day Elliott was back in the same room waiting to see if their man would indeed come back. The door knocked, Philby appeared this time a little more composed than yesterday. He decided to tell his old friend some information:

"OK, here's the scoop. But first you owe me a drink. I haven't had one since my birthday on New Year's Day." Elliott obliged, pouring two large brandies for them both. Philby then prepared to tell him a mixture of truth and lies disguised as a total confession. He confirmed he was a Soviet spy but then lied saying had been recruited by his first wife Litzi. He then told the truth again saying he had recruited both Guy Burgess and Donald Maclean all those years ago before producing from his pocket two pieces of paper with a typed statement upon it, supposedly a written confession. In reality it was a diluted document, supposed to be a detailed account of his work for Moscow but in fact divulged little real detail and virtually no names of interest. Philby admitted to working for Soviet intelligence since 1934 but then said he ceased cooperation with them after the war, playing to Elliott's statement the previous day. Once again and without hesitation he lied to his accuser's face saying that after he renounced his spying he did no more with the exception of 1951 when he confirmed he was in fact the 'Third Man' who tipped off Maclean. He stressed untruthfully that he only did it as a pure act of loyalty. In reference to the names Elliott demanded, he gave away his early Soviet handlers, Arnold

Deutsch and Theodore Maly amongst others, but failed to reveal other intelligence handlers in other cities such as Istanbul, London, Washington and here in Beirut.

Elliott was not totally convinced about it and thought that this traitor may have been linked to George Blake:

"Is Nedosekin your contact?" He asked thinking both men operated with the same KGB handler. Philby told yet another bare faced lie:

"I've got no bloody contact. I broke with the KGB."

Elliott did not believe him. The document he provided was far from convincing, not nearly enough to fulfil the conditions of the immunity agreement. The situation between the two men was now unclear, to Elliott, he was unsure of Kim's game. Obviously he was withholding information even though he had simply admitted his espionage. To Philby, there was no way of knowing if MI5 would ever stand by the immunity deal. For all he knew this was a ploy to get him to come back to London where they could arrest him. Was Elliott still his friend? Or was he his foe? He still demanded answers:

"Our promise of immunity and pardon depends wholly on whether you give us all the information that you have. First of all we need information on people who worked with Moscow. By the way, we know them." He was bluffing, but he needed to pressure Philby into giving up the names. To Kim, just how much did he know? This second duel between the two continued all day, as they drank and discussed one of the worst treacheries of the century until dusk. By the end they were rather tipsy, their public school upper class accents slurring just a little as the two men epitomised the global chilliness of the Cold War in the space of a small Beirut flat. Philby got up and asked Elliott to come to his apartment that same evening for dinner, he was aware that his wife knew of his friend's presence and so would think it be odd if he did not socialise with them. Despite the ruins of their association, they

TEA IN BEIRUT

still found themselves on the same side, portraying a front that nothing outwardly was wrong.

True to his word Elliott arrived at the Philby's apartment a few hours later to be greeted by Eleanor. However they subsequently found Kim on the floor, passed out and drunk after consuming an entire bottle of whisky and clearly in no fit state to socialise. Both helped him to bed before Nicholas stayed awhile, chatting to his wife trying his best to act as if nothing had ever happened.

The next morning Elliott called around once again to invite both Kim and his wife to dinner at one of Beirut's most upmarket restaurants, the Chez Temporal with him and his own spouse as a group. It sounded like a normal social gathering, not much different from those in the past. In reality it was just a front to get Philby to secrete more information. That lunchtime, part two of the great drama between the two officers began. A quiet corner of the restaurant, a table under the white arches overlooking the sea and lit by candlelight was the setting as the food was served, steak with white truffle salad. Both Kim and Nicholas tried desperately to pretend as if everything was normal, it was far from it, Eleanor could see her husband was nervous. It made her relatively uneasy. At one point Philby got up to go to the bathroom prompting Eleanor to turn to Elliott to ask what was going on. Before she could do so, he too had left the table, following his old friend to talk.

Philby had already submitted a partial confession and had admitting to spying for the Soviet Union but now he suddenly felt trapped, an intoxicating suffocation like never before. Over the toilets he handed Elliott a bunch of typed pages, a more concise confession. This was something which he felt he had to do in exchange for his freedom but Elliott was armed with his own paperwork; a single sheet of paper with a list of names all of which were possible Soviet spies. Elliott wanted to know who. Names included Guy Liddell who by now had left the service, Tim Milne,

Tomas Harris. Most notably both John Carincross and Anthony Blunt the fourth and fifth man in the Cambridge network were also on there.

Philby knew that MI6 were going to apply sustained pressure upon him. Elliott was effectively plucking names, everybody who had an association with Burgess and Maclean to try and get him to betray fellow agents. If Blunt had confessed, then surely Elliott would figure that Philby was still lying, especially since he informed him that the entire debriefing would not be over quickly meaning that MI6 were certainly going to bleed him dry on what he knew. But his hands were tied and he knew it. He knew that if he stepped out of line, even slightly, the partial confession would not protect him and the whole immunity deal would be off. Philby was quickly running out of options and it seemed that the lifeline Elliott was handing him was in fact a hangman's noose.

After four days of interrogation, he informed Philby that he had to depart for Africa, the Congo on another assignment, delegating the task of debriefing him to the unsympathetic Peter Lunn the station chief. Inevitably MI6 would ask more probing questions based upon answers he had already given. He knew he was in for a rough time. But even those loyal officers back in London were not going to get off lightly despite their victorious mood that they had finally caught the 'Third Man'. Philby had indeed confessed to Soviet espionage, now the Americans would have to be informed in the manner to which Dick White had dictated. Indeed the head of MI6 was now convinced that they could use the opportunity to exploit Philby to their full potential saying somewhat triumphantly:

"He could have rejected the offer of immunity. But since he has accepted, he'll stay and cooperate."

The job of informing the Americans in the shape of J. Edgar Hoover at the FBI fell to Roger Hollis at MI5 in a memo laced with calming tones:

"In our judgement Philby's statement of the association with the RIS (Russian Intelligence Service) is substantially true. It accords with all the available evidence in our possession and we have no evidence pointing to a continuation of his activities on behalf of the RIS after 1946, save in the isolated instance of Maclean. If this is so, it follows that damage to United States interests will have been confined to the period of the Second World War."

The Americans responded by getting their man in London to draw up their own set of questions for Peter Lunn to ask. They, like the British were not just going to let Philby go by. Everybody wanted a piece of him, another brush with fame in the most negative light:

"What makes you think he will still be there?" They asked:

"He will be, he isn't going anywhere." Came the reply.

While the conversations, congratulations and arguments between MI5, MI6, the CIA and the FBI were rippling between Washington and London, at six o' clock the very next evening in Beirut Kim Philby was standing on the balcony of his apartment with a book in his hand. His Soviet handler Petukhov saw the signal and knew his man wanted to see him urgently.

CHAPTER EIGHTEEN

HELLO COMRADE PHILBY

A few hours later the two men met at their usual haunt, the Armenian bar called Vrej where Philby hurriedly explained what had happened; the British knew everything and possibly the Americans too. MI6 had new evidence derived from Golitsyn and were offering him immunity in exchange for information. He made no mention at all of the confession he had made to Nicholas Elliott, the last thing he wanted was for the British and Americans wanting to prosecute him on one side and the Russians preferring to 'silence' him on the other. Philby told his handler that he was under pressure from MI6 and was only just managing to hold it together but was less certain about another round of interrogation. Realising time was not on their side Petukhov raced back to the Soviet embassy and sent an urgent message to Moscow Centre in the Lubyanka, the KGB headquarters. His cable was received by the head of the British desk, Vassili Dozhdalev and asked specifically for instructions on what to do next. The reply was a question on whether or not Philby would be able to withstand yet another bout of questions. Petukhov how saw Kim's anxiety replied that Philby did not think he could get through another interrogation again. In response to this Dozhdalev issued a direct order; now was the time for Kim Philby to finally defect to the Soviet Union, and he should be extracted as soon as possible out of

Beirut. It may have been possible that Kim was playing up his fears about being abducted by MI6. He was certainly concerned, but it may have been possible that Philby was duping the Soviets just as much as he duped the west in order to force Moscow's hand and hasten his escape. Whatever his motives, it worked, the Russians wanted him out.

During the next hasty meeting Petukhov informed Philby of the decision:

"Your time had come. They won't leave you alone now. You have to disappear. There's no other way. There's room for you in Moscow." He said in a romantic tone. Kim knew exactly what this meant, prepare for life behind the Iron Curtain and the future within the Soviet Union.

Petukhov stressed that to arrange the escape he would have to wait since it would take a while. But when the time came he must be ready to move as fast as possible. They agreed a modified version of their little system of communication; as before Petukhov would walk down the Rue Kantari at a given time, if he carried a newspaper, he required a meeting, if he carried a book, everything was arranged and Philby had to prepare to move.

A few days later, nothing had occurred. Peter Lunn called by to enquire if Philby was ready to discuss the matter in hand but Kim stalled by saying he needed more time. Rather than offering to pressure Philby by questioning him, incredibly he said he was off skiing for the next four days.

Friday 23 January 1963. A cool day marred by a heavy rain storm that lashed the city did not stop Philby from drinking coffee on the balcony despite the weather. The apartment was busy, his youngest son Harry as well as Eleanor's daughter Annie was staying over. While there, Philby saw a figure, strangely familiar walking slowly on the street below. It was Petukhov and he was carrying a book. That day Kim and his wife had received an invitation from a friend, the first secretary at the British embassy,

Glencairn Balfour Paul and his wife Marnie to attend a dinner party. He was invited as a journalist representing the Observer as were many others from other newspapers. It was the first time in weeks Philby had agreed to leave the apartment and Eleanor was looking forward to the event an opportunity to quiz Balfour Paul about Middle Eastern archaeology, but for Kim, he had other business.

Upon seeing his contact in the street, Philby grabbed his raincoat and told his wife that he had to go out to meet someone but he would be back by six o' clock in time for their dinner engagement. Closing the door to the apartment he hurriedly descended the five flights of stairs to the ground and made his way out onto the quiet street of the Rue Kantari, continuously checking to make sure he was not being followed. He was not heading for the dinner party, but for a bar in the city, the St Georges Hotel. While there, distant and alone in thought, he drowned himself in drinks, several of them to be exact before asking the barman if he could use the telephone. Calling his family, it was the thirteen year old who Harry answered it as Eleanor was busy making supper. Kim told his son that he was going to be late and that he would meet his wife at the Balfour Paul's at eight o' clock. Harry's voice could be heard shouting the message through to the kitchen.

By eight, Eleanor was already in attendance at the dinner party and had to apologise for the sloppy attitude displayed by her husband. The other guests were starting to get hungry so the decision was taken by Marnie to begin the meal without Kim after which more drinks were served. As the evening wore on Eleanor was getting steadily drunker and more worried to match, her mind started to wander, had he fallen into the sea, or suffered some other kind of awful accident? The other guests tried to reassure her with the exception of Balfour Paul, that he had obviously been delayed for some reason.

While the curiosity regarding the whereabouts of the missing guest continued to intrigue, the man himself was at the bar where a car carrying diplomatic plates picked him up. In it was Petukhov in the front seat beside the driver and in the back where Philby climbed in was Pavel Nedosekin, George Blake's old handler. He had already let one asset slip into arrest and incarceration, he was not going to let this one go the same way:

"Everything is fine, everything is going the way it should." He assured Philby who wondered if Peter Lunn would ever get into trouble once the realisation of his defection would begin to dawn. The car was heading toward the Beirut docks where a Soviet freighter called the Dolmatova eventually bound for Odessa was waiting. Entering the facility, the car pulled up beside the freighter as it scattered the cargo on the dock. Philby and the minders exited the car and made their way swiftly up the gangplank where the ship's captain shook hands with the defector before welcoming him on board. In a cabin they all took to a waiting bottle of fine cognac especially laid out on a table, raising their glasses in triumphant celebration. Once the bottle was finished off, Petukhov handed Philby his new identity card, Philby was to become Villi Maris, a Latvian merchant seaman from Riga and one of the ship's crew. The real Villi Maris was in fact in a dockside bar, getting extremely drunk alongside an intelligence officer. He had no idea that at this time his identity card had been stolen and that his ship had effectively dumped him.

Back in the cabin on board the Dolmatova Philby found new and warm clothes laid out on the bed to cope with the cold Moscow temperatures.

By the time Eleanor arrived back home, there was still no sign of Kim. By now it had gone midnight so she called Peter Lunn at his home but was told that he was out by his wife Antoinette. Lunn was in fact at the British embassy but within minutes he was on the phone to Eleanor. He asked if she would like him to come round to which she said yes. Upon his arrival he asked if any of Kim's possessions including his passport had disappeared but everything was still there. It was obvious that Philby had no intention of cooperating as part of the immunity deal. He was in the process of defecting to Moscow and was effectively now on the run, meaning the third and most successful link in the Cambridge network had finally been broken.

Eleanor, still worried and oblivious to reality, offered to search the local hospitals and bars but Lunn wanted to do nothing, staying with her for the next two hours. Shortly after two in the morning, Lunn raced back to telephone the ambassador before sending a long cable back to Dick White in London to inform him of what happened. A few hours later the Dolmatova which already weighed anchor and was out at sea carried with it one of the Cold War's and possibly one of the 20th Century's greatest and villainous spies, back to the Soviet Union. As dawn broke Kim Philby watched the sunrise form the deck of the ship knowing that as the coastline receded ever more his final link to the west had been cut and his past severed for good. Philby was to disappear behind the Iron Curtain and would never emerge from it again.

Upon his arrival in Moscow, the newspapers were full of the glory of the defection. The official Soviet newspaper, 'Pravda' ran the headline 'Hello Comrade Philby' however Kim would be in for a shock. Throughout his entire spying career he was led to believe that he had attained the rank of colonel within Soviet Intelligence but upon his arrival he discovered that was not the case, he was no KGB colonel but just ordinary agent 'Stanley'. The Soviets were grateful of sorts, he was thanked, congratulated and appreciated but Philby quickly found that he had very little to do. When he first lived in the Russian capital he was given a thorough medical examination and situated in a small but drab apartment but was soon moved to a more spacious living quarters in the more central regions of the city. It was something he remarked:

"I snapped it up."

The Soviets also gave him a salary, five hundred roubles per month, equivalent to two hundred pounds, a considerable sum. The KGB virtually kept in under virtual house arrest, partly out of fear that he would be abducted, partly out of suspicion that he was a deep cover triple agent for the west who would eventually return to London. Even after all this time and after the service he had committed in the name of the USSR, they still did not completely trust him. To protect him, they screened all visitors and issued him with the alias Andrei Feyodorovich Martins. Ironically Kim Philby defected to escape capture but ended up being a prisoner himself thanks to Soviet paranoia.

A few weeks after his disappearance, Eleanor Philby, who remained in Beirut was still in the dark as to where her husband had vanished. She had already contacted the local police but called them off when she started to receive letters and telegrams from a man purporting to be Kim, originating from the Egyptian capital Cairo. She convinced herself that her spouse was off on one of his many journalist assignments to chase a story but neither the Economist nor the Observer had any idea why he disappeared. The mystery deepened when both publications asked the Lebanese authorities to investigate what happened to their reporter but no records of Kim Philby leaving the country or entering Egypt ever showed up. It was all very curious especially when she received a cable from her husband sent directly from the Cosmopolitan Hotel in Cairo reading:

All going well. Arrangements our reunion proceeding satisfactorily. Letters with all details following soon. All love Kim Philby."

It seemed like a reference to their wedding anniversary which was back on the 24 January, the day after his disappearance but the authorities in Cairo stressed that the Cosmopolitan had no guest registered in the name of Philby. It was also noticed that the signature on the telegraph cable was forged.

A few weeks later Eleanor received a visitor, a badly dressed individual who knocked on the door of her Rue Kantari apartment. In an unmistakable Russian accent he said:

"I'm from Kim. He wants you to join him. I'm here to help."

He put an envelope into her hand and quickly disappeared back down the stairs. She opened it to reveal a three page typed letter from what appeared to be Kim asking her to buy an airline ticket for London and then buy a real ticket bound for Prague from Czech Airlines. He also ordered her to burn this letter once she had read it. Still distraught over her husband's disappearance, she wondered if he had been kidnapped and if so, was she heading into a trap?

After some thought she approached her friend Nicholas Elliott who knew the real truth and asked him about this letter. He told her under no circumstances never to meet any strangers outside the house for fearing she too could follow her traitorous husband behind the Iron Curtain. The speculation mounted regarding Philby's disappearance, a local paper in Beirut even reported that the man in question had indeed been seen in Prague but there was nothing to substantiate the claims. The real awful truth began swirling around the intelligence community; MI6 was criticised for failing to prevent the defection even though Elliott defended himself saying that there was nothing he could had done to stop it happening. Some people, including the MI6 station chief in Spain, Desmond Bristow thought that Elliott might have knowingly left the door open for Philby's escape, engineering it in a way so that Philby would not accept the conditions of the immunity deal therefore allowing him to escape. The scandal from the revelations brought out by a public trial would inevitably cause severe embarrassment to the British government. It would give ammunition to the communists, damage trust with her allies in the US and elsewhere and cause untold damage to the reputation of the establishment. Bristow calculated that perhaps allowing Philby the

Soviet agent to flee was the lesser of two evils for all concerned.

However Nicholas Elliott was not the only one hurt by Philby's deception. James Angleton whom Philby later described as a: *"Brilliant opponent."* was extremely ashamed by his association with the traitor. Between 1949 and 1951 the two had thirty-six official meetings at CIA headquarters, everyone transcribed by Gloria Loomis, his secretary. It was a written record to every official secret Angleton leaked to the Russians via Philby. Then there was the other secrets shared by what he thought were between allies at their weekly lunches at Harvey's. Every secret told in confidence, every one betrayed, all those years of belief, friendship and defence even through the years where Kim denied being the 'Third Man', all utter lies. William K. Harvey was correct in his evaluation all along and he was wrong, an utter betrayal of the worst kind. Distraught at what he unwittingly disclosed, he had all those typed pages burned and later said that if he was the murderous kind he would go so far as to kill Kim Philby for what he did.

The post mortem continued as the Americans pondered just how much he knew. The CIA at that time had interests in the southern USSR, Albania, Turkey and the Baltic. It was now becoming clear with frightening clarity that all those operations, and the operatives sent in were being killed or captured too easily. It seemed as if they were just vanishing as soon as they were deployed and the source of the intelligence was from Philby and the secrets he was squeezing out of Angleton and the rest of the CIA in his most trusted position. Angleton suffered from an obsessive paranoia, refusing to trust anyone fully for the rest of his life, suffering from eventual disillusionment with trust and human integrity.

Fellow CIA agent and journalist who knew Philby in Beirut, Miles Copeland was also shocked. He knew about his meetings with Angleton and so could appreciate the quality of exactly what went out. He came to the conclusion that in relation to the many operations the western intelligence services were running between 1949 and 1951, they would have been better off doing nothing at all. The private fallout and public intrigue into where Kim Philby had gone began to mount in the media. By March 1963 the British government was forced under pressure to announce that Philby had gone missing and by May the Lord Privy Seal and future Prime Minister, Edward Heath issued a formal statement:

"Since Mr Philby resigned from the Foreign Office Service in 1951, twelve years ago, he has had no access of any kind to any official information."

It was a very political type of statement in that it offered no real explanation and very little information. In response the official government newspaper in the Soviet Union, the Izvestia rebuffed this claim, stating publically that Philby had been passing secrets to Moscow for thirty years. Accompanying the article was a sketch of Philby in Pushkin Square. It initiated the 'Great Philby Myth', the master spy who had duped and dumbfounded the west, leaked secrets and aided the development of the Soviet Union before a successful escape to the Motherland. This was true but since the USSR had not formally recognised Philby's defection, was nothing more than a press war waged by the Russians to unease the west.

That same month the press were scrambling all over the story with the same feverish curiosity as the Burgess, Maclean defection twelve years previously. Eleanor Philby had flown back to London where they were waiting for her to get the latest on the defection of the 'Third Man'. She was utterly confused, was he a spy? Had he defected to the east? Elliott had sent a car to get her away from the reporters where afterwards he took her out to lunch. Again he warned her not to go to saying that they probably would not let her back out if she went. Still refusing to accept her husband was a traitor Elliott summoned Dick White to convince her. Over coffee and brandy they all discussed the duplicity of their former associate after which, by the end of the afternoon, Eleanor was in tears. She realised she, like so many others, had fallen victim to a momentous mistake under the charm of a liar.

By July, just over six months since Kim's escape, the Soviet Union officially acknowledged Philby's arrival in Moscow. The very next day in London, Edward Heath announced to Parliament that Kim Philby was actually the 'Third Man' all along and that it was now believed that he was in the eastern bloc.

On the 30 July Moscow formally announced that he had asked for political asylum in the USSR and had been granted Soviet citizenship. It was at this point the Kim Philby finally came clean about his true self. He was in fact a Soviet spy and had been so for thirty years. Through all this admission of guilt, they lay a man embittered somewhat at the fact that throughout all his service he was only just ever an ordinary operative and not the KGB rank he had been led to believe. The same day the Izvestia newspaper announced with some gloat:

"A British citizen, HAR Philby, formally a senior official of the English Intelligence Service, has asked the Soviet authorities for political asylum and for Soviet citizenship. It is learnt that the Supreme Soviet of the USSR has granted HAR Philby's request."

Communication between London and Moscow were now red hot. The search for Philby was on.

One such person who wanted to track him down was Erik De Mauny, a journalist working for the BBC as Moscow correspondent. De Mauny was part of the posse of journalists who had known Kim previously from his days in Beirut and wanted to track him down via a telephone call and social meeting with none other than Guy Burgess. However not long after their meeting Burgess, who had not adjusted well to Soviet life and was now a raging, lonely alcoholic, suddenly died of a heart attack brought on by acute liver failure in Botin Hospital, Moscow on the 30 August. Even though he had no association with Philby, he left him his entire four-thousand book library to him upon his death.

By September, Eleanor received yet another letter form Kim. Clearly he wanted his wife to join him in Moscow but Elliott tried desperately everything to stop her from going but she was unperturbed, finding herself a few weeks later at the Soviet consul where the diplomat happily told her to prepare to fly to Moscow in two days. In addition he handed over five hundred pounds and advised her to buy some warm clothes. Eleanor announced she was leaving to join her husband in the USSR. Elizabeth Elliott, Nicholas's wife tried desperately to stop her from going over tea but Eleanor posed the reverse question to her, what would she do if her husband had defected. Elizabeth knew herself she would probably do the same thing.

By the 26 September 1963, Eleanor Philby flew to Moscow and landed with her hair wrapped up and wearing sunglasses as a disguise. Waiting at the airport was Kim Philby along with his KGB minder. It was the first time they had seen each other since that day in January when he told her he was going out and would be back in time for Glen Balfour Paul's party in Beirut. Now here they were together again where he greeted her with the words:

"Eleanor, is that you?"

A few weeks later Nicholas Elliott received a letter. The author was none other than Kim Philby:

"I am more than thankful for your friendly interventions at all times. I would have got in touch with you earlier, but I thought it better to let time do its work on the case. It is invariably with pleasure that I remember our meetings and talks. They did much to help one get one's bearings in this complicated world! I deeply appreciate, now as ever, our old friendship, and I hope that rumours which have reached me about your having had some trouble on my account, are exaggerated.

It would be bitter to feel that I might have been a source of trouble to you, but I am buoyed up by my confidence that you will have found a way out of any difficulties that may have beset you. I have often thought that there are a number of questions connected with the whole story that might interest you, and it might be helpful all round if we could get together as in old times and discuss matters of mutual interest.

After careful thought, I have come to the conclusion that Helsinki, which you could reach without difficulty, would be a suitable rendezvous – or perhaps Berlin?

I am enclosing an unsealed, addressed envelope. In the event of your agreeing to my proposal, would you post it, enclosing some view of Tower Bridge? On receipt of your letter, I will write again, through the same channel, and make suggestions about the admin side of the rendezvous. As you have probably guessed, I am sending this letter by 'safe hand' to your private address for obvious reasons.

You will, of course, treat this as a wholly private communication concerning only our two selves. At least, I hope you will see your way to follow my advice in this matter. Guy's death was a bitter blow. He had been very ill for a long time, and only his ex-like constitution enabled him to live as long as he did.

What a pity we shall never be able be able to gather a trois at Pruniers!

Let me hear from you soon.

Love to Elizabeth (to whom by the way, you had better not disclose the contents of this letter – nor to anyone else of course)."

It appeared that Kim wanted a meeting with Elliott in East Berlin. Directly contravening the orders of privacy in the letter, he showed it to his superior Dick White. He immediately rejected the idea. Elliott however did reply. He sent him a message regarding his long treachery with a short and blunt tone:

"*Put some flowers for me on poor Volkov's grave."*

With that, their long friendship was finally dead.

Away from the intelligence world, the Philby's associated with fellow Cambridge Spy Donald Maclean and his wife Melinda who herself had come over to join her own husband. Their social life settled into a regular pattern of meeting two or three times a week, undertaking various activities. By 1964 things were changing on both sides of the Iron Curtain. Sir Anthony Blunt was finally discovered as a Soviet agent, after being betrayed by an American he tried to recruit called Michael Straight. He confessed to MI5 on the 23 April and Queen Elizabeth II was informed shortly afterward. Unlike Philby he took the conditions of an immunity deal, a full confession in exchange for protection from prosecution. The fourth man in the Cambridge Spy Ring had been ousted and in reply he also gave up the fifth man, John Carincross amongst others. Finally, after more than thirty years, the most damaging spy ring in western history to date had ultimately been smashed. Meanwhile in Moscow, Eleanor had to return to the United States to renew her passport and to visit her daughter – she would be gone for five months. In those months Philby's charm would not wane and he embarked on another affair, this time with Donald's wife Melinda.

In that time the journalist Erik De Mauny was still trying to track Philby down and eventually managed to do so through the KGB who still vetted all access to their star agent. By March 1965 he had finally been granted an audience with Kim in a strictly controlled but pleasant atmosphere. The two talked, Kim ranted on about communism and how he first became seduced by it, they talked about Eleanor to which he became rather evasive and even defensive. It was more like chat between old acquaintances than an interview.

They remained in contact over the weeks and then over the years, but correspondence was sketchy at best due to the cloud of secrecy the KGB and the Soviet state enveloped Kim in.

After five months away, Eleanor arrived back in Moscow from the Unites States with a renewed passport but it was not long before she found out about her husband and Melinda's affair. Melinda had left Donald and was now living with Kim but it was enough for her, in May 1965 Eleanor left Kim for good, leaving Moscow. Kim had one very special parting gift for her, his old Westminster scarf, the one he carried since school, the one item he held close all his life. The KGB minders escorted her to the airport, furnishing her with a second parting gift, a bunch of tulips to send her on her way. In time Eleanor stated that she would be willing to return to Philby, but not to live in a city where Melinda Maclean was living. Later she summed up her time in Kim's company in a reflective tone that everyone seemed to adopt who came across him:

"He betrayed many people, me included. Kim had the guts, or the weakness, to stand by a decision he made thirty years ago, whatever the cost to those who loved him most. No one can ever really know another human being."

That same year the British tried to gain some kind of small revenge upon their defector by annulling and cancelling the OBE award he had received at the end of the Second World War. This most English of Russians was to be stripped of this most British of honours.

Life in the USSR and in particular Moscow was one that was tolerated. The Soviet capital was polar to the American one and once there he quickly found that he had little to do. The Russians still did not fully trust him, yet they strove to protect him, instead preferring to use him as a propaganda prize to show off to the west. He would be allowed out, taking strolls through the city or even further afield such as along the banks of the Volga River. He did however deliberately try to avoid seeing other westerners. Perhaps he was still afraid here, of all places, of sudden abduction. If he accidently bumped into a westerner for example he would try to get away. If he found one in a place he was, such as a restaurant or theatre, he would immediately leave. By the mid to late 1960's he was suffering from bouts of depression, heavy drinking and a period of brief illness. He attempted to slash his wrists in a suicide bid and tried, perhaps more favourably to drink himself to death. To keep himself occupied and with approval from the KGB, he decided to write his memoirs, a Soviet edited explanation full of truths and half-truths about the mind-set that contributed to his espionage. This included an unburdening admission of guilt that he had been a Soviet agent for thirty years. The result was a book published in 1968 called 'My Silent War', available immediately in the west, but not in the USSR itself until 1980.

But life was relatively disappointing for Philby apart from the socialising with friends which had included after 1966 George Blake who had, in October, escaped from Wormwood Scrubs Prison in London and managed to escape to the USSR via East Germany. Ideological comrades, he associated and became friends with Kim. But despite this and even though he was safe behind the Iron Curtain, he was still out of touch with the intelligence community.

Espionage was like a drug with an intoxicating effect to him, and at the moment he was expressing severe withdrawal symptoms. He had a vast wealth of knowledge to share but thanks to communist suspicion, there was no market for his invaluable expertise.

CHAPTER NINETEEN

A LONLEY OLD SPY

While in exile Philby started experiencing certain nostalgia for Britain. He continued to read his old newspaper The Times which was not available in the USSR so KGB agents had to bring copies back from assignment when they were operating within the United Kingdom. He still followed his beloved game of cricket, usually pouring over scores from matches long since over. One of his main sources of news from the western world came from listening to the BBC World Service on the radio. He also missed Coleman's mustard, something he was always fond of.

By now Philby's depression and drinking affected Melinda so much that even she left him by 1968, returning instead to Maclean. Now Philby was behind the Iron Curtain with no career, and no companionship. He sunk ever further into depression becoming in what one associate termed an:

"Alcoholic wreck."

The 1960's were the height of the Cold War, but Philby had no real part in it anymore. He was a pivotal figure in the early years but now was virtually surplus to requirements. All the service he had performed for the communist cause, his reward of further patriotic service was not reciprocated. These were the darkest days, but as the end of the decade passed and the start of the next one dawned for the aging, greying Philby, the 1960's were as black and white as one could imagine, but the 1970's were to blossom in full colour.

It began in 1970 when he met a young Polish-Russian woman twenty years younger than him called Rufina Invanova Pukhova. The two instantly felt a spark for each other – she found his English charm irresistible. He asked her to marry him after only a couple of dates despite the age gap, she was thirty-eight but he was fifty-nine, to which she accepted and by 1971 the two were living together in marital bliss. He wanted to take her on honeymoon to Siberia to which she though was quite funny. The KGB had a wedding present for Philby and his new wife, an English bone china tea set but despite the new period of settlement she could tell he was still tortured by his life of deceit. He would often suffer from a recurring nightmare where he would imagine himself being caught in the act and waking up in the middle of the night screaming. Philby enjoyed spying, but the risks were less appealing and he was openly upset about how the hardest thing was to lie to people he considered friends.

He spoke to Rufina about how isolated he felt upon his existence in Moscow:

"I came here totally fully of information, I wanted to give everything I had but no one was interested,"

His wife saw just how disappointed he was with what he found in the Soviet capital. He had always been led to believe that the USSR was a great state where communism stood for equality between all classes. This was the very bedrock of the Marxist-Leninist Russian Revolution in 1917, the uprising of the working and peasant classes, united as the proletariat under the doctrine of socialist communism. Instead what Philby saw in the east was so many people suffering. Nikita Khrushchev was no longer in power inside the walls of the Kremlin – that was now Leonid Brezhnev. The USSR under Brezhnev was one of inequality, where Cold War tensions forced Moscow to place emphasis upon military capability. Soviet defence spending as a percentage of GDP was higher than that of America and the west, just to keep up the balance of power. The result was a detrimental effect on the people and consumer goods, of which there were widespread shortages. The Soviet armed forces and nuclear stockpiles received more funding than the economy, agriculture and education and even though this was the middle of the Cold War, life inside the Soviet Union was becoming rather stale. The economic, political and social stalling was known as the Era of Stagnation.

It had a profound effect upon Philby. So much so that he was brought to tears by what he saw, by the disappointment he shared. He drank heavily and suffered from loneliness and once remarked quite poignantly:

"Why do old people live so badly here? After all, they won the war."

By 1974, eleven years since his defection, Philby was still in effect out in the cold. But after more than a decade as a protected citizen, the KGB was about to turn from protector to employer. Finally for the first time Kim Philby, now with grey hair and sometimes requiring glasses, would be walking through the doors of the KGB and into the heart of Moscow Centre.

The Soviets had decided to open a training school for their young operatives. His new job was to train new intelligence recruits at a secret location in central Moscow where he would give lessons on the inner practices of western intelligence agencies. Despite the fact that his did not speak Russian, unlike George Blake who fully integrated into Soviet life, he relished the task. In preparation for briefing officers, he would monitor world events to make his lectures up to date and make notes as they would be arranged in groups of three for their classes; he took it all very seriously, throwing himself wholeheartedly into the job. During classes he would often employ role playing techniques, teaching students that even the way a person spoke could reveal or conceal certain information. At last he was given the chance to vent all his knowledge and experience to a grateful audience. This welcoming in from the cold into the arms of Soviet Intelligence brought him into contact with other rising stars of the service such as Oleg Kalugin who at 34 years old became the youngest general in the

KGB ranks and would go on to play a part in the infamous poisoned umbrella killing of Bulgarian dissident writer Georgi Markov in London in 1978.

Throughout the autumn of his life, Rufina looked after him. They would go on to become great travellers both across the Soviet Union itself and throughout the communist bloc. One of their favourite destinations was Bulgaria due to the cuisine. Kim himself always had a talent for cooking, but there were widespread shortages throughout the USSR, partly due to the effects of the Brezhnevian Stagnation, so therefore was unable to show off his skills to the full. One time the couple had to plead with a shopkeeper to sell them a full goose to cook since only half was the allowed ration. They succeeded and Kim had an entire bird to work with and display his culinary skills.

Even at this stage Philby was still drinking heavily. Rufina tried to help him control it but Kim struggled, all those years of heavy drinking were now beginning to take its toll upon him. The grip of alcoholism had taken hold years ago and now he was in too deep to quit. He could only do his best to control a lifetime habit by employing a two-drink rule, where he could enjoy just two glasses of cognac per night before asking Rufina to hide the bottle for him. Even so he once remarked that drinking was the easiest way to bring life to an end, especially if he broke his rule, usually when he found the bottle. His wife noticed that the drunkenness came on very quickly and he would get increasingly intoxicated. But he never showed aggression, instead just going off to bed to sleep it off.

The increased drinking also had psychological effects upon him. He became paranoid that perhaps Rufina would eventually leave him, getting to such a state where he even took to hiding items of her clothes so she could not leave if she wanted to. At times he would even forget where he had hidden certain items.

It was this fear that actually helped to stem his alcoholic consumption in his later years, but his wife could see that the drink was finally starting to kill him. He promised to give it all up, a promise more substantial that the one he gave to Eleanor that night in Beirut where he smashed he head on the radiator. Faced with the paralysing fear that he would spend the coming years alone, he suddenly declared to his wife:

"I'm afraid I'm going to lose you, I'm not going to drink anymore."

This time he meant it. As sudden as he declared it, he changed. He still stuck to the two drink rule, but the necessity to hide the bottle evaporated. His drinking made up an important part of his daily routine along with other, more benign rituals such as a cup of Russian tea first thing in the morning at 7 am, complimented by a cup of English tea with milk at 5 pm drunken from the fine porcelain cups.

The 1970's drew to a close in controversial fashion for the traitors. In 1979 the Soviet Union formally invaded Afghanistan in support of the communist democratic republic who assumed power after the Saur Revolution in 1978. It would be the start of an almost ten year-long engagement. But for Kim, a more personal event was to occur late in the year. Philby's fellow conspirator, Anthony Blunt was sensationally ousted as the 'fourth man' in the Cambridge Spy Ring, something known to the authorities in the west since his confession in 1964. The immunity deal was still in place and he was allowed to retain all of his honours and academic positions. But by now the world had moved on. A book called 'Climate of Treason' by the author Andrew Boyle had a character called 'Maurice' which closely resembled Blunt. The fourth man subsequently tried to block the book's publication which inevitably drew attention toward him. On Thursday the 15 November, Britain's new Prime minister, Margret Thatcher publically revealed Anthony Blunt as a Soviet spy and issued a second, more detailed statement on the 21 November. Blunt himself was calm but privately shocked as his world collapsed around him. The media tried to track him down and once they did, they dogged his every move. Queen Elizabeth II stripped him of his knighthood and all of his academic honours, including the Fellowship of Trinity

College Cambridge which was revoked. The once revered and admired Blunt was reduced to living as a traitorous pariah in his homeland.

In the Soviet Union, Philby was still living the life of an elderly statesman, by communist standards. He was given a KGB general's pension, more generous than others of the same rank as he continued to travel with his wife. One such trip was to the Volga along with his KGB minder and daughter. At one point Rufina mentioned a remark to the minder, who acted in a rude way by just ignoring her, preferring instead to browse through magazines. Kim, who despite his treachery still upheld rigorous principles, took offence to the way this KGB operative was showing contempt for his wife. Getting up he shouted:

"Whoever is rude to my wife is rude to me!" The minder was visibly shocked.

The 1980's began on a quiet note. In 1980 he was filmed with his wife and KGB enjoying a stroll in the countryside complete with grey overcoat to keep out the cool temperatures despite the sunshine before being helped into a waiting car, a sign perhaps of his frailty in advancing years. However, in 1981 he was given a stage to showcase both his cunning and his experience; an old hand to teach the next generation the subtle art of espionage.

He was giving a secret talk behind closed doors to an audience of enthusiastic agents of the Stasi, the East German security service as a mentor to the spies of the future. This recorded event held in their headquarters was never intended to be publically broadcast, but nonetheless on stage in front of a communist portraits and a slogan in large red lettering, Kim sat alongside a panel of fellow officials. He was introduced by a man named Markus Wolf the spymaster from East Germany – a man so gifted in his craft, western intelligence nicknamed him 'the man without a face'.

After a short introduction given in German during which Wolf reminds the audience that the speaker was a man who had spent three decades working his way up British intelligence so he could pass secrets to the KGB, Kim Philby, under a rapturous applause, stood up and made his way to the wooden lectern complete with large microphone to pick up his words. There he stood in his beige suit, light shirt and a grey themed striped tie – his eyes staring out from the large tinted glasses he wore like some kind of mask in the public. He began by thanking his comrades and making almost an apologetic statement,

"Dear comrades, I must er, thank, comrade general Wolf very deeply for the kind words he said about me in introducing me to you. I must also thank you personally all, you're very noisy and more warm reception. I, I must also warn you that I am no public speaker, almost all my life I've spent trying to avoid publicity of any kind."

He began by talking about his life and how he had taken the path toward communism and treachery against the country of his birth for the sake of ideology,

"Erm, it is perfectly true that I was born into the ruling class of the British Empire. When I was born, my father was district commissioner in India and as such a young man ruling several million Indians. So why am I, his son talking to you like this? Both our organisations dedicated to smashing every vestige of imperialism off the face of the earth."

He then goes on to talk about his recruitment into the secret service, as the German translation echoed in the earpieces of the non-English speaking audience members,

"Er, looking back to my recruitment, the strangest thing about it, is the fact that I was recruited at all."

He went on to mention that he had no real connections except for the fact that he had *'Bourgeois connections'* in his words. He went on to talk about once he was recruited into Soviet intelligence, just how they intended to use him,

"And it was made perfectly clear to me that the best target in the eyes of the centre, in Moscow, would be the British secret service."

Kim also reminisces about the moment he was picked to enter the espionage world,

"I was sitting in my office at The Times with very little to do, and suddenly the telephone rang, and a voice asked me..." Here the German translation began to override Kim's story about how he was asked if he would consider 'war work'. He talks about the interview he had and also, once accepted, how he used his charm and drinking skills wormed his way into the confidence of his colleagues to gain access to archived documents that were not relevant to his work in order to pass them to his Soviet masters,

"It came to the point where every two or three times a week I'd meet him after hours for a drink and he became a close friend with full confidence on me, and so I could ask for papers which had nothing to do with German espionage in Spain or Portugal, but he would nonetheless send me, as a friend to whom he trusted."

Kim then proceeded to reveal just what he did with those papers,

"Every evening I would leave the office with a big briefcase, full of reports I'd written myself, full of files taken out of the actual documents, out of the actual archives. I used to hand them to my Soviet contact in the evening the next morning I would get the files back, the contents having been photographed, and take them back early in the morning and put the files back in their place. That I did regularly year in year out."

Next he talks about how the Moscow wanted him to become the head of the Counter-Soviet section set up in intelligence. By now he was already the deputy head of the team, but the Soviets wanted him to go further by ousting the head, Felix Cowgill and take the lead for himself,

"And er, well, I said er, are you proposing to shoot him or something? And he said no, all the same, you are going to be head of that new department. So I said my instructions from the centre are that I must get rid of my own boss and take his place yes? And he said yes."

'He then went on to explain how he did it,

"This is a very, very dirty story, but after all, our work does imply

getting dirty hands from time to time."

He then moves on to talk about the darker aspects of this so-called 'dirty work', a requirement of the type of espionage Philby was undertaking when he recalled his time in Washington as the liaison to the CIA. He referred to the time when he was helping to insert agents into Albania to overthrow Enver Hoxha and the communist regime and roll back the Iron Curtain. Here he demonstrated the cold ruthlessness required to sabotage the operation,

"As I was erm, a member of the high command, and had all the information about the operation…" He goes on to talk about how he saw all the information relating to Operation Valuable as it was called passing over his desk while handing everything over to the Soviet Union. It contributed in the complete failure of the plan and the deaths of scores of agents and dissidents trying to reclaim their country back. He justifies it by saying that to do so meant the prevention of an escalation that could have led to a third world war,

"If it had been successful, the next target would have been Bulgaria. And if they had started that sort of operation in Bulgaria the Soviet Union would undoubtedly have been immediately involved in world war three."

Philby later talks about his time in Washington and then his discovery of the American awareness of a Soviet spy operating in the British Embassy. Knowing it was Donald Maclean and the whole mess of getting Guy Burgess to warn him only to flee with him and the unwelcome spotlight that put on Philby, Kim admits that the suspicion put upon him would invariably damage his career prospects,

"It absolutely destroyed my position in SIS. And might I think been chief of the whole outfit, I don't know, but erm, anyway, one of the first three you say."

Later he recalls about his time in Beirut and how after he had been found out the sheer incompetence of the officers sent to watch him, Peter Lunn an avid skier,

"Four days after Elliott's departure, my friend's departure for London, reports reached Beirut of a heavy snowfall in the mountains north, Lebanon, and ideal conditions for skiing. And er, he decided four days after my other friend had gone back to London, to take a four-day holiday skiing in the mountains. And he was the only man in Beirut who knew anything about my case. So four days after he left I got the signal for departure. Left my flat, went to the rendezvous and I heard afterwards, that half an hour after I left my flat, Peter Lunn rang up asking for an urgent meeting the following morning. The following morning, I was long way beyond the borders of Lebanon."

Near the end he was taking questions from the Stasi audience members. He was asked how he had managed to get away with it for so long,

"There were many people in SIS who were involved in my recruitment into SIS and my promotion in SIS who would work with me in SIS and give me a lot of information in SIS. Those people would be very, very anxious personally to see me made innocent, including the chief of the whole organisation who made me head of his congress, furthermore, because I'd been born into the British government class, because I knew a lot of people whom had influential standing, I knew they would never get too tough with me. They'd never try to beat me up or knock me around because erm, if they'd been proven wrong afterwards, I could have made a tremendous scandal."

Philby ended the questioning by giving, one last and somewhat useful piece of advice if faced with interrogation from the west, what he referred to as the 'enemy camp',

"So, I ask you is to tell all your agents, that they're never to confess. If they're confronted with a photograph of themselves with a Soviet contact or a German contact, it's a fake. If they're, if

they're confront you with a report in your own handwriting, it's a forgery. Just deny everything. Only admit what is harmless, admit anything you safely can but deny that essential link to any foreign intelligence service, and you're alright."

It was more like a confession than a lecture. But here was Kim Philby, the master spy for the east, giving away his secrets like a wise old man of the intelligence world.

By 1983, personal loss began to get to the elderly Kim. On Friday the 6 March his close friend and fellow spy Donald Maclean died in Moscow and was cremated. Just a few weeks later on the 26 March the shamed Anthony Blunt also died of a heart attack in London. By now only John Craincross and himself were the only surviving members of this once infamous network that had given so much.

By 1984 political events and the Cold War had moved on further. The west was dominated by two figures; Margret Thatcher in Downing Street, and President Ronald Reagen, in the White House. In the Moscow Kremlin, Leonid Brezhnev had already passed away in 1982, replaced by his KGB chairman Yuri Andropov. But by now even he had died less than two years later on the 9 February that year, replaced by his successor Konstantin Chernenko. The state of the USSR had not changed much - in fact it got steadily worse. Despite Brezhnev's death, neither Andropov nor Chernenko could reverse the effects of the stagnation of the past two decades. In April, Philby's old friend Erik de Mauny tried to contact him once again to wish him a Happy Easter and to announce he was going to make another trip to Moscow. He did not receive a reply. However Philby was in contact with another, a journalist for The Sunday Times called Philip Knightly, a man who had known him for at least twenty years. It seemed as if they were preparing to meet up together for an interview.

By 1985 Mikhail Gorbachev assumed the role of General Secretary of the Communist Party of the Soviet Union, replacing

Konstantin Chernenko upon his death. Gorbachev issued radical reforms to reverse to effects of stagnation based around two major policies, 'Glasnost' and 'Perestroika' to encourage openness, transparency and ultimately de-centralisation of powers in the Soviet state. The reforms had a reverberating effect on people and Kim Philby, as well as his KGB escorts were no exception. His supervisor in the organisation was Nikolai Dolgopolov and noticed that the reforms forced the KGB to lift the rather close veil of secrecy surrounding their master spy. Suddenly individuals who were once smothered under the cloud of communist suppression were appearing all over the television and radio channels.

It was throughout the 1980's, at the time when the USSR was reconfiguring itself under the reforms, Philby's home life experienced a period of homely bliss. Regular visits by his son John brought him into contact with his granddaughter, Charlotte where over the next few years the family bonded in Kim and Rufina's central Moscow apartment. At other times the family would go out to sample the Moscow atmosphere such as in Red Square and Bear Park.

By the late 1980's the elderly Philby was now entering his twilight years. He was living through the reforms happening in the USSR seeing it move away from its traditional isolationist stance, taking on a more inclusive attitude. In 1987 Rufina queried Philby about his war work and the contributions he made to the Soviet effort, such as providing intelligence that helped them win the Battle of Kursk in July 1943. Philby answered questions very skilfully. The old charm act had never waned and Rufina wondered how and why Kim had never been bestowed with the USSR's highest honour, to be made a Hero of the Soviet Union? His wife began to campaign for him to be granted the award but perhaps the answer was more political than ideological. By now the war in Afghanistan had degraded to a frustrating stalemate between the Soviet Army, the communist forces and the US backed Afghan resistance, the Mujahideen. The reformist policies were also making progress so Gorbachev, who had much to lose, preferred to stay away from potential tensions with the west at this delicate time. Bestowing a man who was so clearly seen as a traitor there may agitate the British and the Americans so her idea did not win support.

However just like the Old Boy network in Britain, the Russian version suddenly kicked into motion. Shortly after Philby had given an interview, now allowed under the reforms, to Genrikh Borovik, a prominent writer and filmmaker and shown on Soviet television, three students from the city of Kharkov in the Ukrainian SSR wrote a letter expressing their surprise that such a hero had not received such an honour. The letter was addressed to the senior politician Mikhail Yasnov, the chairman of the Presidium of the Supreme Council of the Russian Soviet Federative Socialist Republic. He in turn forwarded it on to the chairman of the KGB, Vladimir Kryuchkov with the message:

"Mr Kryuchkov, please consider the letter attached."

Orders were prepared to begin proceedings to build a case for Kim Philby to receive the Hero of the Soviet Union. It would be the crowing pinnacle of his life it he was to receive such an ultimate honour.

By 1988 the authorities finally allowed him an open interview with a western journalist, Philip Knightly formally of The Sunday Times.

Knightly spent a week in April with Philby, but getting to him was not easy. The KGB was still protecting him and still had the responsibility for his safety. They tried their best to fool the journalist into thinking Kim lived further away from the city centre than he really did. In the arranged car they drove around the city centre to feign distance before taking him to his apartment just off Gorky Street. Once they arrived, the KGB took Knightly up to the floor of his apartment in an elevator. In preparation, no particular instructions were laid out, preferring instead to just prepare for the interviews in a casual way. Kim was allowed full discretion over how to conduct this rare interview to a western journalist. This allowed Philby to use Knightly, just like he had used so many others but in a different way as a propaganda tool, a conduit for his own reasoning out to the other side of the Iron Curtain.

Knightly could see that Philby's main motivation for doing what he did was purely ideological. So strong was not only Kim's, but all the Cambridge spies dedication to the communist cause that they waived all their pensions eligible to them from their war service. This financial loss was more than recuperated by the salary they received from their grateful masters in Moscow.

He publically revealed to Knightly that he had no regrets about his betrayal, an idealist to the end, but he did miss some small things that mattered a great deal such as mustard, Worcestershire sauce, and some of his old friends. Many of these openly criticised Philby about his sheer duplicity over the years. Something which upset him greatly as he told the reporter:

"Friendship is the most important thing of all... I have always operated on two levels, a personal level and a political one. When the two have come into conflict I have had to put politics first. The conflict can be very painful. I don't like deceiving people, especially friends, and contrary to what others think, I feel very badly about it."

Soviet officers continued to bring back for him quintessentially English items such as tweed clothing, the newspapers and the food items. It all helped him feel a sense of familiarity. The main interview Philby had with Knightly was recorded. Here he was, grey haired but neatly combed and porting large, dark rimmed glasses tinted slightly. Just like the charade interview he gave to journalists all those years ago in 1955 in his mother's flat where he flatly denied ever being the 'Third Man', here he was again dressed in a black suit, blue shirt and dark checked tie. He rebuffs claims he was miserable:

"All these stories about living in poverty and longing to go back to England are complete rubbish. How can I be unhappy here? I've got a wonderful wife, I've got wonderful colleagues, not only in Moscow but all over the Soviet Union. Whenever I go, I want to be buried in the Soviet Union. It's a country which I considered to be my own country...ever since 1930....1930 you can say."

For all his staunch belief in the cause, he was disillusioned with communism. There was never any doubt of his loyalty, at least from one side of the Iron Curtain, but he was disappointed in the way it was carried out. He was disappointed with the Brezhnev era, though things got a little better under Andropov and overall though that the future of socialism was quite bright.

Three weeks after he gave the interview to Phillip Knightly, Kim was in hospital in Moscow undergoing a medical examination in a private room, another perk of his hero status. While there he suddenly fainted and fell to the floor, totally unexpected as it was just a regular, routine check-up. He was due to stay in hospital for just a few days then be allowed home.

But he never made it home. Harold Adrian Russell 'Kim' Philby died in the Moscow hospital on the 11 May 1988, 25 years after his defection from Beirut. The officially recorded cause of death was heart failure.

His funeral, held a few days later was an event of grand communist mourning. He was allowed a lavish ceremony, his peaceful looking body on display in a red-lined open coffin surrounded by flowers for crowds of friends, colleagues and admirers to file past and say their goodbyes. His medals which included honours such as the Order of Lenin and the Order of the Red Banner were displayed in front of the casket which was flanked by two Russian soldiers standing as an honour guard. The official obituary stated his,

"Tireless struggle in the cause of peace and a brighter future."

There was something all very Stalinist about the whole sombre event and he was buried in Kuntsevo Cemetery in the western districts of Moscow, in accordance with his wishes to be laid to rest in the Soviet Union.

Upon hearing the news of his former friend's death, Nicholas Elliott, himself elderly and now retired from MI6 but still kept in touch with those in the know, suggested somewhat cynically that Philby should by awarded the Order of St Michael and St George, the CMG. This award was only given to those individuals who render important non-military service to a foreign country, something which fit Philby perfectly in Elliott's eyes. He even offered to write an obituary:

"My lips have hitherto been sealed but I can now reveal that Philby was one of the bravest men I have ever known."

He wanted to make the point that Kim was not in reality a Soviet double agent, but in fact a British triple agent. It would be something that would infuriate Moscow, and the final piece of perfect revenge for all those years of betrayal. MI6 turned the idea down.

Elliott's actions were typical of the bitterness and betrayal Kim left behind to those who believed in him most. James Angleton became increasingly unperturbed, believing that spies were in the CIA, even going on to accuse various world leaders of being Soviet agents. He resigned in December 1974 after a tenure which even accused three of his own colleagues of treason, thus causing the CIA to compensate them after their pensions were frozen. He died, a bitter and suspicious man just one year before his tormentor in 1987 of cancer.

As for Nicholas Elliott, he did live to see not just the end of Philby, but the collapse and dissolution of the Soviet Union just three years later thanks to the weakening of the state from the reforms and the failure of the August 1991 coup. With the Cold War finally over, the elderly Elliott wondered how a man like Kim

Philby could have been so like him, yet so different. The 1990's heralded a time of a new world order, the Soviet Union gone, replaced by the Russian Federation, the KGB dissolved like it's parent state and the focus changing to other world threats such as the turmoil occurring in the former eastern bloc states with the breakup of Yugoslavia. But despite all this, things never changed for Nicholas; in many ways he always kept a part of Kim with him. He once called Philby a:

"Disreputable traitor."

He was right, but the two men were inexorably linked in friendship, comradeship, betrayal and shame. It was a stigma he would carry for the rest of his life until he too passed away in London on the 13 April 1994 aged 77.

Philby was a product of the Cold War, just like his peers, friend or foe. Yet he was an enigma to many, even to those who he pledged his allegiance to. From his initial radicalization and commitment to socialism, he spent the first half of his life hiding his communism and the latter half stressing it to everybody. Was Kim Philby really a traitor? It can be a matter of intense debate. He never betrayed communism or his principles, but he did betray the country and the class he was born into.

This most polarizing of all Cold War double agents, reviled in the west, but revered in the Soviet Union and even modern day Russia, was certainly not the only one to commit treason, but perhaps one of the few to commit such untold damage both to human life and state secrets.

Only one man out of a larger band of idealists could have been so committed as to politically steer the direction of the early Cold War; agent 'Stanley' Kim Philby.

AFTERWORD

The real scale of the damage committed by the Cambridge Spy Ring to both British and American national security may possibly never be fully disclosed or indeed known. After the Soviet collapse many of the archives of the KGB were made available, but a more comprehensive account of the network's activities remain frustratingly elusive, perhaps due to the sensitivity of the secrets leaked.

The members of the Cambridge network managed to inflict a quite profound effect upon western intelligence thanks to how far up and trusted the members actually were, for all their social flaws. They abused the very Old Boy network and class system that elevated them into such privileged power and forced both the United Kingdom and the United States to increase counterespionage operations to weed out moles in both agencies.

The divisions thanks to the influence of the network members almost unwittingly achieved was what the Russians always wanted; to split the west over tensions created by the damage caused. Seeds of incompetence and mistrust were sown and flourished ironically during the event where the spy ring began to fall apart, the detection of Donald Maclean and his eventual defection with Guy Burgess in 1951. MI5 and MI6 fought between one another in a civil tug of war over the complicity of Kim Philby, one of their most admired and suspected members.

Likewise the same effect was occurring in the United States between the CIA and the FBI, albeit in a more fractured way.

Once Philby finally defected in 1963, competitive tensions increased internationally between the UK and the US, each blaming the other over claims of incompetence and not conducting proper background checks on Philby and the others. Scrutiny concerning how the loss of important information was not prevented because the spy ring had not been discovered in enough time embarrassed all the western intelligence agencies. International tensions between two important nations came at a time when the fight to check the spread of global communism fermented as mistrust between London and Washington, lasting for more than a decade. This was perhaps the ultimate, toxic legacy of the Cambridge Spy Ring.

During this time when the Cold War was at its height, the British and the Americans only shared very limited information between each other for fear of even more high level secrets being passed to Moscow. The detrimental effect was only temporary and intelligence relations gradually softened as the years went by, eventually warming to each other and restoring full cooperation by the 1970's. Declassification of documents after the end of the Cold War showed that the Cambridge Spy Ring, while being one of the worst security breaches, was far from alone. The Walker Spy Ring in the US was also severely damaging to US Naval Intelligence for almost twenty years.

However the Cambridge network was far more notorious simply because of the type of people who was in it. All of them upper class, privately educated individuals who came from the same privileged backgrounds and shared the same bourgeois lifestyle, the drink, the clubs, and the social circles. The very class system that was thought to be the very embodiment of what socialism hated actually ended up being their cover. Their credibility gave them all a level of trust they never should have been allowed to have and gave access to a nation's top level secrets. The members of the ring spent years building up respectable reputations to solidify their cover and were effective to different levels. They were all committed idealists, therefore not demanding payment from the Soviets for their services. The one exception was when Philby was in severe financial difficulty and required Yuri Modin to parachute in emergency funds to keep him from bankruptcy.

The Cambridge spies were labelled traitors in the west but were treated as patriotic celebrities in the USSR where they were known as the 'Magnificent Five'. In contrast they were deeply embarrassing to the authorities in their home country and in 1963, the very year Philby defected, the British government was rocked once more by the Profumo Affair. The senior politician, John Profumo engaged in a relationship with a woman who, as it turned out, was herself a Soviet agent. The 'Sex for Secrets' scandal was so damaging that it eventually brought down the government and ended Harold Macmillan's reign as Prime Minister. This was the second time he was undermined by the subversive efforts of the Soviets, having officially cleared Kim Philby of wrongdoing just eight years previously.

Philby throughout his life was an intently proud man, no matter what the act he always accepted he was performing for a greater cause. Perhaps he summed it up in an explanation where he publically stood by the decisions he made:

"Because of the nature of my activities, I had to organize all sorts of operations against the Soviet Union and other socialist countries and then torpedo them myself. I always found support in thinking about the solidarity, the reliability of the rear ...I was also very much helped in my work by the fact that, even in western countries, I continually came across sincere friends of the Soviet people, people whose entire hearts were devoted to socialism...among the members of western countries' intelligence services I know more than a few people like myself..."

Even though he once said he operated on two levels, a personal one and a political one, he always felt more aligned to the latter even to the detriment of his friends and colleagues who accepted him. Even though he never wanted to get caught he was prepared to defend his actions because he thought that what he was doing was the right thing, he never (publically at least) expressed regret or remorse or seeking redemption or absolution beyond the fact that he had to lie to his friends.

The espionage work Kim Philby undertook ultimately contributed to the deaths of tens, perhaps hundreds of western agents, causing revulsion in the light of the full scale of his activities. The Russians prized him as a true hero and never forgot the contribution he made to their nation. The unveiling of a plaque in his honour as a lasting reminder of gratitude at the Lubyanka Building, headquarters of the post-Soviet successor to the KGB, the FSB (Federal Security Service of the Russian Federation) bears testimony to this.

In truth the full scale of Philby's treachery is not truly known. Therefore one can only really generalise about how a man who held such fervent ideals could sign the death warrants of people sent to ferment anti-communist uprisings such as in Albania and the Ukraine. The advance warnings he wilfully sent with no noticeable trace of hesitation or even conscience made him equally effective and dangerous. Global events and proxy wars of the time tells its own story; the Korean War and the Cuban Missile Crisis were instrumental in being prosecuted upon the intelligence Philby provided.

The Soviets never claimed him to be a double agent. They stressed that he always worked for Moscow. In many terms this is actually true, Philby had already embraced communism and was actively spying for the Russians before he entered the British secret service. If anything it is the fault of the security agencies to adopt a man on almost blind trust, the word of a gentleman and the influence of a family friend. The background checks the west conducted on him proved woefully adequate and on many levels, they could not have done much more damage if they just handed details of their secrets themselves to Moscow. If anything the whole Philby and the Cambridge spy story highlighted the very fundamental flaw of trusting another human being based simply on the accent you speak or the colour of your school tie. It was something Philby was aware of and exploited to the full.

Perhaps there is one last, rather important aspect to the life of Kim Philby. Not one person, east or west could ever claim his motivation was money, unlike other traitors. Kim was a committed idealist who harboured such a romantically pure attitude toward the Soviet Union, the country he served for decades and what he truly and sincerely believed in to the end.

ABOUT THE AUTHOR

Christian Shakespeare is a writer on history and espionage novels. He has previously written works on the Second World War including Stalingrad: Struggle in the East and D-DAY: Blood on the Beaches in 2014. In 2013 he wrote the modern day espionage novel Three Faces of West.

Printed in Dunstable, United Kingdom